Ewan Stein is Lecturer in International Politics at the University of Edinburgh, having spent three years as a post-doctoral research fellow at Centre for the Advanced Study of the Arab World, University of Edinburgh. He also has a PhD from the London School of Economics.

REPRESENTING ISRAEL IN MODERN EGYPT

Ideas, Intellectuals and Foreign Policy from
Nasser to Mubarak

EWAN STEIN

I.B. TAURIS

LONDON · NEW YORK

Published in 2012 by I.B.Tauris & Co Ltd
6 Salem Road, London W2 4BU
175 Fifth Avenue, New York NY 10010
www.ibtauris.com

Distributed in the United States and Canada
Exclusively by Palgrave Macmillan
175 Fifth Avenue, New York NY 10010

Library of Modern Middle East Studies 106

ISBN 978 1 84885 460 4

A full CIP record for this book is available from the British Library
A full CIP record for this book is available from the Library of Congress

Library of Congress catalog card: available

Typeset by Newgen Publishers, Chennai
Printed and bound by CPI Group (UK) Ltd, Croydon, CR0 4YY

CONTENTS

PREFACE

On 11 February 2011 Husni Mubarak fell from power after massive popular protests in Egypt. The main opposition forces, not least the Muslim Brothers, were as surprised by the strength of the revolt as was the president himself. Although the protesters' demands were overwhelmingly domestic, behind the calls for democracy, social justice and freedom was an implicit—and sometimes explicit—indictment of a regime that put Israeli interests above those of its own people. Soon a shift in Egyptian foreign policy towards Israel became, for the protest movement, an important bellwether of the revolution's success. In August, the Israeli army killed five Egyptian soldiers in Sinai. Confounding expectations that this would not be tolerated in the new Egypt, the ruling generals took no action. The following month, protesters took matters into their own hands and stormed the Israeli embassy in Cairo. As was often the case, Egyptian domestic politics and foreign policy towards Israel merged into one. For its part, the Islamist movement, a major beneficiary if not instigator of the revolution, remains committed to the 'Camp David consensus' described in this book, opposing Zionism and societal normalisation with Israel while recognising the state's right and need to maintain peaceful diplomatic relations with Israel as a state. What has changed in 2011 is that there is now a newly empowered popular movement that seeks more substantial realignment of Egyptian foreign policy as an integral part of the country's national revolution.

The ideas contained within this book originated from issues related to my PhD research carried out between October 2004 and December 2007 at the London School of Economics (LSE), though its seeds can be traced further back. My introduction to Egypt was initially through language and I first visited the country to study Arabic in 1995. My interest in the politics of Egypt and the broader Middle East developed while I was a Master's student at Georgetown University's Center for Contemporary Arab Studies, from 1998 until 2000. I was struck then and later that there was a sharp divide between work on political thought and intellectual life in the Arab world and theoretical studies of Middle Eastern or Arab international relations. I found this particularly curious given the revival of interest in issues of identity, ideas and culture in international relations in general, and in the politics of the Arab world in particular.

It was because of this that I resolved to do a PhD on some aspect of Arab intellectual life, but to cast it in a theoretically sensitive way. I felt early on that it would be important to focus on the intellectuals of just one state in order to explore the interplay between ideas and politics rather than seek to generalise at the 'Arab' level. I was quickly attracted by the richness and complexity of the Egyptian case, but this study could certainly have been written about other countries too. My supervisor, I recall, held out some hope that I would focus on Yemen, another country I had visited and for which we shared affection.

Reading through Egyptian writings on international issues I soon realised that, implicitly or explicity, the question of Israel was always there, and that Israel was a kind of fulcrum around which ideas about Egypt's national identity and destiny, and theories about the way the world worked, coalesced. It was for this reason that I decided to further narrow my study to an examination of the evolution and, to an extent, 'function', of ideas on Israel in Egyptian political society. I was keen from the start not to restrict myself to just one intellectual trend (the left, say, or Islamism) or to home in on one narrow issue or limited period. Though sacrificing much detail, I hope that this more comprehensive approach has succeeded in showing the interrelationships between intellectual trends and political movements, as well as highlighting important processes like nationalism, revolution and state formation.

Many individuals have provided great assistance and inspiration to me in completing this book, of whom I will limit myself to acknowledging a few here. The first, and most heartfelt, acknowledgement must go to my PhD supervisor Fred Halliday. Fred's passing in April 2010 was a blow to many, and I can only hope that my own work here and in the future does some justice to the incalculable advice, judgement and inspiration that he provided when I was his student. Also at the LSE I am grateful to the support and guidance of Margot Light, Amnon Aran, Michael Cox, Katerina Dalacoura, and my fellow research students. In Egypt, I must thank the staff of the al-Ahram Centre for Strategic and Political Studies, and especially Sayyid Yasin and Adel Abd al-Sadiq, for being so patient and generous with their time. I am grateful to Sa'd Eddine Ibrahim for taking the time to discuss my project with me and supplying references. I also thank Hossam Tammam, also sadly departed, for his friendship and for sharing his encyclopaedic knowledge and sharp analysis of Egyptian, particularly Islamic, politics over the last two years. At the University of Edinburgh I would like to especially thank Marilyn Booth and Tony Gorman for much advice and support. More broadly, I thank the International Relations Department at the LSE and the Centre for the Advanced Study of the Arab World (CASAW) for the financial and institutional support that enabled me to produce this work. It has been a pleasure and privilege to spend three years in Edinburgh University's Department of Islamic and Middle Eastern Studies as a postdoctoral fellow. I thank Roel Meijer and Robert Springborg for their support and comments on the manuscript. Finally, I am eternally grateful to my wife Jennifer for indulging this project for over six years. All shortcomings are, needless to say, my own.

CHAPTER 1

THE SOCIOLOGY OF IDEAS
ON ISRAEL

The land of Palestine, including what is today Israel, has long constituted what may be termed Egypt's 'near abroad'. From the days of the Pharaohs to Egypt's first modern ruler, Muhammad Ali, threats and opportunities have seemed to loom large across the sands of the Sinai Peninsula. More recently, the doyen of Egyptian intellectuals, Mohamed Hassanein Heikal, characterised the historical importance of the area in the language of security and Arab nationalism: 'For the emerging Arab nation, the land bridge that linked the Arabs of Africa with those of Asia was, in terms of community of interests and security, a vital focal point.'[1]

Resistance to Israel has, for students of the Middle East, as well as for the intellectuals of the region, represented one of the central pillars of Arabism. Arabism in general is often viewed as a regional identity, or as the normative standard by which all Arab kings and presidents are judged. Israel has been seen as a motivator for the rivalries of Arab states in their shifting relations with each other, or as the main aggravating factor in an ongoing dialectic between *raison d'état* and *raison de la nation* in the region. Arabism, according to this view, exists in dialectical opposition to sovereignty: as the norm of sovereignty, or public and international respect for the state and states system, increases, so Arabism—and by extension resistance or opposition towards Israel—recedes.[2] Some have recognised that this dichotomy is not so clear-cut and that Arabism can actually strengthen state-building dynamics through legitimating military build-up and economic centralisation.[3] But what is less commonly acknowledged, and what this book seeks to address, are the politically and socially contingent dimensions of Arabism as a set of ideological propositions within states. My contention in this book is that approaches to Zionism and Israel have not remained constant or unified within Egypt, and that they have served purposes for the actors elaborating them that go far beyond explicit foreign policy issues.

Alongside making a general argument about the nature and sources of Arabism, this study sets out more specifically to explain and historicise the 'cold peace' that has prevailed between Egypt and Israel since 1979. Often the cold peace is taken at face value as the Egyptian regime's strategy to withhold implementation of the normalisation components of the Egypt-Israel peace treaty until Israel delivers on its obligations towards the Palestinians. This explanation is sometimes augmented by another that foregrounds Egypt's Pan-Arab goals: in order to reintegrate his country into the Arab fold in the post-Sadat era, Mubarak effectively froze the normalisation process, abiding by the letter but not the spirit of the Camp David Accords and the Egypt-Israel peace treaty.[4]

But while there is some truth to these interpretations, they represent only part of the picture and neglect to integrate the domestic dimension. In this book, I examine in detail Egyptian representations of Israel and argue that deeper, more structural, domestic factors—in close interaction with shifts in the global and regional environment—better account for the onset and persistence of the cold peace. By popularising certain images of Israel, intellectuals and political movements have collectively secured and defended a degree of agency for themselves that is independent of the Egyptian state. It is this division of labour that I term the 'Camp David consensus'. Societal hostility towards Israel has suited, to some extent, the regime's purposes; and intellectuals have largely come to accept the need for Egypt to deal 'correctly' and diplomatically with Israel as a state. Foreign policy is, in this way, 'instrumentalised'.

Intellectuals in Egypt have articulated ideas on Israel using language and symbols derived from broader political and ideological currents in Egyptian society, namely liberal nationalism, Marxism and Islamism, each of which has enjoyed a shifting relationship with the state.[5] An understanding of state-society relations in Egypt is therefore central to the explication and historicisation of ideas on Israel. Critical to my analysis is a conception of Egypt as a country in which there is no straightforward state-society dichotomy. The two spheres are, rather, 'interpenetrated'. At the same time, no social movement has managed to 'capture' the state and inculcate a hegemonic ideological vision through which foreign policy and local worldviews are integrated nationally. Ideologically based societal movements have tended, in the main, to seek maximisation of social power that stops short of overthrowing the state. There therefore exists a multiplicity of normative frameworks through which foreign policy is understood and acted upon as well as, due to the interpenetration of state and society, an implicit consensus that this multiplicity constitutes the natural way of things.

This book, then, has three main objectives: the first is to compare and analyse the dominant ways in which intellectuals of Egypt's main political traditions have represented Israel, or Zionism, from the mid-1930s until the present. The second is to shed new light on an important question in Middle Eastern foreign policy, the 'cold peace' between Egypt and Israel. The third aim is to raise more general questions for the field of international relations—particularly regarding the links between ideas, state-society relations and foreign policy; and on those between norms and identity on domestic and regional levels.

Ideas and state-society relations in Egypt

An understanding of the role, significance and provenance of ideas in Egyptian politics and foreign policy can be enriched by applying insights derived from political sociology and the sociology of knowledge. Karl Mannheim argued that the ideas and ideologies we associate with modernity originated in the experience of social groups, in particular the rising bourgeoisies in the states of Europe that sought to wrest political power from the church.[6] Mannheim saw ideological change (or shifts in national identity) as continuous, and destabilising, processes; with the social mobility produced by capitalism leading elite intellectuals to assimilate the concerns and worldviews of lower strata, while rising groups adopted elements of elite culture.[7] The result is a revolutionary dialectic wherein 'ideology', which legitimises the status quo, encompasses elements of 'utopia' that would, if realised, upset the established order, and vice versa.

A heterogeneous reading of state-society relations in Egypt is also consistent with the Gramscian notion of hegemony. Gramsci provides conceptual tools for understanding the ideological linkages between civil and political society, which, while accepting the existence of two distinct spheres, avoids the sharp Weberian dichotomy between the two. For Gramsci, civil society constitutes the realm in which a dominant or ruling class seeks to organise consent for the existing order, and in which opposition movements also seek to garner support for their own political agendas. The extent to which the state is able to extend hegemony over civil society, and vice versa, varies from case to case, which, for Gramsci, means that an 'accurate reconnaissance' should be conducted of each country.

Integral to Gramsci's theories on the ideological dimensions of the modern state is his conception of the intellectuals. For Gramsci, traditional intellectuals provide the overall intellectual direction in society:

> Every 'essential' social group which emerges into history out of the preceding economic structure, and as an expression of a development of this structure, has found (at least in all of history up to the present) categories of intellectuals already in existence and which seemed indeed to represent an historical continuity uninterrupted even by the most complicated and radical changes in political and social forms.[8]

These 'traditional' intellectuals help explain normative continuity at the state—not necessarily 'national'—level. Gramsci identified a second category of intellectual that links this ideological milieu with civil society. The 'organic intellectual' provides this linkage due to the intellectuals' organic connection (shared interests vested in the production system) to the ruling class. It is the organic intellectual that plays the crucial role of organising hegemony in civil society by making the idea system of the ruling class 'common sense' for the masses:

> Every social group, coming into existence on the original terrain of an essential function in the world of economic production, creates together with itself, organically, one or more strata of intellectuals which give it homogeneity and an awareness of its own function not only in the economic but also in the social and political fields.[9]

A number of scholars have applied Gramsci to the Egyptian case. Asef Bayat, for example, has argued in Gramscian terms that Egypt experienced a 'passive revolution' after 1967. For Bayat, this revolution was an Islamic one intelligible in largely cultural terms. That the revolution Bayat observes is largely one of ideas should not in any way detract from its overall significance. Culture wars have dominated recent Egyptian history and, as the sociologist Michael Mann has aptly observed, the stakes in such ideological struggles can be high:

> Ideological power derives from the human need to find ultimate meaning in life, to share norms and values, and to participate in aesthetic and ritual practices. Control of an ideology that combines ultimate meanings, values, norms, aesthetics and rituals brings general social power.[10]

For Bayat, the ever-expanding 'Islamic phenomenon' in Egypt, led by a variety of societal actors including the Muslim Brotherhood, drew sections of the elite into its ambit and also transformed ideology and identity at the level of the state, but without being able to unseat the incumbent regime. The Egyptian experience thus differs sharply from that of Iran, wherein a largely secular revolutionary trend catapulted the clergy into state power, which that clergy had subsequently to convert into ideological power via a top-down process. Whereas the Iranian Revolution constituted a 'war of manoeuvre', the Egyptian experience embodied an Islamist 'war of position', but one which ultimately stalled.[11]

Robert Bianchi, for his part, employs the concepts of corporatism and pluralism to illustrate the interpenetration of state and society in Egypt. Egyptian society can, for Bianchi, be divided into corporatist, pluralist and hybrid sectors. In the corporatist sectors the state enjoys considerable control, through cooptation and patronage, over actors and resources, whereas in the pluralist sectors societal actors enjoy relative independence from the state. Hybrid sectors combine elements of pluralism and corporatism. Taken as a whole the system represents:

> A persistently heterogeneous system of interest representation in which both pluralist and corporatist structures have played enduring roles, but in which neither mode of representation has attained anything approaching universal or permanent hegemony.

Bianchi concludes that 'the concepts of pluralism and corporatism are most useful when not regarded as diametrically opposed ideal types or as coherent moulds shaping whole political systems,'[12] warns us against thinking of Egypt as monolithic and problemitises the state-society dichotomy. Although the state sets out to control society by deploying corporatist strategies, this corporatism is 'unruly' and societal groups enjoy considerable freedom of manoeuvre.

Nazih Ayubi has also persuasively advanced reasons for the lack of hegemony in Egypt. Rejecting explanations that rest on the cultural specificity of Arabs or Muslims, or those that view the region in terms of 'democratic transition', Ayubi draws on Gramsci and others to suggest that the way in which Egypt encountered capitalism, via colonialism, resulted in the 'articulation' of modes of production. Although rejecting some aspects of the Marxist conception of an 'Asiatic mode of production', Ayubi argues that in Egypt 'the story of the modern state can be regarded in some ways as the political and institutional expression of an articulation between the Asiatic mode of production and the capitalist mode of production, characterised by a rapid move towards the superiority of the latter.'[13] The ruling class or regime may not have established control of the mode of persuasion (politics), and thus ideology or 'identity' as a whole may not reflect purely the world-view of the ruling group.

This reading of Egyptian political economy resonates with that of still more scholars, such as Rodinson, who highlights the difference between a 'capitalist sector' and a 'capitalist socioeconomic formation.' The capitalist sector in Egypt was nationalised after 1952, meaning that the capitalist mode of production adhered increasingly to the state, but that Egypt was not therefore a 'capitalist socioeconomic formation' as large parts of society continued to lie outside of the system and retained their own economic base, and concomitant political and ideo-logical characteristics.[14] Binder and Ansari, though proceeding from different philosophical assumptions, nonetheless reach a similar con-clusion in their analysis of the durable socio-political role of the rural middle class, or second stratum, on which the regime depends to rule, but because of which Egyptian national development has 'stalled.'[15] Likewise, the anthropologist Iliya Harik uncovered the limited rural penetration of Nasserism in the 1960s.[16]

Traditional clientalist forms of political association, particularly in the countryside but also in the recently urbanised cities, and in the linkages between state and society, persist. The 'informal' or 'parallel Islamic' sectors remain the locus of real political dynamism and efficacy in the country—as well as locations of ideological power—while the official institutions of state remain superficially separate, discredited and without real social depth or penetration.[17] The exceptions, one may expect, would be those institutions oriented towards the outside world that must conform to international norms, structures and expectations. But even here, as this book shows, the reality is more complicated and, particularly in its ideological dimensions, heterogeneous.

The lack of ideological hegemony, yet at the same time 'interpen-etration' of political and civil society, produces approaches to Israel that, implicitly or explicitly, encourage a division of labour between state and society in Egyptian foreign policy. There is a relationship between, on the one hand, the idea that Egypt's social movements have failed to seize the state, or that the Egyptian revolution has been 'passive'; and, on the other, the Camp David consensus that holds that state and society have divergent roles to play in foreign policy. The dualism is intelligible in terms of a statism/Arabism divide, as put forward by scholars like Barnett, but importantly this divide does not correspond to that between state and society.

Although Egypt has boasted a relatively open intellectual scene and numerous forms of legal and tolerated opposition, social and political movements have by and large stopped short of seeking to overthrow the state, instead being content to maximise their influence in society. Since the 1970s the regime has encouraged this pluralism, which, even though fake or 'delusional', has—particularly in the context of economic liberalisation—resulted in some decentralisation of power, or the dispersal of political power throughout state and society.[18] Mann defines political power explicitly as *state* power, and it follows for him that the group directing the state, the government or 'regime', enjoys the preponderance of political power.[19] For some, Egypt constitutes a 'bully praetorian state', relying on coercive institutional power and patronage networks to rule.[20] But while it would be foolish to deny the reality—and efficacy—of the Egyptian state's despotic power we should nevertheless expand our definition of the 'political' to do justice to the importance of the informal sector and interpenetration of state and society. If coveted political power does not *only* reside in the state, societal groups may be content with achieving general social power without risking outright confrontation with the state. It is this that explains much of the historical evolution of ideas on Israel, which have tended to absolve the state of responsibility for confronting Zionism.

For Albrecht, Egypt represents a case of 'inclusive authoritarianism'. Egyptian pluralism facilitates, rather than limits, the social control capacities of the state. Egypt's 'authoritarian opposition' serves several purposes for the regime: creating a veneer of legitimacy by providing a modicum of freedom and the suggestion that 'some' democracy exists; attracting rent from abroad based on commitment to political liberalisation; co-opting social groups into elite circles; channelling dissent for information gathering and social control functions; and moderating and de-radicalising potential resistance.[21] As a corollary to this, politics have been 'about' more than simply achieving their stated goals: 'economic and cultural policies are not measured by the policy makers along economic, cultural or social criteria alone. Rather they are weighed according to their impact on the incumbents' grip on power ...'[22]

Attitudes to Israel and Egyptian revolutions

The interpenetration of state and society—and its relevance to shifting representations of Israel—may be illustrated historically with reference to the integrative nature of nationalist revolutions in Egypt. As Abrahamian has noted, the term revolution has become a 'sponge word' soaking up diverse phenomena. For him, revolution means 'a sharp, sudden, and often violent change in the social location of political power, expressing itself in the radical transformation of the regime, of the official foundation of legitimacy, and of the state conception of the social order.'[23] In modern Egypt, three broad overlapping processes may fit this description—though not every change Abrahamian highlights occurred together or necessarily through sharp, sudden or violent movement. Egyptian revolutions have, from an early time, been, if not 'stalled', then certainly partial and limited. But the transformations in ideology, or the 'official foundation of legitimacy' have been significant and reflected in the shifting character of nationalism in Egypt.

Tom Nairn terms nationalism the 'modern Janus' to refer to the fact that societal actors striving to achieve certain progressive goals—industrialisation, prosperity, independence—look inwards and backwards to draw on indigenous identities. Nationalist intellectuals and leaders used these resources in a populist way to mobilise mass support. It is a controversial question the extent to which 'Islam' has constituted the only, or even primary, medium through which nationalism as a social movement can develop in Egypt or the broader Arab world. In the field of Middle East Studies, the backlash against 'Orientalism' sparked by Edward Said's 1978 book has led many to minimise or dismiss religion as a determinant of politics in the region. Work such as that of Benedict Anderson and Ernest Gellner has furthermore been influential in inducing scholars of the region to treat identity as not only constructed, but in a sense arbitrary. Nairn's contribution thus represents a useful corrective to this and allows us to bring Islam back in without returning to the reifications of Orientalism. For Nairn, nationalist movements do not simply 'invent' national identities, though they certainly embellish and frame them for maximum effect. The initial slate is far from blank: 'All that there *was* [for nationalists] was the people and peculiarities of the region: its inherited ethnos, speech, folklore, skin colour, and so on.'[24] In Egypt, a primarily rural society with a venerable Islamic past, that inherited ethnos was heavily tinted with religion and piety. This is not to say all Muslim Egyptians are latent Islamists, but that Islamism represents that trend of nationalism that recognises the centrality of religion to the lives of the people with whom its leaders aspire to connect.

It would be a mistake to interpret Islamic nationalism only in Hegelian terms, as embodying the spirit of the Egyptian 'nation' in the face of foreign oppression, much less Muslim hatred of the West. It also reflects social dynamics. As Nairn makes clear, the ideas of progress, equality and universal prosperity that underpin the philosophy of the Enlightenment were not widely understood as such in the less developed world. Only a tiny westernised elite accepted these ideas at face value. For the rest, progress and secularism really meant imperial domination, and nationalism emerged as a form of resistance to this. Islamic nationalism aimed at leveraging mass sentiment against colonialism and was led and developed by a rising middle class much broader than the narrow elite that accepted the imperialist myth that progress was Europe's gift to the world. As such, it should be treated as much as an expression of class interests as of Egypt's underdevelopment relative to the rest of the world.

Yet revolutionary leaders with specific goals in mind cannot always control the forces unleashed in furtherance of these goals, not least due to the ultimate divergence between the class interests of elite leaders and those of the strata below them. Nationalism thus evolved not only as a way for rising classes to confront imperial domination, but also as a way of enabling those classes to maintain their position in society. It promised freedom yet contained its own safety valves. Mannheim's sociology perhaps describes this dialectic best: ideology, which legitimises the status quo, nevertheless includes elements of 'utopia' that would, if realised, upset the established order, and vice versa. Islam represents in this sense ideology *par excellence*. The perennially debated imperative of *jihad*, for example, can be deferred or directed inwards (the Greater *Jihad*); invoked to justify defence against the external enemy; or seized upon to justify overthrowing an unjust ruler.[25]

The first phase of nationalist revolution in Egypt spanned a period from the 1870s to the 1950s encompassing the Orabi revolt and the upheavals of 1919, which marked the end of Turco-Circassian domination over the Egyptian political system, the rise of the Arabic-speaking middle class and the emergence of nationalism as the language of political action. Whereas from the latter part of the 19th century the language of change in Egypt was that of 'Salafi' Islam, as propagated by Jamal al-Din al-Afghani and Muhammad Abdu, the events of 1919 catapulted the Wafd Party, which would promote a liberal nationalist ideology, to national prominence. The second phase is that marked by the July Revolution of 1952, which saw new middle class officers seize control of the state, the monarchy abolished, the incumbent ruling class displaced, foreign occupation ended and much of the economy nationalised. The revolution would come to be defined by Nasserism, an ideology strongly informed by Islamist as well as Marxist ideology and reflecting not only international influences but also the lasting intellectual echoes of local communist and Islamist activism from the 1930s and 1940s. The third, which is ongoing, is the 'passive revolution' Bayat describes, or what others have viewed as 'counter-revolution',[26] which saw the resurgence of Islamic nationalism, the eclipse of the left and the rehabilitation of the private landholding and old capitalist class disenfranchised by Nasser. Although religion became increasingly prominent in Egyptian politics from at least the late 1950s it was not until Anwar Sadat became president that it came to more or less define those politics. From the 1970s Islamism was advanced by the Muslim Brotherhood and manifold other groups within what has been termed Egypt's 'devout bourgeoisie', elements of which have, especially from the 1990s, developed a qualified autonomy from the state.

1870s–1930s: from Islam to liberal nationalism

The years from the late 1870s until the 1920s saw the rise to political power of the native Arabic-speaking, predominantly Muslim, component of the landowning and bureaucratic bourgeoisie. It saw the consolidation of the economic and political power of this group at the expense of European, Armenian, Jewish, Syrian and Turko-Circassian bureaucrats and mercantilists more closely associated with the Khedival and Ottoman establishments. To the extent this movement involved 'mass' participation it utilised a system of ideas connected with Islam that lower, particularly rural, social strata regarded as meaningful and authentic: as the defence of Muslim land against the infidel, as the return to prominence of Arabic as not only the language of the Egyptians but of Islam, and as the reassertion of Egyptian Muslim interests in the face of Christian and Jewish residents increasingly portrayed as agents for the foreign powers.

The intellectuals around Colonel Ahmad Orabi initiated a pattern, reinforced by the Nationalist Party leader Mustafa Kamil and others in the early 20th century, that would prove both durable and successful: the more politicians and intellectuals felt the need to mobilise beyond the elite sphere, the more 'Islamic' became their discourse even if they were motivated by secular or 'modern' ideas or ambitions. Islamic nationalism provided a seamless link between international relations and culture experienced locally. But tempering populist calls to drive out the infidel in the 1880s we find the moderation of Muhammad Abduh. Abduh initially supported the Orabi movement but turned against it when it began to assume a mass-oriented character. Islamic modernism functioned, among other things, as a way to limit the extent to which Islam could be exploited to destabilise the Egyptian social fabric.[27] This also entailed an acceptance of the status quo internationally. As such, modernists like Abduh or, after him, Muhammad Shaltut, based their ideas on *jihad* 'on the recognition of national states in the Islamic world, belonging to an international order based on peaceful relations.'[28]

Abduh's ideas were, appropriately enough, based not only on Islamic thought but also on the conservative reaction to the Enlightenment in Europe—on Comptean positivism and the need to 'close the revolutionary period' by finding a system of ideas universally acceptable within the context of Egyptian society.[29] This was a language oriented towards reform, not revolution and thus functioned, in Mannheimian terms, as ideology and not utopia. It was not about overturning the social system in Egypt. It aimed at the advancement of the landowning bourgeoisie through modernisation, and sought to find a stable compromise between the unpredictable power of a mass movement and the inertia of traditional society and its worldview. But the overall goals of the populist movements around Orabi and then Mustafa Kamil on the one hand, and the intellectual trend around Abduh on the other, were mostly the same: to increase and defend the political power and economic prosperity of a growing bourgeoisie.

The evolving Islamic nationalism reflected a new middle class's struggle for advancement in the face of colonialism, but it had the potential to be deeply divisive within Egyptian society. Even though championed by an economically dominant class, Islamic nationalism was replete with 'utopian' elements that, if realised, would upset the status quo. Peasant and worker protest, whipped up in the wake of the 'Dinshaway' incident in 1906, for example, spiralled out of hand, producing violence and 'terrorism' against 'foreign' targets.[30] Many who had initially supported the nationalist movement assumed a more critical position vis-à-vis Kamil and his associates.[31]

The risk that Islamic nationalism could threaten the interests of the middle class was thrown into stark relief with the assassination of the Coptic prime minister Boutros Ghali in 1910. If Islamic nationalism could help the elite political parties achieve progress and advancement by leveraging mass sentiment, the assassination of Ghali and subsequent sectarian tensions threatened to undermine this project. Copts, like non-Egyptian Christians (Armenians, Europeans, Syrians) and Jews were prominently represented in political and economic life. As such they could easily be lumped together with the British as the main enemy. But Copts were also part of the rural social fabric and were often large landowners. Unchecked chauvinism could therefore easily lead the nation into sectarian civil war.

According to literary scholar Muhammad Muhammad Husayn, the assassination of Boutros Ghali, more than any other event, was instrumental in convincing intellectuals of the day that a more cosmopolitan Egyptian—rather than Islamic—nationalism was the best way forward.[32] In an early example of 'deradicalisation', Egyptian 'territorial' nationalism took shape in the second decade of the 20th century, articulated by intellectuals like Ahmed Lutfi al-Sayyid and, later, Sa'ad Zaghlul and the Wafd Party. As Vatikiotis puts it, 'more moderate Muslim Egyptian leaders were abandoning [the Islamic] trend in favour of a pragmatic consideration of local Egyptian interests within the context of the social, economic and political conditions of Egypt.'[33] The period following Boutros Ghali's death saw the 'eclipse of the early nationalist movement which hardly distinguished between modern Egyptian national interests and demands on the one hand, and sentiments of Pan-Islamic solidarity on the other.'[34]

The liberal or territorial variant of nationalism was, unlike the Islamic, adopted directly from the West and was largely incomprehensible to the mass of the Egyptian population. Even the Pharaonic heritage that became so central to it was learnt from European Egyptologists. It did not bring with it ideological power, a fact that would render its elite exponents increasingly vulnerable as the Egyptian political community broadened and deepened. Liberal nationalism expressed the elite's acceptance that Britain was very much in charge, that Egyptian sovereignty was circumscribed, and that change would be gradual.

There was certainly no appetite among the landholding class for a general war against colonialism: its economic interests were largely served by the link with Britain and international trade, landowners needed the peasantry to remain on the land, and there was always the danger that a mass-based nationalist movement would move beyond sectarianism and acquire a deeper social revolutionary dimension. Liberalism, as it was understood by many Egyptian intellectuals of the time, was not a value system in which the masses would be able to participate: what was required first was education in order to raise the intellectual level of the population such that they would be able to participate in modernity. Although the Wafd was immensely popular following the revolution of 1919, its prestige stemmed not from any widespread approval for liberal nationalism but from its perceived victory against imperialism. The Wafd was careful, moreover, not to attack Islam,[35] and the political consciousness they were able to exploit had been raised by the Islamic nationalists that preceded them.

Early approaches to Zionism reflected the concerns of Egypt's dominant, though still colonised, classes. Until the 1930s, Egyptian political and intellectual elites—including those of the Wafd—were little concerned with events in neighbouring Palestine. To the extent they were, their engagement centred on the potential of a Zionist threat to Egypt's sovereign interests and the risk that growing public sympathy for Palestinians, as oppressed fellow Muslims, could redound upon the government in the event of inaction or ambivalence, or be exploited in a populist way for support. Concern for the plight of Palestinians was expressed in terms of the rights of Arabs and Jews in Palestine and the desired strategy for dealing with Zionism was one of peaceful diplomacy and gradualism, as with the prevailing Wafdist approach towards Britain. But the government gradually came to express it in Islamic terms as well.

To the extent international relations entered the popular imagination, they did so in Islamic terms bound up with fidelity towards the Caliphate and solidarity with the rest of the Muslim world, the *umma*. Populist intellectuals had portrayed Britain as Christian and infidel since the time of Orabi, with the struggle against colonialism a kind of *jihad*. Hasan al-Banna's Muslim Brotherhood, founded in 1928, similarly conceptualised *jihad* as an obligation in these terms. Zionism, unsurprisingly, was simply 'Jewish' colonialism. Arab solidarities emerged later and were, from the beginning, intimately bound up with preconceptions about the Arabs' status within Islam.[36]

1930s–1960s: the formation and apogee of Nasserism

From the 1930s, the dramatic expansion of the middle class meant that the liberal version of nationalism became unsustainable. In what has been termed the 'tragedy of the liberal intellectual' in the Arab world, the previous generation of bourgeois elite intellectuals, who felt that an undiluted liberal nationalism could bring their states into the modern age, soon ran up against a wall of incomprehension and resentment from the classes below them who, during the interwar period, began to develop their own ideologies.[37] The rise of the Muslim Brotherhood and other more popular nationalist forces in that decade shook the liberal complacency that a secular Europeanised government could survive the ideological disconnect with society—the absence of ideological power at the state level. The power of the Brotherhood was testimony to the enduring centrality of Islam as the common value system in Egypt. Islamic nationalism continued to function as the expression of the aspirations of a rising middle class for economic, political and ideological power in the Egyptian state context, and the need to both create and connect with a mass constituency in order to achieve this. This broad and heterogeneous class is often referred to during the interwar period as the *effendiyya*.[38]

Those involved in the heterogeneous nationalist movement were motivated, at least in part, by resentment and frustration against the Westernised elites that monopolised political and economic power in the country. Nineteen-fifties Egypt was a melting pot of new ideas directed against an increasingly discredited liberal 'experiment.' But most importantly, although the group of officers that seized power in 1952 had been involved, to varying degrees of intensity, in all the major political movements of the 1930s and 1940s, it was not as the head, or in the name, of any one of these movements that the new Egyptian republic was established. As such, the dualism and tension that characterised politics in the age of imperialism continued into the independence period. The ideas developed to underpin Egyptian foreign policy towards Israel represent an oblique reflection of this dualism.

The Muslim Brothers had been probably the strongest popular anti-colonial movement, gathering strength rapidly from the 1930s. By 1952, when the Free Officers seized power, the Brotherhood not unreasonably supposed that they would rule once the military had returned to barracks. So too did parts of the much weaker communist movement. Until 1954 the distinction between regime and Brotherhood organisationally as well as ideologically—and hence the distribution of power between them—was not obvious. Members of the Revolutionary Command Council (RCC), including Sadat and Nasser, had been involved in the Brotherhood, Young Egypt and other Islamic nationalist groupings prior to the coup. The Brotherhood referred to the revolution as their own 'blessed movement' and Sayyid Qutb, who would later become the regime's most potent ideological foe, occupied an office in the RCC's building.[39]

Instead, the Brotherhood was crushed and its members rounded up and imprisoned. While the suppression of the Wafd and the other 'aristocratic' parties can be viewed in conventional 'social' revolutionary terms as the triumph of a rising middle class, the treatment meted out to the Brotherhood (as also, incidentally, to the Egyptian communists) involved a horizontal rather than vertical displacement. The events of 1954 represented the suppression by one part of the *effendiyya* (the military) of another. But once the military consolidated its power a new 'state bourgeoisie' cohered around the regime, which from 1956 monopolised economic and ideological power.[40] Previous class divisions became less salient as closeness to the regime and its patronage networks became the new signifier of socioeconomic standing and the Brotherhood remained, by dint of its opposition and the threat it posed, on the outside.

The state bourgeoisie included the inner circles of the regime as well as those favoured with positions in nationalised businesses, press, the single party and other organs of state. The regime was preoccupied initially with obliterating any independent threat to its own control—namely the Muslim Brotherhood and, to a lesser extent, the communists. Having accomplished this via the simultaneous creation of a mass party (the Liberation Rally) and the physical eradication of the Brotherhood's structures, the regime moved to a phase of seeking to pre-empt any new ideological and organisational challenges (the National Union). Until the creation of the Arab Socialist Union (ASU) in 1961, though, there was no attempt to build an organic connection between the ruling group and the mass of the population. Instead Nasser relied mainly on his own charisma.[41]

Partially because the ideologically based social movements, whose success owed much to their linkage of the international and domestic struggles, did not take power in 1952, the new regime adopted an ambiguous and tentative position ideologically for the first three years of its existence. When Nasserism emerged as official ideology, in which anti-Zionism and anti-imperialism were paramount, it did so largely due to the influence of the external environment and was articulated by Marxist intellectuals that had, prior to the revolution, enjoyed connections with some or other of the Free Officers, but who wrote, worked and remained at liberty solely at Nasser's pleasure.

The end of British military occupation deprived the regime of an historic enemy against which to rally the masses. Intellectuals transferred the anti-colonial, anti-imperialist enmity that had underpinned the national movement prior to 1952 from Britain to Israel (which was, after all, one of the 'tripartite aggressors' of Suez). Anti-colonialism became a unified anti-Zionism and anti-imperialism, with confronting each coterminous with national liberation and socialist revolution. Nasserism as an ideology contained strong utopian elements. But Nasser was never serious about destroying Israel nor achieving the 'unity of progressive forces' across the Middle East. The societal group most eager to hold Nasser to his socialist revolutionary promises—the Egyptian Communist Party—was suppressed then co-opted and was unable to build an independent power base. Arab socialism, much like the liberalism that had enchanted an earlier generation of elites, offered little to those parts of the population that lay outside the regime's patronage networks. This, as much as its supposed lack of authenticity, hindered its development. The values of sovereignty and statism championed by the Wafd and the *ancien régime* continued into the post-revolutionary era, and were tacitly accepted by the leftists and Islamists that accepted to work within the established system.

1960s–2000s: apogee of Islamism?

The 'corrective revolution' of May 1971 may seem a grandiose way to describe a personnel change at the regime level. But if not approached just as an event, but rather as a process over which Anwar Sadat had limited control and likely little awareness, its revolutionary credentials emerge more strongly. Part of the process arguably began towards the end of the 1950s when certain Brotherhood figures (such as Muhammad al-Ghazali and Kamal Abu al-Magd) were tempted into the orbit of the state and contributed to a certain Islamisation of regime ideology.[42] The Brotherhood itself split, into a moderate, accommodating (and mainstream) trend around Hasan al-Hudaybi and a more radical orientation around Sayyid Qutb.[43] The latter's ideas reflected the outrage and impatience of those not only excluded, but incarcerated and tortured by the military regime. Just as Nasserism channelled antipathy to British colonialism to Israel and Zionism, Qutb redirected the Brotherhood's anti-imperialist *jihad* of the 1940s against the Nasserist system, which he presented as an extension or continuation of the Zionist and crusader threat. The rise of radical Islamism at this time is intelligible as a reaction to the absolutism of Nasserism, and as a bid for political and ideological power.[44]

Sadat gave this revolutionary process its needed impetus. Following his triumph over rival 'centres of power' and consolidation of control over the state in May 1971, Sadat adopted policies that would dramatically reconfigure the distribution of ideological and economic power in Egypt. As Kepel has shown, the release of Brotherhood cadres from prison and the space opened up for Islamist mobilisation and proselytising, combined with the significant economic opportunities created by the 'Open Door' (*infitah*) liberalisation programme to allow the Brotherhood and other members of an emerging private sector to gain significant economic and ideological power.[45] The private sector, particularly those favoured by economic links with the Gulf (including many exiled Brothers) and rehabilitated elements of the old aristocracy, formed a part of what has been termed Egypt's 'devout bourgeoisie'.[46] The president adopted a markedly more Islamic posture. The intelligentsia that had laboured to sustain Nasserism as an ultimately superficial ideology gradually gave way, at all levels of political and civil society, to Islamist groups and intellectuals that were sponsored and encouraged by the regime and rapidly rebuilt their popular following.

The Sadatist reforms represented tangible advancement for those sectors of the middle and upper classes that had been excluded from the patronage networks of Nasser's state. But in dismantling the political, economic and ideological underpinnings of Nasser's state, Sadat was devaluing the political power that accrued to his own regime and devolving it to a private sector bourgeoisie, a significant portion of which found political expression in the Muslim Brotherhood. The Brotherhood's enmeshment within the new bourgeoisie ('crony capitalists') created by *infitah* has been convincingly demonstrated and is perhaps epitomised in the figure of the construction magnate Osman Ahmad Osman, Sadat's showcase capitalist and Brotherhood supporter.[47]

Nasser's 'Arabism' had, at least in part, represented an attempt to mollify potential opposition, and maintain the prestige of the Egyptian revolution, while he pursued an essentially statist policy towards Israel, the alleged manifestation of imperialism. Increasing reliance on the USSR, the rise of socialism regionally, and refusal to accept the Muslim Brotherhood as a partner in government combined to encourage the 'left-wing' character of Nasserism. Having turned his back on Nasser's leftwing nationalism, Sadat embraced parts of Islamism and allowed the Islamist social movement to regroup. But at the same time he more explicitly embraced statism, moving steadily away from the pan-Arab revolutionary rhetoric of Nasser. Eventually the revolutionary norms that had underpinned Nasserism—and the state of 'no war, no peace' with Israel—gave way to the Camp David consensus, whereby the state formally ended the state of war with Israel and responsibility for the struggle shifted into society.

From the early 1990s a new generation of private-sector entrepreneurs and businesspeople embraced the more substantial neoliberal reforms initiated by the IMF. Unlike the *infitah* 'cronies' created by Sadat, which overlapped closely with the state, this new group lacked direct links with and often competed with the state. It depended on the state for security, infrastructure and services, yet suffered from the absence of an organic connection. As the rise of parties like *al-Ghad* (Tomorrow) led by the embattled Ayman Nur, and the much broader *Kefaya* (Enough!) movement—as well as the repeated clashes between the regime and the Muslim Brotherhood show—relations could be highly conflictual when parts of this new middle class sought political expression and contestation. Khalil al-Anani has described the relationship as the 'grudging alliance.'[48]

By one estimate, the 'Brotherhood economy' is worth around seven billion Egyptian pounds. This includes companies whose profits go to the Muslim Brotherhood as well as those owned by Muslim Brotherhood members. Senior Muslim Brothers like Khayrat Shatir and Hasan Malik command substantial fortunes and employ many hundreds or thousands of Egyptians, many of whom are also members of the Muslim Brotherhood. They too exist in this grudging alliance with the regime.[49] Most importantly, though, the Muslim Brotherhood offers a parallel structure of belonging, meaning and advancement for middle class Egyptians. Not only does it provide social services for the poor, but it can offer access to employment, sociability and prestige parallel and even superior to those of the state. This is significant for the diffusion of political power in Egypt and helps explain some of the persistent heterogeneity of the Egyptian political system that is in turn reflected in dominant approaches to Israel.

Structural adjustment also involved the privatisation of the rural economy, much of which had been either dominated by the state or subject to restrictions since the Nasser era, particularly via the Agrarian Reform Law. This law was amended in the mid-1980s and again in the 1990s to allow rent to be dictated by market forces, landholdings to grow in size and leases to be terminated at landlords' discretion. The reforms resulted in massive redundancies of peasant labour and the deflation of wages, and the resultant reservoirs of discontent go some way towards explaining the growing appeal of both the *Jama'a Islamiyya* (Islamic Group) and the Muslim Brotherhood in the 1980s and 1990s. Paradoxically, though not without logic, neither of these groups advocates returning to the previous system. Knee-jerk anti-socialism offers only part of the explanation: the more instrumentalist interpretation is the calculation that more landless and miserable peasants would mean more supporters for the Islamists. The Islamist groups were there to provide spiritual and material solace, and security for dislocated rural workers and for villagers and townsfolk against rising crime. The devolution of economic power thus resulted in a dividend of ideological power for societal Islamist groups, away from the state as guarantor of security and employment, and from the established holders of ideological power in the settled agrarian context: Sufi brotherhoods and representatives of the religious establishment.[50] There are even some signs that the regime is encouraging the *Jama'a Islamiyya* [Islamic Group] and other *Salafi* actors to act as, potentially safer, alternatives to the Brotherhood, focussing on moral issues and the societal war with Zionism rather than political confrontation with the state.[51]

While *infitah*, and from the early 1990s structural adjustment, provides one lens through which to view the devaluation of political power at the state level, Sadat's foreign policy provides another. Quickly after the October 1973 war, Sadat moved to make peace with Israel, primarily to remove the main barrier to rapprochement with the United States. The other impediment, Egypt's strategic alliance with the Soviet Union, was also overcome when Sadat expelled thousands of Soviet technicians in 1972 and later abrogated the Friendship Treaty in 1977. By throwing Egypt wholeheartedly into the American embrace, Sadat dealt Egyptian sovereignty a serious blow, or at least that was how many Egyptian intellectuals and political activists saw it: the prize of control over the Egyptian state may have seemed less appealing when the real master was an immovable colonial, or imperial, power. More importantly, Islamists have felt that the risk of sanction, or worse, forcible intervention from the United States and the West far outweighs any possible benefits that would accrue from taking the state.[52]

Conclusion

Approaches to Israel have been elaborated with reference, though have not always been reducible, to broader ideologies and worldviews associated with these revolutionary epochs, specifically liberal nationalism, Marxism and Islamism. They have combined 'statist' with 'societal' paradigms. Ideologies or identities do not emerge fully formed at the nation-state level. They are, rather, digested and elaborated by intellectuals attached to social movements that, if successful, manage to have their version of reality accepted as 'national identity'. A distinctive feature of the Egyptian case is that no socio-political movement has had such success. In this sense national revolution in Egypt is 'stalled' or incomplete, but there also exists a degree of consensus that this dualistic situation should persist, arguably in light of the fact that since the late 19th century it always has. The reality of the Egyptian situation, moreover, has formed the prism through which Egyptian intellectuals have viewed the world, including international relations.

It is thus unsurprising that representations of Israel have constituted a mirror image of Egyptian conceptions of self, but these representations have been dynamic and multiple. Delving deeper into anti-Zionism soon reveals the pitfalls of generalisation at the state level. Attitudes towards Israel have not been so much reflections of state or national identity as they have of the worldviews and understandings of sub-state groupings, social movements and the intellectuals associated with them. Conceptions of Israel expressed, and apparently acted upon, at the state level do not replace or defeat other narratives and understandings within society. They rather form part of a broader composite foreign policy picture. Viewing Egyptian representations of Israel historically reveals a clear link between those representations and group interests at the sub-state level.

This approach not only shows major ruptures, like the 1967 war, in a new light, but also helps explain some of the silences in Middle Eastern international politics, such as the so-called 'cold peace' between Egypt and Israel. Scholars have, for obvious reasons, been far more interested in explaining war and establishing the conditions for peace than in explicating the grey areas of 'no war, no peace' that have often prevailed in the region. The very premise of 'normal' relations between states is itself problematic and there is no reason to suspect that relations between states, or between state and society, in the Middle East are in any sense moving towards any international norm. What indeed, as Anne Mosely-Lesch wonders 'are the natural relations between two peoples and states that have fought bitter wars and that still differ over fundamental aspects of the conflict ... ?'[53] This book provides a framework through which we may begin to resolve such ambiguities.

In the chapters that follow I examine the dominant ways in which Israel has been conceptualised by regimes and intellectuals in Egypt since the beginning of the Nasser period. The book surveys a range of writings from political thinkers and commentators associated with prominent social and political forces in Egypt, as well as the statements of Nasser, Sadat and Mubarak. Rather than scrutinising these works in isolation, or only in relation to each other, it examines them in social and political context. An interpretive work, it is not intended to cover everything written about Israel in Egypt over this long timescale. It is, rather, aimed at historicising and explaining approaches to Israel as they have recurred in Egyptian political discourse and providing a more multi-dimensional analysis of Egyptian foreign policy.

Chapter Two discusses the 'melting pot' phase during which Egyptian intellectuals, political movements and leaders began grappling with the issues of Zionism and Palestine. It examines the emerging positions of the Wafd government, as well as those of the political movements of the new middle class, specifically the Muslim Brotherhood and the communist movement. This chapter also examines the first three years of the Free Officers' regime, up to the Bandung conference of 1955, before the formation of Nasserism as a set of ideas linking domestic and foreign policies.

Chapter Three deals with the decade between the Suez and the Six-Day wars, which may be described as the 'heyday' of Nasserism. It highlights the importance, on a regional level, of sub-state groupings as well as states, to the formation of ideas in Egypt. In addition to highlighting the Marxist categories that underpinned Nasser's conception of Israel as an appendage of US imperialism, the chapter also discusses the characteristics and influence of the Islamist trend under Nasser, elements of statism in regime and intellectual discourse, and the effect this balancing act the regime was forced to play between left and right had on the ways in which Israel was conceptualised.

Chapters Four and Five focus more closely on the 'long' 1970s, from 1967 to 1979. Chapter Four covers the period between 1967 and 1973. This crucial time between the shock of the June War and the partial vindication of October 1973 witnessed a number of influential interventions and shifts on the topic of Israel. The chapter traces the division of the left between Nasserists and an Arab 'new left' and analyses writings on the conflict with Israel from both perspectives. It also examines important liberal and Islamist interventions of the period, the role of the 1972 student movement, and Sadat's own discourse prior to the October War.

Chapter Five examines the process leading up to the Camp David Accords and Egypt-Israel Peace Treaty. It discusses the economic, political and foreign policy reorientations of the period—particularly *infitah* and the dismantling of the Arab Socialist Union, as well as ideological formulations in the 1974 October Paper. It analyses the rise of Islamism and the writings of the Muslim Brotherhood, as well as the interventions of a weakened, but still vocal, Egyptian left. It deals in detail with a number of works that synthesise the diverse traditions on understanding Israel that, in different ways, reflect the Camp David consensus that will come to define the post-Sadat era.

Chapter Six discusses some of the ways in which ideas on Israel evolved during Mubarak's long tenure, under the shadow of revolution in Iran, the rise of Islamic militancy and ongoing domestic struggles on the left and right. The writings analysed in this chapter include those from a 'liberal' perspective, and those that support normalisation. But most reflect the massive cultural influence of Islamic nationalism in Egypt, as well as the considerable synergies between Egyptian social movements that reveal the Camp David consensus at work.

I should stress in closing this introductory chapter that my intention is not to suggest that Egyptians do not care deeply for the plight of the Palestinians or that they are only driven by selfish 'instrumentalist' impulses. Nor is it to imply that the Israel-Palestine issue is merely one of perception or that no 'real' conflict exists. It is rather to show that Egyptian intellectual and governmental attitudes to Israel have been strongly influenced by the prism of Egyptian political, cultural and social realities, as they have been shaped, framed and reinforced by the processes of nationalism and revolution described above. Israel is inextricably a part of the Egyptian collective imagination and self-perception. No understanding of Egyptian foreign policy is complete without recognition of this factor.

CHAPTER 2

THE FORMATION OF IDEAS ON ISRAEL (1936–1956)

The seminal theorist of international politics, E.H. Carr, stressed the importance of the broader, particularly literate, public to the actualisation of foreign policy: it is 'not only professional thinkers' who are influenced by international and foreign policy factors, he wrote, but everyone who 'reads the political columns of a newspaper or attends a political meeting or discusses politics with his neighbour' such that 'the judgement which he forms becomes ... a factor in the course of political events.'[1] The Interwar period marked a general democratisation, or at least popularisation, of foreign affairs throughout the world, and in Egypt the role of Palestine was central.

From an early stage Egyptian approaches to Zionism were as much a part of internal social change and turmoil as they were about international relations. They reflected statist influences as well as newer, more 'ideological', considerations. The paradigms for understanding Israel during the Nasser period represented continuations of ideas and syntheses articulated by intellectuals, from left and right, of a new middle class in the pre-revolutionary period. The Palestinian Revolt of 1936–1939 was pivotal. The proximity of the events, presence of Palestinians in Egypt, and the campaigning of new popular political movements, mainly the Muslim Brotherhood, made the Palestine issue one of domestic political import. There was thus an important linkage established between Egyptian foreign policy towards Israel,

Egyptian public opinion and public policy that continues to dominate the intellectual and political landscape in Egypt today.

In this chapter I chart the changing attitude of the Wafd Party— the most significant political force in the Interwar period—towards Zionism, and particularly its balancing between statism and the need to 'go down' to the masses and engage with the issue of Zionism in religious terms. I then move on to more closely analyse the elaboration of more 'Arabist' approaches to Zionism and Israel from within the Islamist and communist movements, both of which were competing for influence within a growing new middle class in the 1930s and 1940s. Finally, the chapter elucidates the ambiguous attitude of the Free Officers regime towards Israel until 1955 as reflecting a combination of statism and Islamism due to the dual influence of Egypt's external environment and the only significant social movement in the country, the Muslim Brotherhood.

Palestine, Zionism and the Wafd

The two decades discussed in this chapter were of vital importance to the evolution of patterns of political interaction and discourse in Egypt and to the formation of the Egyptian republic's foreign policy fundamentals. Until 1948 the Wafd Party had succeeded in building and maintaining a political consensus around the concept of peaceful change. It won popular support for its gradualist, diplomatic approach to achieving British evacuation (*jala'*), and was widely perceived, because of its mass popularity, to be the only Egyptian political force capable of reaching compromise solutions with Britain. The Wafd sought to replicate this strategy in its approach to the Palestine question, to walk the same thin line between appeasing Britain whilst retaining credibility as the vanguard of a popular nationalist movement. But the politicisation of the issue, and the related decision by King Faruq to declare war in 1948, rendered this gradualist 'liberal' approach increasingly untenable.

In 1936, through the Anglo-Egyptian treaty, Egypt formally acquired an independent foreign policy. Prior to this, Egypt's international relations were dictated by Britain as the colonial power. The new Egyptian government's first point of divergence from British preferences was on the Palestine issue. Prime Minister Nahhas opposed the idea of partitioning Palestine. He justified the stance on pragmatic, legal and emotional grounds. Pragmatically, he argued that the Arabs in the neighbouring lands would not accept the creation of a Jewish state in Palestine. This in turn he linked to the religious and historical rights of the Palestinian Arabs to the land containing the holy places of Islam. This did not, however, compromise the Wafd's essentially liberal outlook, which was predicated on the 'rights' of the people of the region and a relatively inclusive conception of citizenship. Foreign minister Wasif Boutros Ghali, for example, in addition to championing the rights of Arab inhabitants of Palestine, wanted to 'preserve in a special way the rights of Jews living in Palestine, who have become Palestinians just like Muslims and Christians in the country.'[2]

Egyptian premier Ali Maher and the future Arab League secretary general Abd al-Rahman al-Azzam's attendance at the London Palestine Conference in 1939 signalled the beginning of the Egyptian government's intentions to pursue an Arab policy.[3] Seale and other scholars adduce 'realist' explanations for the Pan-Arab foreign policy of Egypt prior to 1952 and see a continuity in Egypt's pursuit of a statist policy to dominate the region.[4] For others, Egypt's emerging Arab orientation, of which Palestine would constitute a central element, was encouraged by the social development of the country since World War One. The expanding bourgeoisie, epitomised by the banker Tala't Harb and others, was seeking new markets and commercial ventures.[5] But this factor alone does not fully account for growing anti-Zionism, as there is no obvious reason why Egyptian capitalists could not just as easily have had dealings with Jews.

The popularisation of the Palestine cause

The formation of a new regional orientation for Egyptian elites, was decisively encouraged by developments on the popular level. As the antagonism felt by Palestinians towards Zionism sharpened, and particularly through the Wailing Wall riots of 1929, Egyptians were alerted to the plight of Palestinians, at first mainly as fellow Muslims.[6] Following these riots, the Wafd Party began a tentative engagement with the questions of Zionism and Palestine, also on a religious basis, depicting Zionism as a Jewish threat to Islam and its holy places. Nahhas recognised that the Palestine issue was one that could rebuild the popular appeal and credibility of the party, and government, in the face of criticism over the terms of the 1936 Treaty. He encouraged newspapers to publish freely on Palestine, which itself contributed to a general increase in Arabist feeling among the Egyptian reading public.[7]

This differed markedly from the situation previously. Until the 1930s, 'neither the press nor the parties represented in parliament, not to mention the general public, took more than a passing interest in the developments in neighbouring Palestine.'[8] The old elites—Arabic-speaking large landowners and professionals connected with the international cotton trade—set the political agenda. Although some Egyptian nationalist historians attribute the Egyptian government's reluctance to engage proactively on the side of the Arabs of Palestine to the influence of Jewish capitalists in Egypt, the ruling class as a whole at that time was not merely ambivalent about the plight of the Palestinian Arabs but fearful of the implications of supporting their revolt.[9] Indeed, as Tariq al-Bishri crisply puts it, 'the interests of the large landowners of Egypt were linked to the idea of Egyptianism isolated from both the Arabs externally and the Egyptian people internally.' The government thus stood 'against the revolution of the Palestinian people,' while a landowner-oriented newspaper, *al-Siyasa,* 'threatened Palestinian nationals in Egypt with expulsion for arousing public opinion, fearing the wrath of Britain on any action that might provoke the Egyptian people to revolt.'[10]

By 1939, the domestic utility for the Wafd of supporting the Palestinians against Zionism had surpassed that of the strategic alliance with Britain and serving the interests of the Egyptian landowning class in maintaining stability. As al-Bishri notes, 'the Palestine cause had entered the fabric of Egyptian political life and become one of the arenas of conflict and competition between the national movement with its different strands and the reactionary powers.' The Wafd, the King and elite intellectuals were playing an increasingly reactive role in politics in general. As 'popular' movements, the Muslim

Brotherhood, communists, Young Egypt and the left-wing 'Wafdist vanguard' naturally foregrounded the role of the Egyptian people in the anti-colonial struggle; while the government prioritised the diplomatic and statist advances it had made and would continue to make, resisting the societal approach because of the revolutionary implications it would have for the Egyptian constitutional monarchy.

Zionism, and ultimately the State of Israel, came to be perceived as a domestic issue with cultural, political and economic dimensions. Popular anti-colonialism was directed not just against Britain but also against Zionism. Following Britain's violent response to the Palestinian Revolt, for the Muslim Brotherhood, 'Britain's position was one of enmity and a clear challenge to the Islamic world and it was not possible, given this, that the relations between Britain and the Muslim peoples would ever improve.'[11] Islamists and other nationalists in Egypt came to perceive a unity of goals and strategies between Zionism, imperialism and the Egyptian ruling elites. As such the *jihad* of Izz al-Din al-Qassam against Jews in Palestine merged conceptually with the *jihad* to oust Britain from Egypt and, perhaps most troubling for the monarchy and parties of the establishment, raised the spectre of violent revolution. Approaches to Zionism reflected the politicisation of Egyptian society in general as elite intellectuals were forced to accept a societal role in foreign policy.[12] Egyptian political culture was in transition from a gradualist, compromising and peaceful approach to securing independence to a more militant revolutionary orientation.

King Faruq's use of the war option against Israel in May 1948 was arguably at least as much about cementing the legitimacy and popularity of the monarchy as it was about protecting Egypt from the Zionist enemy. It was partially intended to demonstrate the power of the Egyptian state and its political system and deflate the popular movement for change by presenting itself as the true embodiment of Egyptian national, and Islamic, aspirations. Thus, the decision to launch the attack was presented in religious terms:

... when in May 1948 Britain withdrew from Palestine and the first Arab-Israeli war broke out, one of the reasons Nokrashy

Pasha, the prime minister, gave in parliament when asking for a declaration of war was that Israel was the vanguard of world communism. He cited the kibbutz movement to press his point. Both houses of parliament, in fact, voted for war against Israel 'in defence of Arab rights and against Communist atheism and nihilism.'[13]

The humiliation of defeat, however, had the opposite effect. It completely discredited the monarchy and the establishment as a whole and hastened the momentum for revolution.

The Muslim Brotherhood

The Muslim Brotherhood, founded by Hasan al-Banna in 1928, developed rapidly in the 1930s and 1940s into a formidable societal force. After the promulgation of the United Nations Partition Plan in October 1947 al-Banna ordered his followers to prepare for *jihad*. But he was, significantly, not exhorting the Egyptian state to intervene:

It was Banna's feeling ... that governments as such should not be involved in the Palestine question beyond the diplomatic and political support they could give the Arabs in Palestine; that if fighting became a necessity, it should be left to the Palestinians themselves and to 'volunteers.'[14]

From the beginning, the Brotherhood was a pragmatic political actor that did not reject everything for which the government stood, and it accepted the necessity of protecting Egypt as a state. Ideas flowed up and down the social and generational ladder. Thus, just as Prime Minister Nahhas—responding to the arrival of an Islamic public on the political scene—spoke out in the late 1930s against the formation of a Jewish state on Egypt's borders,[15] the Brotherhood's discourse was influenced by the more statist and strategic discourses of the Wafd and other parties. The Brotherhood argued that 'historically the security of Egypt had always been linked to that of Palestine. *Any threat* to Egypt had almost always come from beyond Sinai and Egypt's decisive battles had always been fought in al-Sham (historic Syria) and especially Palestine.'[16] In 1938 Hasan al-Banna declared, again in distinctly statist terms, that 'we want to secure our eastern borders by solving the Palestinian problem in a way that meets the Arab point of view and prevents a Jewish takeover of the amenities of this country ... We demand this as it secures our borders and represents our direct interests.'[17]

Given their aspirations to lead a *popular* anti-colonial movement, new political movements like the Muslim Brotherhood were primarily responsible for developing foreign policy paradigms that related international issues (at the top of which was the Palestine question) to their own pivotal roles in the national movement. Through their *da'wa* (proselytising) activities, Islamic activists sought to harness and reinforce the pre-existing cultural dominance of Islam in Egyptian society. But as with any successful nationalist movement, the Muslim Brotherhood combined elements of universalism (serving Islam and the welfare of the entire world) with the particularities of the Egyptian situation. The religious frame through which it viewed its role in the world and the question of Zionism had important implications for the Brotherhood's domestic strategies:

The importance of this attitude cannot be over-emphasised ... its implications were many, for the foreigner—the *khawaja*— was invariably a Christian or Jew; the posture of the Society [of the Muslim Brotherhood] 'in defence of Islam' led necessarily to a view of the foreigner which included religious and cultural as well as political and economic objections. And not the least of the implications of this view was the identification of the foreigner with the *local* Christian or Jew, a relationship between majority religious and cultural inferiority and the minority.[18]

The Brotherhood was also accessing, and modifying, an Islamic discourse on Jews. In the modern Egyptian context, the most politically dynamic part of that tradition was the Islamic reformist trend associated with Rashid Rida and his mentor Muhammad Abduh. Abduh sought to rejuvenate Islam for the modern age both as a means of governance and of resisting European domination. A central assumption of this project was that Islam, or the way it was followed in places like Egypt, had fallen into decay over the centuries since the time of the Prophet. One of the reasons for this decay, *salafists* argued, was that 'it had become distorted during its historical development ... largely as a result of the incorporation of sources at odds with its rational essence.'[19] Of such distortions in *hadith*, *tafsir* and *fiqh*, those introduced via Jewish sources, the *Isra'iliyat*, were deemed to be among the most pernicious.[20] Rida identified two Persian Jews who had converted to Islam as the main culprits[21] and another *salafist* thinker, Mahmud Abu Rayya, 'conflated early Jewish convert transmitters with Zionist Jews in pre-1948 Palestine.' Abu Rayya, Taji-Farouki argues, interwove 'perceptions concerning the *Isra'iliyat* and their 'Jewish' transmitters as a critical problem in early Islam with the contemporary challenge posed by Zionist Jews in Palestine.'[22]

Brotherhood thinkers continued the 'presentist' practice of reading back into history the roots of the Zionist problem. In the 1940s and early 1950s a sympathiser, though not yet member, of the Brotherhood, Sayyid Qutb, elaborated a vision of a 14-century conflict between Islam and Judaism. Qutb's articles on this issue were later collected in a book entitled *Ma'rakatuna ma' al-Yahud (Our Battle with the Jews)*. Qutb suggested that the battle lines were never clearly drawn since,

> Just as in the past, it was the Jews who had disrupted the early Islamic community ... it was the Jews who had more recently undermined Islam by installing a generation of fifth-column-ists in its midst, posing as true Muslims but in reality betraying the Muslim cause ... The Jews have installed ... a massive army of agents in the form of professors, philosophers, doctors, researchers ... some even from the ranks of the Muslim religious authorities ... intending to break the creed of the Muslims by weakening the Shari'a in many ways ... with this and that they fulfil the ancient role of the Jews. [23]

This picture of the nature of the Jewish, and by extension Zionist and Israeli, threat to Muslim societies was one to which Qutb and others would return, and which would resonate strongly during the Nasser and Sadat periods. But, as Nettler has pointed out, for Qutb, 'the State of Israel was a part of this universal Zionist conspiracy, but by no means was it the whole.'[24] Israel represented a manifestation of an eternal Jewish threat, under whose umbrella was placed the entire colonial project, Orientalism and all cultural and political threats to Egypt.

It is a matter of some debate the extent to which the Muslim Brotherhood and other groups helped create a popular antipathy towards, and conflation between, Jews, Zionists and Israel, as opposed to merely responding to pre-existing collective prejudices. Awatif Abd al-Rahman notes that whereas the Muslim Brotherhood's sympathy with the Palestinians emerged from the group's conception of Arab and Islamic solidarity, that of Young Egypt—the quasi-Fascist group led by Ahmad Husayn—was 'spurred by a racist impulse deriving from their hatred of Jews.' The group did not distinguish between Jews and Zionists and called for boycotting them in their newspaper.[25]

Some, like Brynjar Lia, suggest an essentially realist dynamic whereby nationalist and security concerns at the level of the state actually led to the adoption of more culturist analyses of Zionism:

> [M]any Egyptians expressed their apprehension that the future security of Egypt and its favourable position as a cultural and economic focal point in the Middle East would be endangered if a Zionist state were to be established on its borders. These and other considerations produced a definite change in Egyptian public opinion—from indifference in the late 1920s to a deep sympathy for the Palestinian Arabs in the late 1930s. This strongly reinforced the shift of public opinion from secular Egyptian nationalism and Westernisation towards an Arab Islamic orientation, thus closer to the position of the Muslim Brothers.[26]

Lia thus suggests that the Muslim Brotherhood were interacting with a sympathy for Palestinians and concomitant suspicion or fear of Zionism and Jews, sentiments themselves derived from Egyptian security concerns, and that the Arab Islamic orientation was a result, rather than the cause, of the hostility. Walid Abdelnasser reaches a similar conclusion in arguing that the Muslim Brotherhood was responsive to 'dominant sentiments among the Egyptian population which was opposed to the establishment of a Jewish state in Palestine,' and, adding a social element, that the Brotherhood 'made use of the public hatred of Jews in Egypt, who, to a large extent, constituted an integral part of the upper stratum of the Egyptian bourgeoisie.'[27] Or, as Talhami posits, 'resentment against this high profile maintained by Egypt's Jews [in political and economic spheres] resulted from the Jewish community's open sympathy for the Zionist effort in Palestine.'[28]

These latter arguments are weakened by the fact that they themselves are based on propaganda. Research has shown that although disproportionately represented Jews nonetheless constituted a tiny minority of the upper Egyptian bourgeoisie and tended not to be especially Zionist.[29] As previously discussed, Zionist activity in Palestine was not a central political issue for any Egyptian elites until the late 1930s: Jews and non-Jews alike had reasons to fear anti-Zionist activism. Other historians, primarily Marxists, insist that the Brotherhood itself was guilty of stirring up anti-Jewish hatred and xenophobia in Egypt through the obliteration of any distinction between Zionists and Jews, using ethnic chauvinism to divert the national movement from its true revolutionary course. Thus, for Abdel Malek: 'By fostering a psychosis of fear, they [Young Egypt and the Muslim Brotherhood], made every effort to create out of nothing an anti-Jewish sentiment hitherto unknown in Egypt.'[30]

In 1937 and 1938, the Brotherhood called for boycotts of Jewish merchants and 'vitriolic attacks on Zionists and on Jews *qua* Jews (Jews as Jews as opposed to Jews as Zionists) were published in the society's newspaper, describing them as a "societal cancer."'[31] Lia again ascribes the Brotherhood a reactive role these in anti-Jewish campaigns, absolving the Brotherhood of responsibility and instead placing the blame on the Egyptian Jews, arguing that 'Anti-Jewish sentiments were kindled by the unwillingness of Egyptian Jews to support the Palestinian Arabs and the involvement of Egyptian Jewish associations in the financing of Zionist organizations in Palestine.'[32]

Rather than dismissing the Muslim Brotherhood as anti-Semitic, or placing the blame on Egyptian Jews, it is better—following social movement theory—to conclude that the Muslim Brotherhood was engaged in a process of cultural creation, centred around an anti-Semitism they were able to 'frame' within the terms of pre-existing sensitivities. As E.H. Carr saw it, the usefulness of 'propaganda' for domestic consumption is limited by 'the necessity of some measure of conformity with fact.'[33] In less positivist terms, propaganda must be at least in conformity with established understandings and percep-tions. Rather than inventing something out of nothing, the Muslim Brotherhood saw an opportunity in the rise of Arab-Zionist conflict in Palestine to increase their profile and spread support for their pro-gramme within Egypt itself. Clearly it helped that a particular view of Jews and the nature of Zionism seemed to match Egyptians' expe-riences of—and prior interpretations of—British *Christian* colonial-ism, which could then be triangulated with what was happening in Palestine. The result was to sustain a view of international relations and foreign policy in which religion was the primary driver.

The Muslim Brotherhood was not, as some, as Orientalists might imply, a manifestation of Islam's intolerance towards Jews, Christians or the West. Nor was it, as Marxists have tended to insist, irretrievably reactionary and conservative. A more nuanced Gramscian approach is helpful. As a political activist, Gramsci was in favour of engaging with religion for progressive goals, as his frustration with Marxist politics in Sardinia in a letter reveals:

> All they ever teach you here is a stupid anti-clericalism, quite mis-guided intellectually and politically. I don't go to church either, because I'm not a believer. But we must recognize that the major-ity of people are believers. If we carry on ignoring everyone but the atheists, we'll always be in a minority. There are plenty of bourgeois atheists who make fun of priests and never go to church, yet they are anti-socialist, interventionist, and wage war on us. But though these kids go to mass, they aren't industrialists; all they are asking is to work with us to stop the war as soon as possible.[34]

In Egypt also, the reality was more complex. The Muslim Brotherhood's main contribution to the discourse on Israel in 20th century Egyptian political and international thought as a whole was indeed its essentialist conception of Jews, its equation of Jews and Zionists and its reduction of Israel (in line, it must be noted, with Israel's own founding narrative) to a concrete manifestation of Judaism and Zionism. This concentration on cultural and 'civilisational' elements was in part to distinguish its own programme from that of the communists and socialists.[35] Marxist writers have long reflexively placed the Brotherhood on the side of reaction and colonialism. But Brotherhood thinkers were nevertheless influenced by the political economic preoccupations of the latter groups. The intersection of the communist and nationalist movements in the 1940s meant that a Marxist-Leninist conception of imperialism became familiar to all the new political movements. As such, the Muslim Brotherhood, although it tended to stress the religious component of the Zionist threat nevertheless incorporated Marxist categories in the 1930s and 1940s when arguing that a Jewish state 'would be an outpost of Western imperialism and a weapon for stabbing Arab countries.'[36]

Although deploying distinctly Islamic symbols, Muslim Brotherhood and other religious-based activism in the 1930s and 1940s must be seen in the context of the Egyptian national movement as a whole, which was itself part of a global anti-colonial trend. The general thrust of this was to conceptually and programmatically link international and regional relations with the popular struggle in Egypt. Brotherhood calls for the restitution of the Caliphate can be seen as direct responses to the colonialist partitioning of the Arab world, particularly in Palestine. Tariq al-Bishri has famously revised an earlier dismissive view of the Islamist contribution to Egyptian nationalism. He cautions against viewing Caliphate schemes as purely reactionary even though they were often associated with rulers, such as the Egyptian King Fu'ad, and represented attempts by those rulers to extend their influence in the wake of the Ottoman Empire's collapse:

> It is certain that those calling [for the Caliphate] were not rulers and did not have organic links to colonial or governmental bodies. They were youths calling for a wide movement of comprehensive popular unity. It was a unifying call directed

against the fragmentation of Arabs and Muslims, whose rulers had fallen to European and general Western colonialism. It was a call for unity and confronting imperialism. It is framed as an Islamic slogan that it will defend against the Zionist project and Western hegemony. Islam will not become a force of *jihad* unless it manifests politically in the context of a popular movement.'[37]

The fact that Islamists were using Marxist categories is understandable. Although certainly not for class war or peasant revolution, the members of Muslim Brotherhood were not mere right-wing extremists, but the organisation became an authentic and resonant social movement with deep roots in Egyptian society. Moreover, even if Marxism, like liberal nationalism, was an imported 'foreign' ideology, as an existing ideology of protest against imperialism and oppression it was available to the Muslim Brothers for adaptation. And if Marxism and Islamism were poles apart in some ways, in others they were more compatible. As Wilfred Cantwell Smith reminds us:

> To regard the Ikhwan as purely reactionary would ... be false. For there is at work in it also a praiseworthy constructive endeavour to build a modern society on a basis of justice and humanity, as an extrapolation from the best values that have been enshrined in the tradition from the past. It represents in part a determination to sweep aside the degeneration into which Arab society has fallen, the essentially unprincipled social opportunism interlaced with individual corruption; to get back to a basis for society of accepted moral standards and integrated vision, and to go forward to a programme of active implementation of popular goals by an effectively organised corps of disciplined and devoted idealists.'[38]

For Eric Hobsbawm, 'anti-imperialism and the colonial liberation movements inclined overwhelmingly to the Left,' because 'the Western Left was the nursery of anti-imperialist theory and policies.'[39] Both Islamists and the secular left sought to attract the same followers by linking the inadequacies of the Egyptian government to British imperialism, and identifying the solution as the removal of both. Despite the Muslim Brotherhood's aversion to 'imported' doctrines, many of its categories derived from those of a global, overwhelmingly leftist, anti-colonial phenomenon during and after World War Two. Egyptian communists can take much of the credit for introducing this global discourse to Egypt and it is to their views on Zionism and Israel that we now turn.

Egyptian Communists

The communist movement's approach to Zionism saw significant development over the course of the 1930s and 1940s, due to the shifting social, and 'ethnic', orientation of its leadership as well as its complicating external links. The main substantive contribution of the Egyptian left to discourse on Israel was to put forward a non-religious interpretation of Zionism that linked Israel's existence and actions to the same forces of imperialism and local capitalism that oppressed Egyptians and other Arabs. Communists also recognised in the 1940s that it was the United States that would inherit the imperial mantle from Europe. The communist movement began in the *mutamassir,* or Egyptianised, community, but became progressively more 'Arab' in orientation. Many prominent members of the various communist groups were Jewish.

From the mid-1930s the Egyptian communist movement came to enjoy closer integration with the new middle class national movement, mainly through the process known as *tamsir,* or 'egyptianisation'. There were distinct class divisions within the communist movement, that tended to correspond to evolving 'national' and religious schisms within the Egyptian body politic. In the political climate of the 1930s and 1940s, egyptianisation meant engaging with the issue of nationalism, a thorny one for individuals like the Egyptian Movement for National Liberation (EMNL) leader Henri Curiel who, although viscerally sympathetic to the plight of the Egyptian poor, was upper class, spoke little or no Arabic and, as a 'foreigner' and a Jew was increasingly regarded as intrinsically suspect. At school Curiel recited 'Our ancestors the Gauls' and studied nothing of Egyptian history beyond the Pharaonic period.[40]

Curiel's concern was not to show how Egyptian culture could be accommodated to foreign ideas but to impress upon Egyptians the notion that Marxism could solve the problems of Egyptian society, as it could any society, thinking 'how could they fail to become communists when Marxist doctrine so exactly fitted the situation they had discovered?'[41] But despite what nationalist revisionism would later assert, the Jewish leaders did not necessarily feel themselves to be 'foreign' to the Egyptian situation. As Curiel's biographer notes:

> What distinguished and will always distinguish their little body of activists from the hordes of European militants was the fact of being born in the Third World (as it would come to be called), into a supremely cynical system of production that had achieved the ultimate in the exploitation of man by man. Theirs was no theoretical awareness based on some ideological opus or clever calculations of surplus value. It was a gut reaction that permeated their being and shaped their consciousness for ever.[42]

Until World War Two, leadership of the communist movement in Egypt was largely restricted to the Jewish and international community. The egyptianisation of the communist movement marked its transition from the elite *mutamassirin* to the Egyptian *effendiya*, the same social class from which the Muslim Brotherhood and other organisations emerged.

Perhaps the communist activists' most important contribution at this stage was to link national liberation with class struggle on the grounds that 'it is not possible to liberate the working class without liberating Egypt from imperialism.'[43] The linking of the class issue with the nationalist movement related to the question of the egyptianisation of the communist leadership and the question of how Egyptian communism should relate to the national movement as a whole. The socialist thinker Rashid al-Barrawi translated Lenin's *Imperialism: the Highest Stage of Capitalism* in 1945. From Lenin, Barrawi 'provided a theoretical basis to the growing tendency to equate capitalism with imperialism and ascribe the retardation of the Egyptian economy to the domination of foreign firms.' As Roel Meijer suggests, the popularity of Lenin's book in Egypt can be attributed to 'the rise of a radical nationalist movement and of the economistic, secular trend within it.'[44]

After World War Two communists found it easier to attract supporters on their own terms. The post-war international milieu was conducive to the development of Leninist critiques of imperialism in many colonised countries, including Egypt. But, as Curiel himself put it, '[i]f the salvos of October brought Marxism to China ... those of Stalingrad brought it to Egypt.'[45] Although it had been largely overlooked by the Egyptian nationalist movement prior to the war, the Soviet Union became markedly more attractive following it, both as a developmental model and as the major power in the world opposed to British colonialism. The successes of the Soviet Union during the war, in addition to those of the communists in China, attracted many Egyptian Muslims and Copts to the communist groups. Egyptian communists followed the lead of the USSR when it came to their approach to Zionism and up until 1947 this was not much of a hard sell: Zionism for the USSR prior to 1947, and hence for communist groups in the Arab world, was a 'reactionary national-bourgeois ideology.'[46]

The communists in Egypt were, in line with the international communist position, overwhelmingly opposed to Zionism and the creation of a Jewish state in Palestine. In 1946, the *al-Fajr al-Jadid* (New Dawn) group condemned Zionism in internationalist terms as the 'instrument of world imperialism which resorted to lying to the peoples of the world and the toiling Jews and resorts to terror today, enslaving the Arab people.'[47] New Dawn actively sought to disassociate Zionism from Judaism and to universalise the conflict in revolutionary terms:

> ... the immediate danger which not only threatens the toiling people in our Arab sister Palestine, but also threatens the lives of the toiling people in the Middle East in particular and the peoples of the world in general. It threatens the cause of world peace because Zionism is the rotten colonial Jewish capitalism which misguides the toiling Israeli people, whether workers or agriculturists, to exploit them ... It puts poison in the honey by

raising the racial persecution complex ... blinding their sight
from the truth in the interest of a group of tyrannical Zionist
capitalists.[48]

For another communist group, Iskra, Zionism was also a threat to the
Arab world due to its colonial imperialist nature. This interpretation
would have lasting influence in Egypt across the political spectrum:
'it is a territoristic colonialism, totally tied to the world imperialists.'
As such, 'its danger is not confined to Palestine alone but threatens
the independence and freedom of all other Arab countries.' The group
was clear to distinguish between Zionism and Judaism and called on
Jewish workers, peasants and intellectuals to 'form a united front to
struggle against colonialism and its Zionist instrument.' The optimum
solution was the establishment in Palestine of 'a democratic government in the shadow of which Arabs and Jews cooperate.'[49]

The Soviet support for the 1947 UN Partition Plan provoked an
abrupt volte face in the international communist movement's attitude toward Zionism and sounded the death knell for communism
as a popular movement in Egypt. The Egyptian communists, in following the Soviet line on partition, exposed themselves to charges of
both Zionism and subservience to the Russian Communist Party. The
USSR had come to view Zionism as a potentially progressive force in
an Arab world dominated by reactionary regimes. Batatu suggests that
the Soviets supported the establishment of Israel because 'most of the
Arab states have thrown themselves into the arms of the Anglo-Saxons'
and the 'unfriendliness of most Arab governments to the Soviets and
the communist parties.'[50] Or, as Mohamed Hassanein Heikal saw it,

> Stalin seems to have believed that the creation of a Jewish state
> might help to solve the Jewish problem in Russia and might
> also inject into the backward area of the Middle East a new pro-
> gressive element. This thinking was probably influenced by a
> superficial knowledge of the kibbutz movement, by the number
> of Zionist leaders who came from Russia, and by the prominent
> positions held by Jews in the new communist regimes then estab-
> lishing themselves in Eastern Europe. Moscow saw everything in

terms of the struggle between communism and western imperialism. Jewish groups were in arms against British imperialism
in Palestine. Jewish and Arab proletariats would march forward
shoulder to shoulder towards the new red dawn.[51]

From 1947, most Marxists in Egypt 'accepted the Soviet Union's determination that the first priority for advancing the anti-imperialist
struggle in the Middle East ... was to expel British imperialism from
the region.' In supporting partition, and hence the establishment of
a Jewish state, communists thus came to view Zionism as a 'powerful anti-imperialist force in the Middle East.'[52] Most communists
opposed the 1948 Palestine War on the grounds that it was intended
to 'stop the trend of the rising nationalist movement and turn our
holy war against the imperialist into a religious and racial war' and 'to
divert the attention of the toiling masses away from the struggle for
an improved standard of living to an outside matter which neglects the
battle.'[53] Although this mirrored the Muslim Brotherhood's resistance
to statism, after the defeat of the Arab armies in 1948, communists
were the only Egyptian political current to argue in favour of Israeli
self-determination. But the questions of Palestine and Zionism had
become so integral to Egyptian national politics that downgrading
them amounted to political suicide. The Brotherhood, in particular,
was quick to vilify its main political rivals.

At the time of the Egyptian revolution in July 1952, then, the communist stance was to support the rights of Israelis to their state, albeit
only in the land designated for the Jewish state in the UN Partition
Plan. Although the communists still perceived Zionism to be an imperialist ideology and accused the imperialist powers of colluding with
the Zionists to establish Israel, they saw the creation of the Jewish
state as a *fait accompli* and considered Israel itself legitimate. In spite
of the now complete unpopularity of this position, interestingly, the
Egyptian regime was, until 1955, apparently willing to accept Israel:
secret communications between Egypt and Israel were carried on, and
the solution to the conflict was envisaged to be the return of the refugees and the establishment of a Palestinian state on the land allotted
by the Partition Plan.

Statism, Islamism and the new regime

The young officers that seized control in 1952 were involved to varying degrees in the new middle class political movements that formed in the 1930s and 1940s. They recognised their significance when they took power in Egypt in 1952. They constituted a key source of potential support as well as opposition, and included most Egyptian writers, academics and journalists. The Muslim Brotherhood, Young Egypt and the communist movement all hoped to assume control if and when the military had returned to barracks. Gaining the support of the middle class, or at least weakening its links with potential opposition movements, was thus an early priority for the new regime. From the end of the 1940s, not least because of the boost in popularity it gained through the Palestine War, it was the Muslim Brotherhood that most threatened the survival of the military regime. As Shukri notes, the Free Officers, even in seeking to undercut the Brotherhood, had to win favour among its 'masses.'[54]

In the first two years of the revolution there was close cooperation between the Revolutionary Command Council (RCC) and the Muslim Brotherhood, as well as with Sayyid Qutb, who, strikingly given his later assessment of the president, frequently met with Nasser.[55] Qutb was given an office in the RCC's building and charged with reforming education. He was 'considered one of the intellectuals of the revolution' and more extravagantly, for some, 'the father of the Revolution.'[56] The Brotherhood evidently shared many of the new Egyptian regime's goals and policies. From an early date, it was foreign policy that drove a wedge ideologically between the regime and the Brotherhood: the Muslim Brotherhood expressed its opposition in 1954 to Nasser's agreement with Britain allowing for the return of troops during wartime.[57] But the influence of Islamist ideology on the regime's conception of Israel was evident in 1954 even as Nasser tightened the noose around the Muslim Brotherhood itself. In 1954, Nasser claimed that the communists were the greatest supporters of Zionism and attacked Curiel personally as both the biggest communist and the biggest Zionist in Egypt.[58] Nasser's equation of Zionism with communism at this stage was, as with Nokrashy Pasha in 1948, completely in line with that of the Brotherhood. Anti-Zionism was thus instrumentalised to discredit the communists.[59]

The first three years of the new regime were characterised by general ideological ambiguity and retrenchment, and a 'conventional' statist approach to foreign policy. The influence of the international environment obliged the regime to govern Egypt as a sovereign state among other states. Like the communists, with which the Free Officers had had contacts of varying closeness, the RCC felt the immediate priority was to remove British colonial control rather than confront Israel. But although the Free Officers had been involved in the *effendiyya* political movements of the post-war period, they were not reducible to any of them and as such lacked an organised or coherent support base: neither President Nagib nor Nasser were leaders of a social movement. What we can see is the combination of, on the one hand, statism imposed by the external environment and Wafdist inheritance, and, on the other, a deference to elements of the Muslim Brotherhood's reading of Israel and international relations.

The regime rode a wave of approval—helped by the Brotherhood's support for the coup—to pursue a number of diplomatic compromises with Britain, engaging in the similarly statist approach of the Wafd, which had also been caught between the desire to avoid antagonising great powers while preserving its domestic popularity. While the regime brought most publishing and press organs under its control, it did not have an agreed-on message to publicise via these organs and Nasser had yet to establish himself unequivocally as leader. A diversity of political opinions was thus allowed for the first two years of the revolution. This initial laissez-faire attitude to ideas on the part of the military officers owed more to factionalism within their own ranks (particularly those around the titular leader, Muhammad Nagib, and the strongman of the younger generation of officers, Nasser) and lack of strong ideological consensus at the regime level, than to any principled commitment to freedom of speech.[60]

As far as attitudes to Israel were concerned, this ambiguity was manifested in a wary openness to relations with that state and a conception of the issue between Egypt and Israel as primarily a border dispute rather than existential struggle. This tentative openness and lack of programmatic clarity—unusual perhaps for a 'revolutionary' government—must be seen in light of the large question mark hanging over the United States' post-war role in the Middle East. In the context of the Cold War doctrine of 'containment', countries hostile to communism could count on US support. And, as Beattie notes, the 'Free Officers acted with an awareness of American support for a coup and the absence of British support for [King] Faruq.'[61] The United States was instrumental in facilitating the Anglo-Egyptian 'Head of States' agreement in 1954 securing the withdrawal of British troops from Suez, which had itself produced a distinct warming of Anglo-Egyptian relations, as evinced by Nasser's assessment that 'After the Suez settlement there is nothing standing in the way of our good relations with the West.'[62] Through the coup of 1952 Nasser inherited the substantial popular approval, and mandate, of the Wafd. And he initially put it to similar purpose—to implement a realistic policy of compromise deemed to serve Egypt's best interests under difficult circumstances. It is worth recalling the terms under which Egypt had secured British withdrawal:

> no Egyptian pasha—not even a master of manipulation such as Ismail Sidqi in 1946—could have consented to the loss of the Sudan or to a military treaty giving Britain the right of *automatic* re-entry in wartime. Nasser did both, in 1953 and 1954, as the price of evacuation.[63]

In 1950, the United States had announced its 'unalterable opposition to the use of force or threat of force between any of the states in the area,' a principle on the adherence to which Washington conditioned the supply of arms to the region.[64] Nasser's recognition of this condition, and his aspirations for US military support, also affected his regime's attitude towards Israel for the first three years of the revolution. In the context of seeking to maintain good relations with the United States, the RCC was keen to stress that it was not interested in war with Israel. Although the idea that peaceful relations could be established was shaken by the Lavon Affair in 1954, when Israeli saboteurs exploded bombs in British and American cultural targets within

Egypt to scupper Anglo-Egyptian agreement, the affair lent credence to the idea that Israel acted as a dangerous state in its own right, rather than as an appendage of US or Western imperialism.

The cautiously optimistic stance of the United States towards the new regime stood in stark contrast to the USSR's attitude, which was to immediately denounce it as a dictatorship. According to the Marxist Khalid Muhi al-Din, Nasser could not understand why communists around the world were labelling the regime fascists when the officers had worked so long with Haditu, the main communist formation in Egypt prior to the coup. Muhi al-Din later recalled that

> The result was to make the left-wing officers very vulnerable and hand the trump cards to the right-wing officers. My opinions were well known. How could I defend them and get people to agree when every day saw us insulted by the communist press all over the world?[65]

There was, shortly after the coup, a debate about Egypt's national identity, which would have significance in later years as the regime's foreign policy goals increased in coherence and adapted to changing circumstances. Egypt had already, as we have seen, entered into the Arab fold strategically and intellectually via Palestine. Intellectually, Arab unity was envisaged as a stepping-stone on the way to Islamic unity or a vision of a loose federation of Arab states. Writers such as Ali Amin Abd al-Rahman Azzam, Muhammad Ali Alubah and Sati' al-Husri championed a Pan-Arab orientation, but in the form of a 'United Arab States.'[66] Nasser himself, who published his *Philosophy of the Revolution* in 1954 stressed that Egypt belonged to three circles: the Arab, the Islamic and the African, with the Arab circle the closest to Egypt. But the emphasis was on the strategic benefits of such a conception for Egypt as a state. The Arabism articulated by intellectuals and officers was one of federation, rather than of borderless organic unity, and justified in terms of Egypt's interests and strategic security rather than in historical-ideological terms.[67] It was a unity embodied in the Arab League and dedicated ultimately, and theoretically, to securing the implementation of UN resolutions, particularly Resolution 181, the Partition Plan, (i.e. not eliminating Israel) through international diplomacy.

Until 1955, elite political discourse remained largely focussed on Egypt. The nation-state had become more or less hegemonic as the pre-eminent unit for political mobilisation by the time the Free Officers carried out their coup, as some of the communist groups ignored to their detriment.[68] The international extension of this was the concept of 'national interest,' as distinct from, and superior to, all other group interests. Thus the Palestine question was not considered to be of existential import for Egypt, particularly as compared with the imperative of ending the British occupation. Although Egypt had serious issues regarding the borders between Israel and Egypt, the regime was not overly concerned with Israel's existence as a state.

At the time of the Egyptian revolution, Nasser and others viewed Israel as a product of British colonialism in the Middle East: the Palestinians and Egyptians had faced a common enemy. According to Nasser in *Philosophy of Revolution*:

> It has been clear that imperialism is the most prominent force in this region. Even Israel herself is not more than a product and manifestation of imperialism. Had not Palestine fallen under a British mandate, Zionism could not have found the needed assistance to realise its idea of a National Home in Palestine. It would have remained a madman's fantasy, with no hope of ever materialising.[69]

But this view of the roots of Israel's existence, and the blame the British had to shoulder for its birth, was not consistently integrated into a broader theory of imperialism. Whereas many on the left had been quick after 1945 to identify the United States as the new imperialist threat to the Middle East, Nasser was prepared to give America the benefit of the doubt. Similarly, 'he did not pass the death sentence on Israel. Rather he speculated on what this new state was, represented or could become.'[70] Indeed, Vatikiotis goes so far as to suggest, in the late 1940s Nasser had 'perceived both Zionism and Israel as "progressive" elements in contrast to the "rotten" Arab regimes in the Middle

East,'[71] a view not unlike that held by some Egyptian communists at the time. Nasser perceived the Free Officers' enemies prior to the revolution to be 'our own superior officers, other Arabs, the British and the Israelis—in that order.'[72]

The Free Officers, and Nasser in particular, were prepared to countenance reaching some kind of peace agreement with Israel, even if, as some Israelis at the time believed, President Nagib was adopting a conciliatory—or at least not overtly hostile—position towards Israel as a tactical ruse in order to win military and economic support from the West.[73] In meetings between envoys of Israel and the RCC in Paris, Nasser sent a letter saying 'public opinion in Egypt and the Arab world made it prudent for the RCC to build its policy towards Israel gradually and that avoidance of aggressive statements against Israel was the first step in this direction.' The Israeli government itself was apparently optimistic about the prospects for constructive relations with the Free Officers' regime, hoping that it would adopt an 'Egypt-first' position in which it realised there was no reason not to further good relations with Israel.[74] The Israelis viewed the RCC not as 'collaborators' but as Egyptian nationalists that would see building bridges with the Jewish state was in Egypt's best interests. Shlaim's research indicates that the RCC was in fact willing to move forward on talks with Israel, that Nasser was privately reconciled to Israel's existence and that he saw Israeli prime minister Moshe Sharett as an honest man.[75]

Despite the strong statist inheritance and leaning of the RCC, the officers nevertheless depended, until 1954, on the support—or at least passivity—of the Muslim Brotherhood. The Brotherhood was initially opposed to joining the government after the Free Officers seized power for 'fear that the Society would lose its "popular" quality' and for fear of 'bringing down the wrath of foreigners and minorities on the regime and thus complicating its problems.'[76] But they did want to serve as the regime's revolutionary party in society. The regime, however, had its own plan for restructuring the political architecture in Egypt, which involved the institutional exclusion of the Brotherhood. In a bid to neutralise the Brotherhood's social power, replace the old political parties and pre-empt the organisation of opposition to the regime, the RCC established the Liberation Rally (LR) in 1954.

But the LR, while it effectively neutralised the scions of the old bourgeoisie as a political force at the top, left intact the traditional power structures, and hence ideological framework, at the bottom of the organisation. Perhaps most importantly, the LR aimed at absorbing the extensive reservoir of support—and as a functional replacement— for the proscribed Muslim Brotherhood and as such was not intended to disseminate a revolutionary ideology. Due to the preoccupation with winning over the Brotherhood's masses, it deferred to religious principles, teaching religious observance and orthodoxy to youth.[77] The brand of Islam taught was Hanbali, closely matching the doctrine of the Muslim Brotherhood.[78]

Even when the United States ultimately refused to support Nasser in the way he hoped, the blame was laid at the feet of Zionism or Jewish influence rather than imperialism or intrinsic American hostility. The United States would, Egypt's new rulers appeared to believe, be a potential support for Egypt if it were free of Jewish manipulation. In 1955, Nasser drew a link between US reluctance to arm Egypt and the Israeli raid on the Egyptian-controlled Gaza Strip, concluding that the responsibility for both lay with Israel, and the influence of its supporters (Jews) in the United States.[79] Linking this to the Gaza raid, he concluded that America 'was trying to keep Egypt weak and that this resulted from Jewish influence.'[80] Significantly, Nasser was still using part of the Brotherhood's conceptual framework on Israel – which was to see it as Jewish and controlling the United States. But at the same time he treated Israel as a state with which Egypt could deal, and which could be contained, using accepted diplomatic means.

The Bandung Conference in 1955 marks the high point of the statist paradigm under Nasser. After this point, Nasser's desire to maintain stature in the global anti-colonial movement encouraged a view that the principal contradiction for Third World states like Egypt was that with imperialism, which linked combating Israel with revolution at home. As such, it made strategic sense for Nasser to portray Egypt's confrontation with Israel, which had heated up with the latter's raids on Gaza in 1955, as part of this countervailing struggle, to which the Soviet Union would be prepared to contribute. It is notable, however, that at this point Nasser requested arms not to confront imperialism, but to defend Egypt against Israel. In a section on 'Other Problems', the Bandung Resolution on Palestine, which Nasser drafted, was couched in the language of international law and called on Israel to abide by UN resolutions:

> In view of the existing tension in the Middle East, caused by the situation in Palestine and of the danger of that tension to world peace, the Asian-African Conference declared its support for the rights of the Arab people of Palestine and called for the implementation of the United Nations Resolutions on Palestine and the achievement of the peaceful settlement of the Palestine question.[81]

The implication was that should Israel comply, there would be no obstacle to full recognition by the Arabs.[82] Israel was not reduced to imperialism and Nasser's approach matched the international consensus on Israel, which was to recognise it as a legitimate—if errant—state in the region.

Ironically, Nasser's conception of Israel as reflected in the Bandung Resolution was also compatible with Soviet thinking on Israel at the time, just as bilateral relations were being established, but for the last time until 1973. It is often assumed that weak or developing states adopt the ideologies and worldviews of their international sponsors. This assumption underpinned the policies and doctrines of both sides of the Cold War: allies were claimed and the world divided into the forces of imperialism, or freedom, and progress or communism.[83] But the case of Egypt reveals the influence of great powers on their protégés to be more ambiguous and contingent, particularly on specific issues. Nasser's turn, following Bandung, towards a more intractable position on Israel flew in the face of his new Soviet friends. The Soviet position on Israel was, like America's, to support Israel's right to exist.

The foregoing discussion has illustrated that by 1955 there were a number of distinct approaches to Israel present on the Egyptian political scene. Most importantly, the conceptions elaborated by the Wafd, the Muslim Brotherhood and the communists related to these groups' domestic political situations and strategies. The original 'statist' approach of the Wafd government to the events in Palestine from 1936 inexorably transformed to incorporate elements of the Islamic worldview prevalent in society and magnified by the activism of the Muslim Brotherhood and other Islamic nationalist worldviews, although particularly after 1945 the political and intellectual initiative devolved to the new middle class nationalist movement. The early years of the revolution combined this statist inheritance, reinforced by the international context, with elements of the still resonant Muslim Brotherhood worldview. The conception of Israel that would become most closely associated with 'Arabism' in the era of Gamal Abdel Nasser combined insights generated by Egypt's communist intellectuals as well as the pan-Arab sensitivities created by the Brotherhood, each prominent new political movements among the rising middle classes. In this, the evolution of Arabism prior to the Suez War speaks as much about social and political transformation on the Egyptian domestic scene as it does the formation of the Arab states system or Egypt's evolving quest for regional dominance.

CHAPTER 3

THE ANTINOMIES OF NASSERISM (1956–1967)

The termination of British occupation in Egypt posed a peculiar problem for the Egyptian regime. The Revolutionary Command Council (RCC) saw itself as the culmination of a revolutionary narrative that had, since 1882, been oriented primarily around ridding Egypt of colonial control. With that goal apparently accomplished in 1956 the revolution required a new *raison d'etre*. Nasser's solution was to assert that the revolution was incomplete until Zionism, imperialism and Arab reaction were fully eradicated from the Arab world, and, especially from 1961, until socialism was further advanced in Egypt. The link between confronting Israel and revolutionary change was relatively clear: the debacle of 1948 was due to the fact that the reactionary Arab regimes were actually agents of the British, who had presented the Zionists with the Balfour Declaration in 1917.[1] A priority for the regime, as outlined in the 1962 National Charter, was to build a powerful national army, which would be necessary to defeat Zionism, and which could only be realised through economic, social and political development embodied in the revolution.

Nasser also needed a foreign policy doctrine that would connect him to a broader international society without sacrificing intelligibility at home. With the global rise of socialism and Third-Worldism, Nasser clearly saw the value in tapping into the left-wing strand of the Egyptian nationalist movement, particularly in light of his destruction of the Muslim Brotherhood as a potential structure linking state and society via the idiom of Islam and desire to construct an ideology that was distinct from that of the Brothers. Israel was thus cast in the terms of international socialism—with one key difference: Egyptian leaders no longer countenanced the idea that any agreement could be reached with Israel on its own, strategically, as was the prevailing internationalist position.

But the socialist discourse was not one that permeated society as a whole; and as such it did not provide the regime with tangible ideological power. The Liberation Rally was replaced by the National Union in 1957, which although intended more explicitly as a mechanism to structure new political support for, rather than just neutralise opposition to, the revolutionary regime, also did not act as a transmission belt for new ideas and there was, as with its predecessor organisation, no attempt to restructure existing patterns of social control at the lower levels of the National Union structure. This meant that local sources of intellectual authority and informal patronage networks remained intact, as did the traditional ideological framework of Islam.[2]

International society and the left

The theorist of the 'English school' of international relations, Hedley Bull, has noted that a multiplicity of normative frameworks have existed globally; that there was not always a universal 'international society'. Whereas until the end of the World War Two the dominant framework reflected the supremacy of the West and expressed its interests, Bull writes that 'as Asian, African and other non-Western peoples have become stronger relative to the Western powers, they have become freer to adopt a different rhetoric that sets Western values aside, or at all events places different interpretations upon them.'[3] This Third-Worldist international society influenced the resonance of ideas domestically in Egypt and acted to encourage a more left-wing political discourse.

The Bandung Conference in 1955 marked the beginning of Nasser's association with the Afro-Asian People's Solidarity Movement, of which he came to be regarded as a leader, which was important in encouraging the regime to frame foreign policy issues, including those pertaining to Israel, within the terms of socialism and anti-imperialism. Nasser's appraisal of Israel as a 'fabricated state' (*dawla mulaffiqa*) reflected a desire to connect with the global discourse of anti-imperialism that had been consecrated at the conference. In a speech in Cairo, alongside President Sukarno of Indonesia, Nasser announced:

> Israel today does not represent for the Egyptians, nor for the Arabs, nor for the Afro-Asian bloc, nor for the world's conscience, only a military aggression toward Egypt or the Arabs, or this region of the world. Rather, it represents something else. It represents the attempt to dominate us by way of this state. Israel represents foreign pressure on the Arabs. It represents the attempt to divide the Arab forces and spread division among them, to prevent them from joining and uniting and benefiting from the fruits of their country and their land.[4]

Nasser adopted the doctrine of 'positive neutralism' that would be associated with the Afro-Asian People's Solidarity Movement. According to Sayegh, although positive neutralism presupposed nonalignment, 'a country may trade with countries belonging to the two cold-war blocs or receive aid from them; but, in order to qualify as "positively" neutral, it must avoid aligning itself with either bloc.' But in practice positive neutralism for Egypt did not mean equidistance between the blocs. It rather called for 'safeguarding national independence against imperialist aggression' and solidarity with other neutralist countries in Africa and Asia and '*the socialist countries* as the parties most interested in the preservation of peace ...'[5] The regime was willing to push the boundaries of positive neutralism to the 'outer edge' and to risk dependence on the Soviet bloc, a factor that placed it squarely within the 'radical' camp in the Afro-Asian movement.[6]

The USSR itself had revised its negative opinion of the Egyptian regime by 1955. The passing of Stalin in March 1953, and Khrushchev's support for national liberation movements meant that the USSR was by 1955 willing to lend *unconditional* support to Egypt. The USSR apparently accepted 'Nasser's own belief that he could build socialism without a proletarian revolution.'[7] Especially given the scorn with which the coup in 1952 had been received in the Soviet Union, this more conciliatory tone not only allowed Nasser to accept aid, but also increased the political salience and utility to the regime of Egyptian leftists.

An important combination of factors – the Americans' refusal to authorise a $27 million arms request in February 1955, and Israel's raids on the Gaza Strip that year – marked the beginning of Egypt's attempts to seek military assistance elsewhere. Other Western actions in the region encouraged Nasser to turn to the Soviet Union. Britain was in the process of negotiating the defence agreement with Iraq, Iran, Turkey and Pakistan that would become known as the 'Baghdad Pact'. Nasser vehemently opposed the pact and launched a press campaign against Western alliances.

The USSR's keenness to build bridges with nationalist forces in the Middle East had contributed to a reversion of its own position on Israel. As we have seen, the USSR historically considered Zionism to be an imperialist movement, but revised this stance through its support for the UN Partition Plan of 1947 and the creation of the State of Israel in 1948. Its recognition of Israel's existence *and* approval for Zionism as a progressive anti-colonial force, however, persisted only until the early 1950s. Israel had clearly placed itself in the Western camp of the Cold War and after this point the USSR reverted to its previous anti-Zionist position. This reversion did not entail the rejection of Israel's right to exist as an independent nation-state, but rather a rejection of the ideology undergirding that existence and corresponding pro-Western orientation.[8] In Soviet thinking, Israel was aligned with the imperialist United States, but through socialist action within Israeli society could be detached. It was, in other words, Israel's current class basis rather than existence *per se* that was problematic.

Soviet international relations thinking had, since the 1950s, been underpinned by three apparently contradictory concepts: proletarian internationalism, anti-imperialism and peaceful coexistence.[9] The USSR conceptualised Israel within the terms of these three broad concepts. Thus, the internal Israeli social struggle would, in the long run, resolve the Arab-Israeli conflict (proletarian internationalism). Israel should thus be engaged with the goal of detaching itself from the US orbit, as with all other US clients (anti-imperialism). But the Soviet view on confrontation with Israel was strongly hedged by its concept of peaceful coexistence. As such, they were not against, and indeed encouraged, the Arabs to seek rapprochement with Israel on favourable terms, including through relinquishing territory, and they upheld the right of Israel to exist as a legitimate nation-state.

On the international plane, the most significant country to view Israel, and not just Zionism, as a manifestation of imperialism, was China. The Chinese position from 1956, like that of Egypt, was to regard Israel as an 'instrument of Western imperialism for exerting pressure on the Arab countries and for maintaining tension in the Middle East.' The Chinese position radicalised further in the 1960s, when they took the view that

> the principal and antagonistic contradictions existed now between the Arabs on the one hand, and Israel together with the United States on the other. Since antagonistic contradictions were in their view irreconcilable, the Chinese now rejected any suggestion that the Palestine question should be settled peacefully, and advocated instead a people's armed struggle as the only way to settle the Arab-Israeli conflict.[10]

Arabism, socialism and the Suez War

The changed international context encouraged the formation of a socialist intelligentsia in Egypt after 1955, which would contribute to an evolving discourse of Arabism. The regime felt the need to distance itself from the worldview and programme of the now banned Muslim Brotherhood, and slow its cultural agenda of societal mobilisation and reform via Islam. Ideas, in the absence of a strong popular-based ideological movement allied to the regime, filtered into the Egyptian public sphere from the external environment, which for Egypt at this time was strongly coloured by socialism. The burgeoning links with the USSR and the Afro-Asian Solidarity Movement thus had an important effect on political discourse, although because of the lack of effective mobilisational or educational structures, socialist ideas were hesitantly and superficially promoted in society at large.

Many liberal intellectuals of the urban bourgeoisie left Egypt, withdrew from public life or adapted their discourse to suit the new realities. After 1954, with the old liberal parties and the Muslim Brotherhood banned, leftist thinkers increasingly dominated the intellectual field. They staffed the press, publishing houses and universities, forming not only an ideological resource for the regime, but also framing issues of policy for the domestic audience.[11] This socialist intelligentsia was enriched by the reintegration of Marxist thinkers into civil society. Nasser's participation in the Bandung Conference, as well as the Czech Arms Deal, had delighted Egyptian communists who, though tortured, wrote letters of support for Nasser from their prison cells. Many communists were released in 1955 and 1956 and the main groups united in their support of Nasser. The Suez nationalisation intensified the support that Nasser had won from communist intellectuals after Bandung, with even the most intractable communist opponents tending to support the nationalisation of the canal as 'a new blow received by the imperialist camp from the Egyptian people.'[12] In the mid-1950s the regime encouraged the re-establishment of a left-wing press, free enough to come up with creative policy analyses but nevertheless operating under state auspices and with the regime's blessing. Communist-run publishing houses were opened and communists began to write for mainstream daily newspapers such as *al-Jumhuriya (The Republic)*, *al-Misa (Evening)*, which was edited by the previously exiled Free Officer Khalid Muhi al-Din, and *al-Sha'b (The People)*.

The trend towards radical Arabism was not inevitable and nor was it part of a grand plan. The reality was more one of improvisation. The Suez War, arguably inadvertently, altered the demographic context in Egypt, which made the intelligentsia as a whole more uniformly 'Arab' in ethnic composition. In addition to nationalising the Suez Canal, which precipitated the invasion, the Egyptian regime sequestered assets and nationalised businesses of foreigners, particularly French, British and Jews, in its aftermath. Most Jews, indeed, had already left after 1948. For Mahmoud Amin al-Alim, the signs were that when the fighters returned from the Palestine War of 1948, they had a wish to 'get even with the Jews', which encouraged many to leave.[13]

After Suez, the vast majority of 'foreigners' left the country, either because their businesses were gone or through the fear that this would happen. Greeks, Jews and others who left may have considered themselves Egyptian on account of their permanent residence, often for generations, in the country, even if 'native' Egyptians had increasingly viewed them as outsiders and resented them due to their perceived complicity with the coloniser. Though they were later celebrated as evidence of Nasserism's revolutionary character, the sequestrations and subsequent departure of foreigners may not have been planned, but rather represented a reflexive reaction to the shock of the Tripartite Invasion.[14] Either way, the exodus of foreigners had the effect of vastly increasing the ethnic homogeneity of the cities. After Suez, to be Egyptian more than ever meant to be 'Arab'.

The exodus of Egypt's non-native Arabic-speaking communities after the Suez War marked the disappearance of a constituency that was more comfortable with a Mediterranean—and state-centric—version of Egyptian national identity and, by extension, less given to an ethnocentric view of Israel. The ideological approval Marxist intellectuals granted to Nasserism marked the final abandonment of internationalism in favour of Pan-Arab nationalism as a feature of communist, and thus general, political discourse.[15] Many Marxists embraced their new role as Gramscian 'traditional intellectuals' in the service of what they perceived to be the new progressive regime. The accommodation was consecrated by the expulsion in 1957 of the staunchly cosmopolitan, and Jewish, leader of Haditu, Henri Curiel.[16]

The Egyptian left provided the vocabulary of a societal paradigm for representing Israel. The Communist Party, which had hitherto distinguished between Zionism and Israel, transferred its assessment of Zionism as an imperialist movement to Israel as a Zionist state and manifestation of imperialism, thus denying its legitimacy and linking its ultimate defeat to Egypt's national and social struggle. It was left-wing intellectuals, including, from their prison cells, communists, who provided the theoretical support for Nasser's new approach to Israel. For the United Egyptian Communist Party in 1955, 'American imperialism ... has made Israel its spearhead in its Middle Eastern policy directed against Egypt, Syria, Lebanon, Jordan and Saudi Arabia—a springboard for extending its influence and domination over the economy and politics of the Arab countries.' 'Imperialism is the principal enemy' stated a 1956 report by the Party, while the Marxist-edited paper *al-Misa* announced soon after the Suez War that Israel was an 'imperialist base' and 'tool against the Arab liberation movement.'[17]

The transition was gradual. Some prominent thinkers proceeded from Islamic nationalist viewpoints but adopted less narrow postures and, after the nationalisation of the Suez Canal, were at least initially inclined to see a future of Egyptian and Arab strength in the face of Israel. The former Nationalist Party leader and Minister of Culture, Fathi Radwan, had, shortly after the Revolution, written a novel entitled *Muhammad al-tha'ir al-a'zam {Muhammad the Greatest Revolutionary}*, which contained thinly veiled comparisons between the Free Officers Revolution and the birth of Islam.[18] In 1957 he published *Hadha al-sharq al-arabi* [*This Arab East*]. The latter work included a long treatise on the history of the Suez Canal culminating in its nationalisation. It also incorporated a lengthy discussion of Israel, based on Alfred Lilienthal's *What Price Israel?*, which debunked the Zionist claims to religious entitlement in Palestine.

Radwan's book also celebrated the discovery and exploitation of oil in the Arab World. Oil, for Radwan, was the source of modern civilisation: it fueled industries and generated the electricity that powered 'the printers that produce books'. Oil, in short, was 'life.'[19] And it was no coincidence that the world's oil resources were concentrated in the Arab East. The spiritual dimensions of hydrocarbons were as important as the economic. The presence of oil revived the universalist destiny of the Arab East, which during the Middle Ages was the locus of spiritual and intellectual, as well as material, dynamism for Western civilisation.

Radwan's Arabism, put forward in the post-nationalisation euphoria, led him to the more internationalist conclusion that the oil-rich Arabs could play a civilising role in world conflicts, mediating between Jews, Christians and Muslims and contributing to a more inclusive world civilisation. This was what had happened in the past when Aramaic, Persian, Indian and Greek influences enriched what became known as Arab culture, because 'it is not just ideas that create civilisations and culture, it is the atmosphere in which these ideas are received, the hands that gather them, and the minds that synthesise them.'[20] Radwan's intervention represents an interesting example of a self-confident and cosmopolitan form of Arabism, perhaps more redolent of an earlier, more optimistic Egyptian intellectual, Rifa'a al-Tahtawi (1801–1873) whose thought was free of the defensiveness that would characterise later Islamist interventions on international affairs.[21]

The Suez War seemed to offer bald proof of Israel's imperialist nature through its collusion with the old colonial powers, Britain and France. Long-held anti-colonialist sentiments were exploited. The Suez War refocused national resentment against Britain as the coloniser, and Israel as the conqueror of Palestine, into a unified hostility towards the West 'provoked by the appearance of intimate links between Zionism and Western power'.[22] This chimed with the nationalist consensus that had linked Egyptian domestic and foreign policy since the late 1930s. After Suez, many intellectuals considered the West as whole as the real enemy—an enemy that used Israel to perpetuate its domination. This interpretation served a useful purpose for the Nasser regime. It meant that Nasser could justify not confronting Israel militarily again by insisting that war against imperialism was futile: only a popular revolution could succeed in defeating imperialism, and that would clearly take time and be predicated on the Egyptian revolution's successful export and concomitant unification of the Arab peoples, as well as the continued economic and social development of Egypt.

The National Charter

Left-wing influence increased following the Syrian secession from the United Arab Republic (UAR) in 1961. The secession was blamed on Syrian 'reactionaries' and capitalists, supported by the 'Syndicate of Kings' Husayn of Jordan and Sa'ud of Saudi Arabia, in league with the CIA.[23] Nasser launched a new foreign policy doctrine known as 'Unity of Objective' (*Wahdat al-Hadaf*), defined as the continuous struggle against 'reaction' in the Arab world and the strengthening of progressive elements supporting Arab unity. Echoing the tension in Soviet ideology between peaceful coexistence and proletarian internationalism, Heikal, in 1961, famously drew a distinction between Egypt as a state and Egypt as a revolution: 'If as a state Egypt recognises boundaries in its dealings with governments,' he wrote, 'Egypt as a revolution should never hesitate or halt before borders.'[24]

Under Unity of Objective, the salient divisions in the region were seen not to be vertical (between states) but between progressive and reactionary forces in state and society. In this formulation, Israel, rather than constituting a hostile state in its own right, a distinctive and alien presence in the Arab world, merged with the latter camp. In July 1962, the doctrine was enshrined in the UAR National Charter, which defined the UAR as 'the vanguard, base and fighting fortress of the Arab progressive struggle.'[25] The Charter called for moving beyond the stage of 'political revolution', since '[i]mperialism has now changed its attitude and has become incapable of directly confronting the people. Its natural hideout was within the palaces of reaction.' It was thus 'incumbent upon the people to strike at them and defeat them at one and the same time to assert the triumph of the political revolution in the remaining parts of the Arab Nation ...'[26] Explicitly rejecting sovereignty, the Charter continued:

> The United Arab Republic, firmly convinced that she is an integral part of the Arab Nation, must propagate her call for unity and the principles it embodies, so that it would be at the disposal of every Arab citizen, without hesitating for one moment before the outworn argument that this would be considered an interference in the affairs of others.[27]

The Charter did not, in line with its internationalist vision, concentrate on the Palestine question. The threat of Israel was instrumentalised in the context of the need to develop the army of the United Arab Republic, the 'vanguard of the progressive Arab struggle, its base and fighting fortress [and] the natural enemy of all the enemies of the Arab nation and its progress'. Developing the army would require scientific progress, which was in turn the main target of 'world imperialism and its monopolies'. The crowning achievement of imperialism was the 'seizure of a piece of Arab land in Palestine, the heart of the Arab nation, and its usurpation without a shred of right or law in the interests of a fascist military presence that would not live without the military threat, whose real dangers come from Israel's identity as a tool of imperialism.' The UAR, for its part, was the only Arab state capable of building an army that would 'deter the Zionist, imperialist, aggressive plans.'[28]

There was no mention of liberating Palestine or destroying Israel. The Charter and the Unity of Objective framework it laid out reflected the Egyptian communist perception that the real enemy was imperialism, that Israel was simply a local manifestation of imperialism and that consequently to tackle Israel directly would be to dilute revolutionary energy. Israel needed to be contained or 'deterred' (*radi'*), not destroyed. Instead the priority should be to deepen the revolution in Egypt and broaden it throughout the Arab world in order to defeat imperialism. Achieving a military capable of confronting Israel, then, was dependent on the further development of society.

The regional left

Arabism, in much literature on the region, has tended to be approached either as a set of primordial common values hanging over the Middle East, as something cynically manipulated by state leaders in furtherance of *raison d'état*, or as a normative framework for regional order created through the interactions between states. Although some of these interpretations are helpful some of the time, Arabism as a set of regional norms also owes its development to social dynamics which had a transnational character. Since the end of the 1930s, Egypt had sought to dominate the emerging Pan-Arab movement, of which Palestine had become the focus, as a *state*. But the rise of a Pan-Arabist—and Palestinian—orientation on the popular level in Egypt had much to do with the prominence of the Muslim Brotherhood and other middle-class groups that stressed the Islamic component of the Arab-Zionist struggle, and which organised volunteers to fight in Palestine.

Egyptian control of the Gaza Strip made it impossible once again to ignore the Palestine question and sharpened the domestic impact of regional change. Although Nasser was keen to avoid military confrontation with Israel, Israeli incursions in Gaza and Palestinian infiltration from 1955 made this increasingly difficult. Nasser's answer was to use proxies. He created battalions of Palestinian border guards for the purpose of channelling Palestinian resistance while shielding Egypt from Israeli reprisals and tipping the new regime into war. As Sayigh notes, 'This marked the beginning of a difficult and ultimately unsuccessful balancing act, as the government sought to defuse Palestinian discontent with the status quo on the one hand, and keep the peace with Israel on the other.'[29] Nasser justified the proxy approach, which by its nature was not intended to result in military victory over the short term, with reference to Israel's status as a part of imperialism. Speaking in Gaza in May 1956, Nasser predicted that:

As [the Egyptian and Palestinian] army grows strong, those who created Israel will support it with arms. It was announced in Paris yesterday that France will give Israel 12 new planes, but this talk does not alarm us. We knew before that we do not face Israel alone, but we face those who created Israel.[30]

Nasser's enmeshment with the Palestinian resistance meant that different intellectual strands within Palestinian and Egyptian politics were also intertwined in complex and often contradictory ways. Schisms within the Palestinian guerrilla movement in the second half of the 1950s reflected the uneasy tension between recognising a specific Israeli—or Zionist—threat and dissolving the conflict with Israel into the broader revolutionary struggle against imperialism. For the Arab Nationalists' Movement (ANM), which shaped its policy according to that of Nasser, the goal of liberating Palestine 'could not come about unless the Arab countries were free from Western colonial control and therefore able to concentrate their resources against Israel.'[31] For Wadi' Haddad, one of the group's leading lights, 'the road to Tel Aviv passes through Damascus, Baghdad, Amman and Cairo.'[32] Fatah, on the other hand, leant more strongly in favour of a 'Palestine-first' position that viewed Arab regimes with some mistrust and promoted the idea that the liberation of Palestine was a priority that should exist independently of socialist revolution or unity in the Arab world. Rather than predicating the liberation of Palestine on Arab unification, Fatah argued for the establishment of 'an autonomous political entity,' insisting that 'there are Arab parts of Palestine, and it is on those parts that a leading, revolutionary national Palestinian rule should be established to act in cooperation with the Arab states to save Palestine.'[33]

Fatah's orientation was similar to that of the Muslim Brotherhood, and it is significant that many of its founding members—including the Cairo University student Yasir Arafat—had Brotherhood backgrounds. As far as the Islamist conception of Arab Unity was concerned, Zionism, in addition to usurping a part of the Islamic homeland, impeded the unification of the Arabs, which was in turn a prerequisite for Islamic unity. The Brotherhood had called for mobilising Arab and Muslim publics in a *jihad* for Palestine. For the Brotherhood's Salih Ashmawi in 1948, shortly after the declaration of State of Israel, defeating Zionism was an immediate priority, rather than—as was the later Nasserist position—a task dependent on the achievement of Arab unity: 'The blessing of Palestine will not stop merely at achieving Arab unity, it will also achieve Islamic unity.'[34] In this way, the Brotherhood's discourse on Palestine anticipated the later argument of Fatah, and ultimately the PLO, which viewed the liberation of Palestine as the key to, rather than the goal of, Arab unity.

This illustrates the importance of sub-state groupings to the transnational circulation of norms and ideas. Both Fatah and the Muslim Brotherhood were, for similar reasons, interested in liberating Palestine through popular action and reluctant to grant Egypt and the other Arab states more than a supporting role. Ironically, they may have been truer revolutionaries that the ANM, which had tied its fate to the Nasserist state. And the Fatah-Brotherhood, society-centric, stance suited Nasser's actual reluctance to endanger the peace with Israel, and risk the security of his regime, for the sake of Palestine.

The Pan-Arab Ba'th Party, for its part, developed an infatuation with Nasser after Suez. As Munif al-Razzaz, who would become secretary-general of the Ba'th's National Command in 1965 phrased it, 'So great was the excitement he generated that it was supposed that he could realise all our aims at a stroke, by a decree from the top. Rather than struggling for twenty-five years, it was tempting to let an officer such as Nasser do the job overnight.'[35]

Syrian Pan-Arabists had come to view Egypt as the 'nucleus state' from which Arab unity could spread. Sati' al-Husri, a Syrian Arab nationalist who was the director of the Arab League's Higher Arabic Studies Institute in Cairo, was particularly successful in arguing the point that Egypt was a central part of the Arab nation, against those intellectuals who rejected Egyptian 'Arabness'. Al-Husri contended that although geography and population were important, the concept of the nucleus state depended primarily on Egypt's revolutionary 'socialist' political system. The Ba'th were also pioneers in advocating neutralism as a foreign policy stance for the Arab nation, anticipating Nasser's adoption of the doctrine,[36] which further enhanced the ideological fit. Nasser's success in making this ideology synonymous with his leadership owed much to the appeal of socialism and anti-imperialism throughout the region, since 'many of the underlying social and political causes that gave rise to the Free Officers' coup—and later, revolution—also prevailed in the Fertile Crescent countries and may help to explain the meteoric rise of Nasser to the position of idol of the masses.'[37]

Whereas Palestine had for two decades formed the heart of the Pan-Arabist and popular Islamic-nationalist political trend in Egypt, it was not until after Suez that the Egyptian regime began routinely casting Palestine as the end goal of Arab *socialist revolution*. The regional rise of socialism was transforming the political landscape. The Ba'th Party and others sought to synthesise socialist principles with more 'traditional' idea systems and established precepts.[38] Michel Aflaq promoted a view of Israel, which, while prioritising socialism and revolution, also recognised a more specific 'World Zionist' threat, which was in line with the party's simultaneously Pan-Arab and Islamist inclinations. In July 1957 he wrote:

There are in fact two views of imperialism and Zionism, and each of them is inadequate and deviationist: it is known that the rightist front concentrates on Israel to divert the attention from imperialism. On the other hand, there is a liberation view which is not quite accurate when it makes Israel and imperialism two names for one entity. This partially conceals the danger of world Zionism which is undoubtedly an imperialist movement but an independent one. On our part, we consider Israel an imperialist base, beyond a doubt, for it is imperialism which has created, defended and fed it for this purpose. But ... Israel is also an expression of the power of world Zionism, but world Zionism is capable of making use of imperialism itself. The success of the Arabs in shattering imperialism will solve the largest part of the problem but will not solve it in its entirety.[39]

For Aflaq, imperialism could not be defeated without also prevailing over the independent force that was World Zionism.

The Islamist trend under Nasser

The suppression of the Muslim Brotherhood in 1954 did not mean that the Islamic current disappeared completely from public view. Both the Brotherhood and the Islamist paradigm with which it was associated were still very much alive. With most Brotherhood members in prison after 1954 and the Society's organisational structure decimated, those remaining activists, in coordination with imprisoned Brothers adopted a lower profile. From about 1957 'nuclei' of former Brothers and new sympathisers had emerged throughout Egypt.[40] The Brotherhood continued to quietly gather members on the basis of a gradualist approach focussing on Islamic education and not revenge (*intiqam*), though the movement would split to include a more militant trend.[41]

The perspective popularised by the Ikhwan and other *effendiyya* groups in the 1930s and 1940s continued to resonate among intellectuals despite the socialist turn. In two volumes, Alexandria University professor of Arabic literature Muhammad Muhammad Husayn's *al-Ittijahat al-Wataniyya fi al-'Adab al-Mu'asir (Patriotic Tendencies in Contemporary Literature)* provided a rich intellectual history of Egypt between 1882 and 1945.[42] The book stressed the integral and continuing salience of

Islam in the evolution and symbolism of the Egyptian national struggle. One implication of Husayn's literary research was that Israel, like Britain, represented above all a manifestation of a broader Judeo-Christian threat to Islam, which could only be resisted by putting religion at the centre of the Egyptian national struggle.

Husayn's book would provide a rich resource for those who saw Egypt's relations with Israel and the West in terms of cultural imperialism, or the 'intellectual invasion'. One of Sunni Islam's most prominent clerics, the Saudi scholar Safar al-Hawali, has recommended Husayn's work, among others, on his web forum in answer to a request to 'please guide us to some books that refute destructive ideas so that we may be aware of them—specifically, secularism.'[43] Husayn was also a prominent reference for the ideologues of the violent *al-Jama'a al-Islamiyya* in the 1980s, as will be discussed in Chapter 6. While the Muslim Brotherhood had, in the prerevolutionary period, laid out an Islamic case for opposing the coloniser and Zionism, on the grounds that each was threatening the land of Islam, Husayn's detailed textual analysis presented the case that this trend was the natural and authentic expression of Egyptian nationalism. Husayn made frequent use of the Khaldunian concept of *'asabiyya* (group feeling) to highlight his point, and in his estimation Islamic and Arab *'asabiyyat* were natural and inevitable, unlike those based on the fake borders established by colonialism. Arabism in Egypt, for Husayn, was inextricably connected to Islam and the deeply rooted Islamic piety of Egyptians. The British occupation was significant primarily because for the first time it was Christians ruling over Muslims in Egypt.

Husayn presented each 'tendency' in the Egyptian national movement in turn and bemoaned the statising dynamics of modernisation in Egypt. The author scorned states and the states system altogether: they were colonial constructs aimed at weakening Islam. Egyptian politicians were essentially duped or driven by ambition to accept this new framework. He bemoaned the fact that Wafdist leaders viewed Arabism largely as a question of independent states cooperating in order to secure particular interests. Husayn described the arbitrary carving up of the former Ottoman lands into states following World War One as being second in danger only to the fact that the Arabs have started to believe in these fake boundaries. Husayn did not deny that Egyptian patriotism existed, but insisted that this represented just one of many loyalties people felt, such as to their villages, provinces or to others of the same trade or profession. Proponents of narrow nationalisms, like Ahmad Lutfi al-Sayyid, erred in expecting patriots to renounce all these other loyalties, particularly that to the broader Islamic *umma*.

Rather than accepting the need for Egyptian and Arab elites of the time to grapple with modernity, Husayn derided their blind subservience to colonial dictums. Such subservience was reinforced in literature and visual art imploring the Arabs to return to pre-Islamic (*jahili*) *'asabiyyat*. The promotion of Phoenician, Babylonian and Pharaonic imagery and solidarities was, for Husayn, the work of the Europeans themselves who were driven solely by the desire to keep the Arabs weak. It was a non-Muslim project to rewrite the history of the Arabs by downgrading or erasing the Islamic component. Husayn cited the plans of American philanthropist John D. Rockefeller to finance a new Egyptian museum as evidence of this, highlighting Rockefeller's Jewish religion and the 'Zionist-American' money behind the project.

The goal of the West was ultimately, for Husayn, to detach Egyptians and Arabs from their religion, which was their real source of strength. Israel was part and parcel of this unified threat to Islam. Prior to 1948 the West's goal was to create a Jewish state in Palestine and afterwards to ensure it faced no resistance from Muslims:

> the opposition of the Arab states to the ambitions of the Jews in Palestine is attributable to Islam and Arabism. If the Egyptians, for example, are separated from Islam and Arabism, and adopt Pharaonicism, the incentive to fight (*mujahidat*) the Jews and oppose their state in Palestine will die.[44]

Tackling Israel was never, then, for intellectuals during the Nasser period *just* about facing down imperialism, understood in political economic terms. There was also a religious and cultural dimension to political discourse. Nasser feared political challenges—domestically and regionally—from the left as much as the right. A pragmatist, his priority was to protect and preserve the independence of his regime. With the rise to power of Abdel Karim Qasim in Iraq, which brought communists there close to the levers of power, Nasser elevated the anti-communist components of Egyptian political discourse. Links between the Egyptian and Iraqi communist parties were close.[45] On 23 December of that year, Nasser made a speech in Port Said attacking the communists and in early 1959 launched a wave of arrests that encompassed thousands. The Marxist-oriented *Al-Misa* was also closed in that year.

The Arab-Zionist conflict was instrumentalised to embarrass, and legitimise the suppression of, the left. The rift between Egypt and Iraq, and between the regime and Egyptian communists, prompted Nasser to turn to an old slur against communism, that it was synonymous with Zionism, long a Muslim Brotherhood assumption. Nasser accused Qasim of being a Zionist as well as an ally of the British and the communists. The Iraqi communists had, he alleged, been vocal in their attacks on Arab nationalism, while remaining silent on Zionism. Nasser's use of the concept of imperialism at this time also reflected his adoption of an element of analysis that contradicted that of the left (albeit excepting some of Maoist or Trotskyite persuasions) but reflected that propounded by the Muslim Brotherhood. Following the challenge from Iraq in 1958, according to Hasan Hanafi, Nasser described imperialism as the same whether it came from the East or the West.[46] As a 'neutral' state, Egypt was against both forms of imperialism.

The influence of Islamism—and depletion of Soviet influence— marked a subtle reversion to views on Israel that were resonant in Egypt prior to the Czech Arms Deal, when Jewish influence in America was blamed for US hostility to Egypt. Heikal opined that the problems with US policy in the region were due to a lack of understanding or awareness of the essential conflicts in the Middle East. This shortcoming, which he termed the 'greatest tragedy of our age in this region', was due largely to Zionist influence in the United States and the importance of the 'Jewish vote.' The American people, Heikal lamented, were unaware of the extent to which their government served Israeli interests and were ignorant of the plight of the Palestinians.[47] The implication was that if this misunderstanding could be rectified, the United States would be a force for good in the region. The result of such analysis was to strengthen a culturist view of the conflict that legitimated the Islamist, rather than leftist, components of the Egyptian intelligentsia and downgraded the idea of regional socialist revolution as a prerequisite for defeating Israel.

During this time, Nasser also recruited some Muslim Brotherhood members, notably Kamal Abu al-Magd and Abd al-Aziz Kamil, to inject an Islamic component into regime ideology.[48] Many of the officers still identified with Brotherhood ideology from their pre-1952 activities, and the regime was conscious that the mass public enthralled by the Muslim Brotherhood had not yet fully transferred its loyalty to the new order.[49] In 1960 the regime established the Supreme Council for Islamic Affairs (SCIA), which published *Nasser's Encyclopaedia of Jurisprudence {fiqh}* as well as the monthly periodicals *Studies in Islam* and *Islamic Books*. The SCIA was instrumental in presenting Nasser's shift to socialism in the 1960s in Islamic terms, and also represented an important foreign policy instrument. The monthly magazine published by the SCIA, *Minbar al-Islam*, was multilingual and designed to export a rejuvenated version of Islam 'for a new era' internationally. Also, the Islamic Research Academy (*Majama' al-Buhuth al-Islamiyya*) was set up to confront the Saudi Islamic World League (*Rabitat al-'Alam al-Islami*). In addition, a Qur'anic radio station was launched, religion was made a compulsory subject in schools and a programme of mosque construction was launched.[50] Perhaps most important was the nationalisation of al-Azhar, the Islamic world's most venerated university, in 1962.

Marxists were, moreover, not the only intellectual force behind the Nasser era's definiting political document, the National Charter. For the sake of preserving the independence of his regime, as well as due to an ongoing suspicion of communism, Nasser continued to court and co-opt Islamist thinkers and religious ideas remained prominent at the highest levels. The march towards socialism was slowed by the concomitant resurgence of Islam in Egyptian political life. Debates within the Preparatory Commission for the National Charter, chaired by Anwar Sadat, bore this out. They revolved around the extent to which Egypt should adopt 'Arab socialism' or the 'Arab application of socialism', with the former constituting, for Mahfouz, a 'right-wing' position and flowing from assumptions about Egyptian and Arab specificity.[51] In May 1961, Sadat led a UAR delegation to the USSR, where Khrushchev belittled the Egyptian strategy of fusing socialism with Arab nationalism, chiding that 'you do not know much about socialism.' Sadat responded with an explanation of Arab socialism, which can only be furthered 'in a framework of national unity.' He added that 'we also believe that there are a number of spiritual factors, including religion, which have their effects in addition to the accepted basis of material development.'[52]

The former Muslim Brotherhood ideologue Muhammad al-Ghazzali addressed the commission to condemn 'atheist socialism' and presented a thesis on Muslim socialism founded on ideas of social justice. As Mahfouz points out, this was identical to the thesis Ghazzali had already presented in his Muslim Brotherhood capacity in 1950 entitled *Islam and Economic Systems*. Ghazzali's recommendations were published without opposition from within the commission and were greeted with a critical article in *al-Ahram* entitled 'Religious Reaction Rears its Head Again.' The response to this article was the first incidence of violent demonstrations Egypt had seen since 1954 as Azharites and students took to the streets in protest.[53]

Although the language and tone of the National Charter was heavily tinged with Marxism, it explicitly condemned dialectical materialism because of its antipathy towards 'God and His prophets and their sacred messages of truth and salvation.' The Charter ascribed a positive role to religion in society and in guiding the individual and reconciles the teachings of Islam with socialism: 'The All Powerful in his wisdom has placed equality of opportunity before all human beings as a basis of the final judgement.'[54] Other aspects of the Charter were also in tune with the programme of the banned Muslim Brotherhood. The rejection of political pluralism corresponded with the Brotherhood's condemnation of political parties in the name of a 'monolithic Islam'; the refutation of the dictatorship of the proletariat and the principle of class struggle were also fully in line with Brotherhood thinking.[55]

Thinkers of and associated with the Muslim Brotherhood published works reviving the 'intellectual invasion' (*ghazw fikri*) theme that had been popularised in the 1930s and replicated by Muhammad

Muhammad Husayn in the 1950s. Thus, for Muhammad Jalal Kishk in 1966:

> I believe we are living in the third crusader war. The first was that which the Pope Urban II called for in November 1090. The second began with Napoleon's landing in Alexandria in July 1798. As for the third, it is hard to define its beginning because it does not depend on military campaigns so that we can date it to a day of invasion. Rather, its main impetus is the intellectual invasion, and this is a complicated factor, hard to define: maybe its roots go back to the first crusade. In confronting it we have no weapons other than our religion.[56]

For Kishk, Islam was the primary enemy of Israel, as well as the communist and capitalist 'West', due to the fact that Islam was the only viable basis of unity among African and Asian states. This was expressed in strategic terms: 'Israel, as a national enemy, wages a war against us in Africa with a war against Islam and Muslims, and attacks the Islamic states, because they know that Islam is our only way to Africa and nothing else.'[57]

Communism was, for Kishk, an ideological weapon used by the West, as was Zionism. And the two were inextricably linked:

> All communist parties in the Arab world, without exception were established by Jews in the Mashriq and by French in the Maghrib. The greatest danger threatening the Zionist presence in the Mashriq is Islam. This is the force that ended the French direct presence in the Arab Maghrib. It is still the main force that opposes the remains of this presence and is able to end it at the same time.[58]

The limits of Islamism's usefulness to the regime

More threatening to the interests of the regime in the mid-1960s were the subversive and influential writings of Sayyid Qutb. Via Zaynab al-Ghazzali and other women, the regrouped Muslim Brotherhood groups were in contact with imprisoned leaders, including Qutb. Chapters from Qutb's *Milestones* were distributed among Brotherhood study groups from 1962, and published shortly after Qutb's release from prison in 1964. The study groups aimed at convincing '75 percent' of Egyptians of the necessity of an Islamic state through a series of 13-year educational cycles.[59]

Meaningful rationales had to be provided for this, some of which were spelled out in *Milestones*. But the link between the 'near' and 'far' enemies was perhaps drawn more concretely in Qutb's direct political activism than in his writings. As Eccel has written, 'the politically most radical part of the tradition is largely oral, passed on in small teaching circles and private discussions, as one might imagine due to the penalties for the written or public verbal expression of some of its assertions.'[60] Ali Ashmawi, the young leader of the Brotherhood's 'Special Organisation' [al-tanzim al-khas] and participant in the study groups at this time notes that 'Sayyid Qutb was to bring about a great change in people's orientation and the organisation, and a complete reformation of thought. I see that that stage was completely new, and had its influence on the progress of work in the next stage.'[61]

Qutb's ideas and the political programme he inspired are exemplary of the way in with Israel and Zionism have been instrumentalised for countersystemic purposes. It will be recalled that the position of the Muslim Brotherhood from 1936 was that Arab peoples should join in the *jihad* against Zionism in Palestine, while the Arab states played a supporting diplomatic role, and that the Brotherhood opposed joining the government after 1954 for fear of provoking foreign intervention. Inspired by Qutb's ideas, however, elements of the Muslim Brotherhood abandoned this faith in the Arab regimes to provide a protective umbrella and moved their overthrow to the top of the agenda—including above liberating Palestine.

Qutb had already written about the 'intellectual invasion' and laid the bulk of the blame at the feet of the Jews. This holistic view of the Jewish threat would continue to underpin his understanding of both Israel and Egypt. Israel was instrumentalised not to legitimise and build a social movement, as was the case with the left and the 'moderate' Hudaybi wing of the Brotherhood. It, or, to be more precise, *Judaism*, was now being leveraged to lend credence to a more radically countersystemic project. The radicalised, and radicalising, elements of the Brotherhood in prison were increasingly reacting against Nasser's authoritarianism and what was perceived to be the forcible imposition of an alien ideology on Egyptian Muslims, with one of Qutb's main intellectual contributions being to articulate an Islamic rationale for overthrowing an 'unIslamic' regime. The crux of Qutb's originality lay in his elaboration of the concept of *jahiliyya* (literally, 'ignorance') and its application to existing Muslim societies as well as his call for the removal of so-called Muslim regimes. For Qutb, the message of God had been simple and clear from Noah to Muhammad—there is one God. Christians and Jews lost sight of this fundamental precept and therefore their societies were *jahili* societies. But, crucially, Muslim societies had also been led astray and were Muslim only in name. For Ali Ashmawi,

> This was a new thing for us because it led ... to the feeling that you are far from the beliefs of the people and that the people have grown away from their religion and you are able to feel that you are in one valley and they are in another, and that they are genuinely not Muslims. In correspondence with this feeling are many dangerous things like considering people to be infidels (*kufra*) and that you shouldn't eat their slaughtered animals or marry them and isolate and avoid them. This was a dangerous direction, but we took it.[62]

Qutb's views on Israel and Jews as expressed in the 1960s were coloured by his paramount preoccupation with the state of *jahiliyya* in which Muslim societies found themselves, a state that could not be reversed so long as infidel rulers remained in place. For Qutb, the Jews 'recruited' Nasser in 1948 and used the Free Officers' coup as a way of subverting Egypt, the lynchpin of the Arab-Muslim world. It is for this reason that Ashmawi considers Qutb's views on Zionism to be at the very heart of his political philosophy:

> We discuss the opinion of Sayyid Qutb regarding the World Zionist Movement and its domination over the Eastern and

Western camps as an entry from which will follow a discussion on the rest of his political opinions, because this precept is what governs, in my opinion, his political view, and is the wellspring of his thinking.[63]

Qutb considered Israel and Egypt to be on a par – both creatures and tools of a broader Jewish plot. He took a long historical view that saw an age-old Jewish conspiracy aiming at world domination. For Qutb, in common with Muhammad Husayn, many Jews embraced Christianity following the Spanish inquisition and aimed to subvert it towards that goal. Sephardic Jews also embraced Islam, 'but retained their Jewish religiosity, and those had a big influence on the plans to dominate the Islamic movement and destroy Islam, as they had worked to do with Christianity.' This Jewish-inspired venture was manifested in Christian missionary operations in Islamic countries, whose failure to convert Muslims resulted in a change of tack whereby Orientalism would attempt to destroy the underpinnings of Islam 'by way of Westerners that had converted to Islam, or had not converted but wrote about it.' The 'Jew, Gibb' was mentioned specifically. Orientalist work criticising Islam in turn gave way to Western scholarship that praised it— but this only represented a more subtle, insidious, way of undermining the religion and people's faith in it by destroying 'tiny parts until the reader is convinced without realizing.'[64]

The chief instruments of the Jews in their quest for domination over the world, and destruction of Islam, were, for Qutb, control over money and information. Once they had gained control of 'most European states' and America, they set their sights on Russia. The means by which the Jews gained control of Russia was the communism of the 'Jew, Karl Marx'. The communist 'coup' in 1917 was a Jewish plot: 'many of the leaders of the coup were Jews, or married to Jews.'[65]

For Qutb, then, Jewish domination 'extended to the Eastern and Western camps' and aimed primarily at 'war with Islam, besieging it and striking it in every place.'[66] The Jews facilitated the fall of the Ottoman Empire and were behind Ataturk's revolution. After prevailing over Turkey, Egypt was considered the key to the Islamic world, and the initial approach to destroying Islam in Egypt was via its women. The movement for women's rights in the early 20th century and the 'throwing off' of the *hijab*, were manifestations of this strategy, which also underpinned the social policies of Gamal Abdel Nasser.[67] His regime's policy of industrialisation and the employment of women in factories in the countryside, which inevitably brought them into contact with men, was designed to destroy Islamic values in rural areas, specifically because it was there that 'Islamic values were strongest.'[68] The ultimate goal in all of this was, and for Qutb in the mid-1960s, remained, to sustain a *jahili* society in Egypt and facilitate Zionist and crusader domination.[69] As such, the way of resisting this was to work incessantly towards reviving Islam in the souls of the Egyptian people.

In his final testimony, *Limadha a'damuni {Why Did they Execute Me?}*, Sayyid Qutb blamed 'Zionist and crusader' forces for the regime's suppression of the Muslim Brotherhood in 1954, and explained why he resolved to rebuild the Islamic movement: 'I saw the real results in the life of Egyptian society from the great spread of atheist ideas and moral decline as a result of the destruction of the Muslim Brotherhood and the end of its educational activities.'[70] He wrote:

> The issue is much greater than the simplifications of those who see what happened as simply development. It relates to Zionist and imperialist crusader plans to destroy the fundamentals of the human elements in the region in order that these millions will become broken debris that cannot resist even if you put the strongest weapons in their hands.[71]

Qutb continued that while in prison in the 1950s, he realised that:

> After a long review and study of the Muslim Brotherhood movement and a comparison with the first Islamic movement in Islam it became clear in my thinking ... that the Islamic movement today faces a situation similar to that faced by the human societies the day Islam emerged for the first time from ignorance ... It is not just the distance from the Islamic system (*al-nizam al-islami*) and the Islamic *shari'a*—at the same time the Zionist and

imperialist crusader camps are strong, fighting every attempt at Islamic proselytising and working to destroy it by way of local regimes and apparatuses.[72]

Qutb also condemned communism in *Ma'alim fi al-Tariq* [*Milestones on the Road*],[73] which should be understood as an oblique reference to the system that Nasser was seen to be following. Islamist critiques of communism thus flowed directly from their attacks on Nasser, ironically given Nasser's recourse to the same slurs. The fact that Nasser was perceived to be the leader of a communist regime that had led Egypt into a humiliating defeat against Israel in 1967 could be seen to confirm the Islamist link between communism and Zionism.

It is worth dwelling on the deeper political significance of the regime's experiments with the Muslim Brotherhood. Nasser's initial swing back towards the left after the Syrian secession from the UAR in 1961 revealed the serious pressure actually putting revolutionary rhetoric into practice placed on the regime. Nasser had dispatched Egyptian troops to fight on the republican side in Yemen. But the Yemen campaign drained Egypt financially and the country was already suffering from serious food shortages. As with later moments of acute economic hardship, notably in 1977 when Sadat withdrew bread subsidies, the regime grew alarmed about the prospect of a revolt of the poor, for whom it turned out the revolutionary regime was unable to provide.

This pressure eventually led Nasser to seek reconciliation with Saudi Arabia, which was supporting the royalist side in the Yemen war, which in turn necessitated a reformulation of foreign policy doctrine. Egypt also sought further aid from the United States. The Brotherhood, along with Saudi Arabia and other regional actors, stood for a new conservative form of Arabism based on adherence to Islam—with the Wahhabis and the radical wing of the Muslim Brotherhood standing for a particularly austere form of Islamic state. The Brotherhood in general had enjoyed support from the Gulf States, particularly Saudi Arabia, since its proscription in 1954. Nasser's rehabilitation of the Muslim Brotherhood in the early 1960s, along with the other Islamising steps he took, can be seen in regional terms as part of moving away from the revolutionary socialist forms of Arab nationalism and towards a more conservative status quo Islamism aligned with the United States.

These regional considerations were inextricably linked to domestic concerns in Egypt, as elsewhere. The general atmosphere of anti-communism—demonstrated most brutally, with apparent CIA support, by the Iraqi Ba'th in 1963—reflected the persistent fragility of post-revolutionary states in the face of societal grievances and pressure from below. The new Iraqi president Abd al-Salam Aref, who oversaw the butchery of Iraqi communists in the country's poorest areas, strove to present himself as a pious Muslim.[74] He was a supporter of Sayyid Qutb and lobbied to have him released from prison on health grounds in 1964. Islamism was viewed as a potential solution to faltering state hegemony over society. The trouble was that the Islamism of the Brotherhood, as it had evolved under Qutb's guidance, also represented an ideology of revolt against political oppression and absolutist state power.

Statism

Resurgent Islamism thus reinforced, rather than eroded, statism and its terms of reference were compatible with those of many secular intellectuals. From the early 1960s, leftist newspaper editors were removed, to be replaced with less 'ideological' individuals, the most significant of whom was the appointment of Mohamed Hassanein Heikal, Nasser's close friend and advisor, as editor-in-chief of *al-Ahram*, the Arab world's largest circulating newspaper, as well as a prominent pre-revolutionary liberal Fikri Abaza, as head of the Dar al-Hilal publishing house and editor of *al-Musawwar*.[75] The journal *al-Ahram al-Iqtisadi* (*The Economic Ahram*) was established following the closure of *al-Misa* under the editorship of Boutros Boutros Ghali, which adopted a markedly less radical, though still socialist, tone on domestic and international issues.[76]

Nasser's approach to the ideological threat from Qasim, and broader revolutionary tendencies across the region, was, at the beginning of the 1960s, to downplay the need for revolutions in Arab states as a step towards unification in favour of building a broader front against Iraq.[77] Islamic solidarity was one framework revived to give meaning to the shift, but the language of sovereignty and statism was also deployed. The regime espoused a state-centric view of Arab nationalism under the slogan 'Unity of Rank' (*Wahdat al-Saff*),[78] bolstered intellectually by such figures as Abd al-Rahman al-Bazzaz. Bazzaz served as director of the Arab League's Institute of Higher Arab Studies in Cairo and would, in 1965, become prime minister of Iraq. In 1960, he published *Al-Dawla al-Muwahhada wa-al-Dawla al-Ittihadiyya (The Unitary State and the Federal State)* in which he argued for a federal state as most appropriate given the heterogeneity of Arab political systems. 'Total union of the whole Arab world', he wrote, 'would necessitate the destruction of all monarchies.' This would be unacceptable because 'certain countries, because of their present situation or of the services rendered them by their kings, do not wish to change their status.'[79]

Bazzaz's embrace of political heterogeneity and unity resting on states' shared ethnic identities, and the concomitant downgrading of socialism, magnified the exceptional status of Israel. The idea of a heterodox 'Middle East', for Bazzaz, was a form of 'intellectual imperialism', implying that:

> Israel is in the Middle East; it is an established fact, being actually there and no longer merely one of the goals of Zionism; it is there to stay. It remains for you Middle Easterners to live together and to find ways and means for friendship and cooperation leading to peace.[80]

A similarly excluding perspective was put forward by the journalist Ahmad Abd al-Muti' Hijazi in his response to one academic's suggestion that Israel was proof that states and nations could be established on a religious basis: 'the Professor believes that the establishment of Israel on the basis of religion has nothing queer or abnormal about it ... and believes further that Arab unity should be built on this same foundation.' Bazzaz called on Arabs to insist on the term 'Arab world' for their homeland, 'thus wiping out Israel intellectually, and affirming that the Israelis are people who are foreign to us and usurpers of our land.'[81]

As we have seen, Egyptian foreign policy discourse shifted leftwards following Syrian secession from the UAR in 1961, but actually putting revolutionism into practice was incompatible with the maintenance of economic stability and social harmony at home. Before long, the doctrine Unity of Objective that was enshrined in the Charter became 'Unity of Action.' Under the new formulation, Egypt would work with all Arab states—reactionary and progressive—under Egyptian leadership to secure common goals,[82] postponing unification and Arab socialist revolution. Marxist thinkers attempted to reconcile this new stance with Egypt's role at the vanguard of Arab revolution. As Lutfi al-Khuli wrote in *al-Tali'a*, 'in the first stage, Egypt will appear in the map of the [Arab] social forces as a separate entity, but later on it will become [an integral] part of the Arab nation [and thus could] lead the over-all battle against imperialism.'[83]

The apparent embrace of sovereignty and statism contributed to a distinctly warlike atmosphere. As a consequence, Nasser found himself cornered into bellicosity towards Israel. Under Unity of Action, the issue of Israel rose to the fore in Arab politics in a way it had not since Suez. Israel, rather than imperialism, returned as the essential adversary of the Arabs, and for the first time the 'liberation' of Palestine and the 'liquidation' of Israel became official Egyptian policy goals. Against the backdrop of Israeli plans to divert the Jordan River, conservative states like Jordan and Saudi Arabia, as well as pro-Western Lebanon, signed up to an Arab League declaration pledging to 'liquidate' Israel.[84]

The Unified Arab Command that would theoretically liberate Palestine was never more than a chimera, but the Egyptian regime found itself caught between an overriding reluctance to engage in military conflict and the need to deal with states that were calling for interstate war with Israel. Intellectually, accepting the idea of Israeli specificity led to the conclusion that tackling Israel militarily was a separate task from the struggle against imperialism and one to which the UAR should be more than equal. One part of Nasser's approach to this conundrum was to seek, as he had done in 1955, a Palestinian solution. Following the Arab League summit in May 1964, the Palestine Liberation Organisation (PLO) was established, essentially becoming an arm of Egyptian foreign policy.[85] Under the demagogic leadership of Ahmed Shuqayri, who famously called for the Jews to be pushed into the sea, the PLO shifted the onus away from Egypt and onto the Palestinians themselves.

In addition to giving support to the PLO, the regime and its spokesmen also started talking about people's war to liberate Palestine, recognising that there was a specific Israeli problem but again shifting expectations away from the idea that the UAR or any other state army would be there to solve it. In September 1964, Heikal argued that 'those who established Israel' did so not just to create a Jewish national home, but to create a base in the Arab world for the furtherance of imperialist interests. Success in eradicating (tasfiyat) the Israeli aggression and furthering socialism, freedom and unity among the Arabs were thus two sides of the same coin.[86] Nasser threatened to launch what would be essentially a people's war against Israel in 1965: 'one day the Arabs will recruit two to three million men in order to liberate Palestine and restore the rights of the Palestinian people regardless of how many arms Israel receives from the West.'[87]

Caveats inserted into Egyptian, or Arab, socialism which highlighted the specificity of Egyptian, Arab or Muslim culture, coloured—directly or indirectly—approaches to Israel. They supported the emerging consensus that state and society had different roles to play, and that Israel and imperialism were distinct threats to be dealt with differently. The dualistic narrative that underpinned Heikal's 'Egypt as state, Egypt as revolution' formulation was echoed in his analysis of Israel. In January 1963, Heikal maintained that 'Israel [was] a tool of imperialism, which created it'. But he added that Israel had its own special plans and goals that transcended those of imperialism. He argued that while Israel may have been a 'tool' it was not a puppet, and he used the analogy of a hired killer whose employer finances and arms him, but who has his own ambitions, views and dreams. Especially in times of danger, he warned, the hitman may act on his own initiative. Heikal warned that Israel was beginning to feel cornered, by the successes of the UAR on the one hand, and the increasing tendency of the United States to overlook Israeli concerns in favour of its own national interests—itself a result of the Arabs' success in convincing the United States that it could not ignore Arab interests—on the other.[88]

Heikal's discussion of Israel in *al-Ahram* after the second Arab summit in May 1964 also attempted to reconcile the two perspectives. He elevated Israel as a more specific threat than imperialism in general, but continued to conceptualise the threat as emanating from Israel's role as a tool of imperialism. Heikal warned of future *'nakbas'* [catastrophes] that would threaten not just the Palestinians but all Arabs, 'expelling [them], on account of their abiding opposition [*al-ta'arrud al-'abadi*] to imperialism and to end for good the hope for unity and the cause of progress [*al-khuruj min siyaq al-taqaddum*].' In justifying the regime's decision to build bridges with 'reactionaries' in order to form a united front against Israel, Heikal explained that the summit was possible due to the beneficial effect the progressive camp, primarily the UAR, but also revolutionary Algeria, Yemen and Iraq, were having on the Arab world: 'Cairo is no longer alone,' he exclaimed. Heikal applauded Kuwait for conditioning its foreign relations on countries' stance on Palestine as well as their commitment, enshrined in the summit's final resolution, to fighting British imperialism in the region. The 'new powers' in the Arab world, Heikal happily concluded, were having a positive effect on the old.[89]

An emerging liberal thesis

The summitry period encouraged the idea that Israel was distinctive and exceptional, not just part of imperialism. As we have seen, such a view had its echoes in Ba'thist and Islamist thought, instrumentalised as a weapon to embarrass or move away from the left. But another form of instrumentalisation was also present. The thesis of Israeli distinctiveness also furthered a liberal agenda, albeit one that was tentative and respectful towards 'Nasserism' at this stage, but which was characterised by a commitment to political and economic modernisation in Egypt and an emphasis on strategic statist interaction and active public diplomacy. Since 1956 a conception of Israel as part and parcel of imperialism had driven the Nasser regime's strategy of avoiding war with Israel through an argument that protecting and spreading the Egyptian revolution must come first. This went hand-in-hand with a narrative of Israeli insignificance: the Israeli state was simply a group of Zionist 'asabat (gangs), without substance, power or independent existence outside of its imperialist protectors. By the mid-1960s, however, as the Arab states set themselves against Israel *specifically*, some intellectuals began to pay more attention to the particularity of Israel, and even to suggest that Israel may be a more powerful challenge to Egypt and the other Arab states in and of itself.

In March 1965, during the period of Arab summitry, Dar al-Hilal published a book by the Egyptian journalist Ahmad Baha al-Din entitled *Isra'iliyat*.[90] Baha al-Din would return to the main theme raised in the book after the Six-Day War in a series of articles in the liberal journal *al-Musawwar*. Baha al-Din noted in the introduction to this book that even though Israel was never out of the Arab media, the Arabs knew little about it. He complained that Israel was too often interpreted at face value, as an invading, occupying state, carrying out the will of foreign forces in the Arab world and eager for further expansion. What was rarely acknowledged though, for Baha al-Din, was 'Israel as a civilisational challenge to the Arab nation.'[91]

Baha al-Din stressed the Zionists' skill at using American politics as an instrument and analysed Ben Gurion's speeches to show how the Zionist movement succeeded in mobilising 'World Judaism [al-yahudiyya al-'alamiyya' behind Israel. Baha al-Din was clear in highlighting the differences between Zionists and Jews, noting that 'Israel is afraid that the Jew will follow religion and not nationalism.' To reinforce this, he pointed out that no religion required that its followers return to the source of the religion (all Christians were not expected to live in Jerusalem, nor all Muslims in Mecca). 'Jewish emigration,' he concluded, 'was nothing but a political, reactionary, imperialist and extremist objective.'[92] Baha al-Din dismissed the view that the conflict between Israel and the Arabs was a reflection of a religious struggle between Judaism and Islam since 'Israel is a state established by people with no relation to religion'.[93] He argued that Zionism was a political 'religionist' movement (*haraka siyasiyya dinawiyya*) and not a religious movement (*haraka diniyya*). It was Zionist political action that populated Israel, not Judaism, and Jews did not of their own volition flock there after the establishment of the state.[94]

In Baha' al-Din's book, it was not imperialism *per se* that made Israel distinctive but modernity. As such, its terms of reference diverged from those of the Charter and Nasser's left-wing nationalism. Although he celebrated the revolution of Gamal Abdel Nasser, the word 'socialism' (*ishtirakiyya*) does not appear in the book's 257 pages. The real source of Israeli power lay in its modernity, and its 'civilisation', particularly as compared to Arab 'backwardness'. For him, 'The establishment of Israel itself was an expression of the weakness of the Arab region and its civilisational backwardness.'[95] Baha al-Din drew a parallel between the ineptitude of the Mamlukes in confronting Bonaparte's invasion in 1798 and that of the Arab kings in 1948. In each, backward 'reactionary' leaders were powerless in the face of European 'modern' civilisation.[96] 'Zionism', for Baha al-Din, 'represents the West and all its power, with its modern political, scientific and civilisational tools.'[97]

Confronting Israeli modernity was thus dependent on Egyptian political and economic development. Baha al-Din described the Egyptian revolution as having national, social, cultural and industrial dimensions, marking the turning point in the Arabs' development, and breathing life into their struggle against Israel. Since Nasser, 'half the world opposes Israel and supports us.' This was to be explained by the Arabs' modernisation and, particularly, the fact that they now had people 'who understand the logic of modern international politics.'[98] It was the Arabs' continued modernisation that would define the 'clash of destinies' over the long term, since 'backwardness is the only thing that guarantees Israel can remain on our land forever.'[99]

Despite the praise for Nasser, Baha al-Din's intervention constituted a veiled critique that would be made more explicit two years later. While Baha al-Din was clear to defend and celebrate Nasser's role in accelerating Arab development in his 1965 book, after 1967 this author, and others, attributed the defeat in the Six-Day War to the same backwardness that had lost Palestine in 1948. Baha al-Din's preoccupation with Israel's 'modern' and 'civilised' characteristics, including its ability to pursue its interests rationally through modern international diplomacy, would be echoed in a form more directly critical of the Nasser experiment by Tawfiq al-Hakim (in 1972), and helped support Sadat's rejection of an 'adventurist' foreign policy and focus on economic and political development at home. The liberal trend thus came eventually to instrumentalise Israel for democracy.

1967 and the failure of the revolutionary paradigm

Nasser again turned to the left, partially because the refusal and then highly conditional offer of the US Congress to grant further aid to Egypt on 14 July 1966 demonstrated to Nasser the West's unreliability as a guarantor against societal unrest. The proposed 'Islamic Pact' (*al-hilf al-islami*) between Saudi Arabia, which had just secured a $350 million arms deal with the West, and Iran, moreover threatened to marginalise Egypt on a regional level, and led Nasser to declare once again that co-operation with these 'reactionary' forces was impossible.[100] Nasser openly aligned Egypt with Brezhnev's Soviet Union. Egypt's left-wing intellectuals were able once again to draw on the previous logic of the Charter to make Arab unity contingent on social revolution:

> The fundamental meeting point revolves around social action which is responsible for building unity of struggle for all the revolutionary Arab forces without exception. ... It is a mistake to ignore or disavow the level of ideological differences, whatever they may be.[101]

The editor of the left-wing journal *Ruz al-Yusuf,* Ahmad Hamrush, sought to lay out 'the Road to the Unity of Progressive Forces' in the Arab world. 'The unity of progressive forces,' he wrote, 'must flow from their realisation of the truth of their role in the societies in which they exist and an honest appraisal (*wuzn sadiq*) of their influence over the masses, and with a complete awareness of the possibilities for confronting the imperialist and reactionary forces surrounding them.'[102] In the following issue he continued on this theme, repeating Nasser's call that the union of all 'revolutionary forces' was necessary to break completely with imperialism, remove its remaining bases in the Arab world and confront the danger of Zionism: 'Cairo was and remains the base of the liberation struggle. Nasser declares always his support for

liberation causes, not just in the Arab countries, but in all the countries of the world.'[103]

It is notable that in Ahmed Hamrush's editorials around this time,
as in the 1962 National Charter, the threats of Israel and Zionism
were discussed only tangentially as Egypt's struggle was universal-
ised on a global scale. When Israel was mentioned, it was largely to
highlight the complicity of 'reactionary' states in the Jewish state's
continued survival. In March 1966, Hamrush denounced the Islamic
Pact as 'imperialist' and accused its prospective members—Iran, Saudi
Arabia, Pakistan, Turkey, Tunisia and Morocco—of not being concerned with Israel. He pointed to the dubious Islamic credentials of
the Shah and Bourguiba of Tunisia and drew attention to the strong
economic and financial ties that existed between Israel and Iran, going
as far as to suggest that since Israel had a controlling interest in many
important Iranian companies, it was impossible for the pact to be
aimed at confronting Israel.[104]

The rejuvenation of anti-imperialism was also encouraged by the
Syrian coup in February 1966. The new Ba'th government was markedly more radical, subscribing to a 'Maoist doctrine of people's war
against Israel ...'[105] On 27 July 1966, marking the fourteenth anniversary of the Egyptian revolution, Nasser addressed the Arab Socialist
Union with a clear statement of his reluctance to pursue a military
course with Israel. He said that 'when the Syrian army asked us to
participate with them in fighting Israel, we said to them that the battle is greater than Israel. There is a reactionary conspiracy inside Syria,
and the battle is an expression of the alliance between Zionism, imperialism and reaction.' He pointed out that because Israel was able to
match the Arabs plane for plane, tank for tank, the Arabs' most valuable advantage was people. 'If we wanted to liberate Palestine we could
arm three, two, or four million and go and liberate Palestine without
thought for the victims.'[106]

The politics of summitry had, for Nasser now, been a mistake:
though the Arab kings could help confront Israeli aggression, they
could not help to liberate Palestine, since 'the only way to liberate Palestine is revolutionary action.' Nasser returned to an old
theme—reminding his listeners that it had been the connivance of

the reactionary King Abdullah of Jordan with the Zionists and the links of the Arab regimes with colonialism that had led to the loss of Palestine in the first place. He stressed, 'I do not imagine in any case that Saudi Arabia can fight in Palestine when it has an American base in it and a British base. Saudi Arabia first has to be able to liberate itself from the Americans and the British, then after that it can turn to liberate Palestine.' Nasser complained that after three years of summits, 'Arab reaction has shown its true colours ... We found that Arab reaction hates us more than it hates Israel, we found that there is coordination between Arab reaction and Israel. We found that the same [people] who support Arab reaction support Israel.' In concluding his point, Nasser stated:

> This is our position. We discover Arab reaction in all corners of the Arab nation. Arab reaction works with imperialism and Zionism works with imperialism. So how can Arab reaction fight Zionism? ... We cannot coordinate our efforts for Palestine with Arab reaction, because Arab reaction which betrayed us in 1948 is the Arab reaction present today in 1966.[107]

Nasser's obsession with remaining the vanguard of Arabism, and being seen to defend Arab causes, is often held to explain the disastrous descent into war with Israel in 1967.[108] Egged on and mocked by radical and conservative Arab states alike for his impotence, according to this view, Nasser took the steps that ultimately brought Egypt past the point of no return. But we must also acknowledge domestic considerations and see in the brinkmanship of June 1967 the exposure of the irreconcilable contradictions within, and ultimate failure of, 'Egypt as state; Egypt as revolution' as a formula linking state and society towards a common endeavour and enabling Nasser to give Egypt's neutralised society a sense of agency without threatening the stability of the regime. As Kerr notes, war with Israel came as a surprise to many: 'the conflict to which all signs seemed to point ... was between Arab revolutionaries and conservatives'.[109] And with Ba'thists in Syria calling for immediate people's war (against Israel/imperialism), it was the prestige and authenticity of the Egyptian *revolution*—as the embodiment of societal agency—that was also at stake. As with 1948, though, the gamble of 1967 ended badly for the incumbent regime. And it took around the same amount of time—four years—for the 'corrective revolution' of 1971 to inaugurate a new social and cultural experiment.

CHAPTER 4

INTERBELLUM (1967–1973)

The six years between 1967 and 1973 mark an important period in the evolution of Egyptian foreign policy discourse. They were significant as Egyptian intellectuals and leaders sought to recover from, explain and readapt to the defeat in 1967, but before the 'victory' of 1973 restored some measure of self-esteem and set in train the process that would lead to the Camp David Accords and Peace Treaty in 1978–1979. Sayyid Yasin has argued that from 1967 the conflict with Israel shifted from one over existence (*wujud*) to one over borders (*hudud*). The fact that Egypt had lost its own territory (Sinai) as well as that part of Palestine under its control (the Gaza Strip) clarified the Palestine issue and cut through much of the symbolic posturing over 'liquidating' Israel or fomenting region-wide revolution. Statist narratives, never absent, thus came resolutely to the fore, as Egypt lost its actual 'foothold' in Palestine and part of its own national territory.

After 1967 interstate war became a more salient and plausible option than it had been before. Soviet arms supplies and personnel assistance skyrocketed and Nasser quickly launched the War of Attrition in the Canal Zone. Some intellectuals, and many students, were spurred by the humiliation of defeat to protest and campaign for, variously, more democratic freedoms, deepening of revolution and the restoration of Islam to the centre of political life; as well as returning to a war footing with Israel. But unlike the aftermath of 1948, defeat in war did not catalyse societal violence against the regime. Protest and demonstrations in 1968 were, as compared to those taking place concurrently in Europe and elsewhere, tame. Later, the leftist student movement of 1972 called on the regime to arm the people and allow them to fight against Israel, while also ridiculing Sadat for his reluctance to field the Egyptian army against Israel. But despite Sadat's protestations about the diversion of world attention elsewhere, it remained important to the regime to demonstrate that Egypt, as a state, was capable of responding militarily to Israel. The surprising Egyptian success in the early stages of the October 1973 campaign thus restored prestige to the idea of Egypt as a state.

The left after 1967

The defeat of 1967 threw the Egyptian, and Arab, left into two broad camps. The first sought to defend the Nasserist experiment and argue that the 'setback' had occurred as a result of imperialist forces supporting Israel, or even instigating the battle, but that because the main aim of imperialism in the region was to destroy the Arab revolution and topple its regimes, the fact that this had not happened meant that Israel had not won the war. This position was adopted by the writers of the Marxist journal *al-Tali'a*, as well as externally in the pro-Nasser ANM. The second saw the defeat as indicative of the failure of the Nasser regime to mobilise the population, itself due to the fact that the socialist revolution in the region was in its infancy, stalled or a fiction. This position was associated with a 'post-Nasserist' Arab left, and was strongly represented within elements of the Palestinian guerrilla movement and its supporters, including many Egyptian students.

The Nasser regime continued to identify Israel with imperialism after 1967. Soon after the June war, President Nasser announced that 'liberating the homeland from Israel would be no easy matter, because Israel did not stand alone. It operated as a stooge of world imperialism and colonialism.'[1] Domestically, an acceptable reason for Israel's resounding victory had to be provided to the Egyptian public and portraying Israel as imperialism allowed the regime to absolve the state of some of the responsibility for the defeat, as well as introduce a note of caution regarding the prospects of 'erasing the consequences of the aggression' quickly—something the stalemated 1969–1970 War of Attrition over the Sinai bore out.

Although in his endorsement of the Rogers Plan, based on the United Nations Security Council Resolution (UNSCR) 242, Nasser effectively accepted the existence of the State of Israel, in 1970, he continued to associate Israeli designs with American imperialism, remarking that 'Israel is America's forward base in Western Asia,' and that US strategy 'has been to overthrow all progressive Arab governments ... and they use Israel as their instrument in the execution of this policy.'[2]

The Marxist journal *al-Tali'a* was quick to defend the regime's version of events, which held that the war was an all-out imperialist assault on the Arab revolution spearheaded by the United States, and that since its objective had not been achieved, Israel could only claim to have inflicted a superficial 'setback' on the Arabs. In the first issue after the war, Isma'il Sabri Abdullah argued that 'Israel is nothing in all of this other than the evil guard dog unleashed by the American master colouring the holy land with blood hoping that its owner would leave it some bones.'[3] Ibrahim Sa'd al-Din argued that US imperialism had failed to destroy the Arab revolution through economic and psychological means, and so had used external aggression instead. He called for the unity of the forces of liberation and peace to defeat imperialism, referring to the socialist countries, and referred to the division in the ranks of this support reservoir caused by the Sino-Soviet split, arguing that this had allowed imperialism to do what it had done.[4] In August 1967, *al-Tali'a*'s editor, Lutfi al-Khuli, remarked that the 1967 war showed Israel in her true light—as nothing more than an arm of imperialism. Israel's interests, like those of American imperialism, lay in toppling the revolutionary regimes and establishing a 'Greater Israel' (*isra'il al-kubra*) project whereby the boundaries of the Jewish state would extend from the Nile to the Euphrates.[5] That Israel failed to achieve these objectives in the Six-Day War revealed that the war against Israel and imperialism was ongoing. Lutfi al-Khuli and other contributors also argued that strengthening socialism in Egypt was essential in order to erase the consequences of the aggression and to ensure the 'presence and continuation of the revolution.'[6]

The transition from Nasser to Sadat in 1970 initially left this interpretation intact. In January 1971, Sadat argued that 'we face today world Zionism supported by the power of the United States.' World

Zionism's aim, he averred, 'has made for its objective "Greater Israel" from the Nile to the Euphrates.' In furtherance of this goal, 'Zionism never abandoned its main principle and its original objective. It wants to make itself an agent for any big power that emerges in this world so that it may be able to realise through this big power, its dream of establishing "Greater Israel".' Sadat indicated that 'Israel—according to the declarations of its ministers—is the first line of defence for American interests in the region.' He also pointed out that after 5 June 1967, 'Goldberg, the US delegate was a Zionist and declared that he was proud of being Zionist' and concluded that 'the problem is no longer Israel. The problem is America.' He added that 'Israel took its requirements from the budget of the US Defence Department. This means that Israel is part of the United States.'[7]

Some Arab leftists were highly critical of the Arab regimes that had led their countries to defeat. Sadiq al-Azm was an important figure in the 'Arab New Left' after 1967 and formulated a critique of the defeat that would be influential among leftist intellectuals in Egypt, particularly within the student movement.[8] Since al-Azm's work represented a real shift in Arab left-wing thought in the wake of 1967, and was an important influence on Egyptian intellectuals, it deserves attention here. In his *al-Naqd al-Dhati ba'd al-Hazima*, *{Self Criticism After the Defeat}* published in 1968, al-Azm noted a contradiction on the part of the Egyptian and Syrian regimes and their apologists in the call to 'erase the traces of the aggression,' as well as to pursue negotiations. Negotiations legitimised the pre-1967 borders of Israel, while a war to recover the occupied territories would not be able to stop at that, since victory against the Israeli army would require military action inside Israel proper. In this he noted the parallel with Vietnam. The North Vietnamese had penetrated as far as Saigon. The Arab forces would, necessarily, have to take the battle to Tel Aviv in order to win a war with Israel.

But for al-Azm the Arab world was no Vietnam, Cuba, China or Korea. In the latter cases, scientific socialism was advanced to the extent that the entire population could be mobilised in the war effort. In addition, these societies had reached the degree of technical and scientific sophistication and exhibited the 'national feeling' that would be necessary to confront imperialism. For al-Azm, the socialist revolution in the Arab countries was in its infancy, if not completely stalled, and as such a war could only be waged if this revolution were accelerated and deepened. Those who called for a more limited campaign were not serious according to al-Azm. Egyptian and other Arab officials, he pointed out, blamed the 1967 defeat on Israel's links with American imperialism. If it was impossible to defeat imperialism then, he enquired, how would it be possible in any renewed struggle, no matter how well-prepared the Arab states were militarily? But a popular liberation struggle—the only type of war that would be successful against imperialism—could not be won at this stage.[9]

Al-Azm chastised the Arabs for not admitting a degree of responsibility for the defeat, accusing those who blamed imperialism, or Soviet inaction or lack of faith of shirking this responsibility. He was particularly scathing about those who sought to portray the conflict in religious terms, including the notion that Jerusalem was more important than the rest of occupied Palestine. For al-Azm, this attachment to Jerusalem was yet another indication of the Arabs' backwardness and their lack of national feeling and attachment to the land as a whole. Religious thinking also led to paranoid conspiracy theories about world Zionist domination, in which the Jews were seen to control the United States and the West and the strength of an enemy which was seen to manipulate the course of history in its favour was exaggerated. This line of thought was particularly dangerous because it exonerated the United States and the capitalist world of blame. Innocent of any wrongdoing, so this interpretation went, the West was simply in thrall to the global Jewish conspiracy, and was a 'natural friend' of the Arabs. The Arabs, by this reasoning, must try to win over the United States in the same way as did the Zionists.

For al-Azm, this constituted a rightist, reactionary, position that exaggerated Jewish influence in an essentially 'WASP'-dominated US political system. The argument that Jews controlled America could not explain the latter's response to the Suez Crisis and its less-than-helpful attitude towards Jews during World War Two. And ultimately, this theory ignored the fact that it was *capitalism* that drove American policy in the region. That American oil, strategic and cultural interests in the Middle East corresponded to the goals of Zionism constituted a happy symbiosis, not the control of the world's major capitalist power by Jews. American interests in the Middle East were to support Israel and the reactionary regimes, and to suppress liberation movements. The June defeat thus represented a major success for the United States and Israel in the region. It reinvigorated the reactionary regimes, reinforced Israel's strategic importance and, crucially, did not harm oil or other major interests. Any battle to liberate the land, then, for al-Azm, must go hand in hand with the struggle against imperialism through building socialism in the Arab world.

Al-Azm also lambasted those who, in blaming the defeat on imperialism, argued that the Arabs would have beaten Israel had they been able to fight it 'on its own' but not against the United States and Europe, which armed and supported Israel. For al-Azm, this line of thought ignored the fact that Israel was always linked to colonialism and as such, barring a radical, and unlikely, shift in international power configuration, there would never be such thing as fighting Israel 'on its own.' The resort to blaming imperialism was, he argued, just another way of shifting blame and allowing the Arabs to continue as they were. Al-Azm did not dispute that Israel was organically linked to imperialism; his point, rather, was to stress that Arab society must change in order to be able to confront imperialism as a whole.

Some Egyptian leftists after the war maintained the view that the struggle against Israel formed part of the broader anti-imperialist struggle and should thus constitute an integral part of a general Arab progressive movement in terms similar to those of Sadiq al-Azm. In 1973 Saad Eddine Ibrahim published a book, actually a collection of papers published in left-wing Arab journals and delivered at conferences in the Arab world and United States following the war. Ibrahim was in June 1967 president of the Arab Students' Organisation of North America (*munazzamat al-talaba al-arab*) and had been vocal in his criticisms of the regime's handling of the conflict, a stance that had him stripped of his Egyptian citizenship.[10]

Ibrahim's terms of reference were also similar to those of Baha al-Din and Fathi Radwan, in that he rejected out of hand the notion that Israel and Zionism where somehow outgrowths of Judaism. Zionism,

Ibrahim argued, constituted an ideological amalgam of elements of the Jewish religion and European ideas of social Darwinism crafted in such a way as to appeal to 'the religious among them, as well as secularists; the ordinary people and the intellectuals.'[11] It also incorporated the principle of permanent expansion (*mabda' al-tawassu' al-da'im*) and domination as prerequisites for Israel's survival. Ibrahim also analysed Arab approaches to Israel, which he noted had since 1967 emerged mainly from the al-Ahram Centre for Political and Strategic Studies, the PLO and the Institute for Palestine Studies in Beirut. The first, the 'traditional view' was widespread in the 1930s and 1940s and viewed Israel not as part of imperialism, but as a 'racial, religious entity.' The only stance to take towards the Jewish state, in this view, was to pursue *jihad*, as the Arabs' forefathers did against the crusaders. All enemies of the Jews, in this reading, were friends of the Arabs and vice-versa, even if this meant siding with Nazis as did Kaylani in Iraq and Aziz al-Masri in Egypt.[12] Ibrahim pointed out that 'the traditional viewpoint is not wrong, but it is limited and partial,' since Israel was not solely to be understood in terms of religion. The 'progressive conception of the Palestine question', which flowed from the Bandung Conference and positive neutralism was favoured by intellectuals in the 1950s and 1960s and was one with which he agreed:

Israel is an indivisible part (*juz'un la yatajaza'*) of Western imperialism—and the battle between the Arabs and Israel is—or should become—an indivisible part of the world liberation movement ... Consequently, striking world imperialism in any place and inflicting disaster on its armies in any land is a step toward the liberation of Palestine.

The problem from the Arab point of view, for Ibrahim, was that 'the Arab information apparatus never changed its view from the traditional conception with the same speed or degree. As such, the ordinary Arab individual did not change his views of the nature of the conflict.'[13] Ibrahim concluded that as part of imperialism Israel wanted to keep all of Palestine and conquer yet more Arab lands. He called for a return to a war footing in which Egypt and Palestine would face Israel in a 'people's war' of attrition.[14]

The influence of this new left, largely embodied in the student movement, but with some supporters in the older generation of intellectuals, notably the Marxist thinker Mohamed Sid Ahmed, placed the onus on region-wide revolution against imperialism to defeat Israel, magnifying the role of social movements and intellectuals, and opposing the defeatist reformulation of the conflict as one of borders and states. But the difference between before 1967, when the regime sought just to contain Israeli aggression and roll resistance into a broader anti-imperialist programme, and after the war, was that Nasser and then Sadat did actually want to recover the occupied territories and regain prestige. And this was not something that could be achieved through ideology and rhetoric. There was a strong sense after 1967 of 'getting real.' Israel was increasingly conceptualised as a state, rather than appendage of imperialism, and was also accepted as a permanent, albeit illegitimate, feature of the regional landscape within its fifth of June borders. From 1967 until 1973, the Nasser and Sadat regimes continued to describe Israel as a forward base for US imperialism, but neutralising it ceased to be the end goal of a broader regional revolutionary process, as the new left were arguing.

Nasser, increasingly sceptical of the Marxists' certainty that Israel was nothing more than imperialism's guard dog, grew more sympathetic to the notion that if nothing else Egyptian thinkers and decision-makers had been poorly informed about Israel before the war. The view of Israel encouraged in Egypt and other Arab countries was revealed to be dated and inaccurate and perspectives like that of Baha al-Din became more useful. Nasser argued soon after the defeat that the Israeli army did not distinguish between 'left-wing' and 'right-wing' nationalism in the Arab world and that all Arab states must stand together in the face of the Israeli threat.[15] Even though it was still part of the broader imperialist firmament, it had characteristics that deserved to be studied and understood. With a view to remedying this, the al-Ahram Centre for Zionist and Palestinian Studies, which was subsequently renamed the Centre for Political and Strategic Studies, was established in 1968. Heikal was in charge of the Centre, which was housed in the al-Ahram building in Cairo and gathered together many of Egypt's most prominent intellectuals.[16] From the regime's perspective, the intellectuals' role was to research and provide information about Israel that would help Egypt regain its territory and return to the status quo ante.

In the early 1970s Heikal recruited a young scholar to the al-Ahram Centre to conduct an in-depth study of Israel and Zionism, the first fruits of which were published in 1972. Abdelwahab Elmessiri would spend the next four decades examining Israel, most significantly through his *Encyclopedia*, which will be discussed in subsequent chapters. Elmessiri had been a member of both the Muslim Brotherhood and the Communist Party, and his work reflected a convergence of both culturist and political economic perspectives. Elmessiri's work did much to popularise, and intellectually substantiate, the long-standing Islamist contention that Israel was in reality a symptom of a much larger cultural and civilisational challenge from the West.

Not unlike Sayyid Qutb, whose travels in the United States did much to harden his attitude to the West, Elmessiri's days as a graduate student of comparative literature at Columbia and Rutgers universities appear to have played an important role in forming his critical attitude to Western civilisation. It is undoubtedly significant that Elmessiri was resident in the United States at the time of the 1967 war, when he witnessed the near-euphoric celebration of Israel's victory. Also reminiscent of another comparative literature student, Edward Said, whose path Elmessiri crossed briefly at Colombia University, and who has also referred to the 1967 war to explain his interest in the relationship between the West and the Middle East, Elmessiri developed an obsession with the critique of European and American culture.[17] Elmessiri developed the view that Zionism (and Nazism) were not extremes or aberrations in the history of Western civilisation but were rather, like imperialism, reflections of its true nature.

Complications to statism

Any hopes the Egyptian regime may have harboured of restricting relations with Israel to an interstate basis were dashed by the rise of the popular Palestinian national movement, which, as it had in 1936, seemed to rouse a hitherto 'depoliticised' Egyptian population. The Six-Day War had proved for many Palestinians that the Arab states were not up to the task of liberating the land occupied by the Zionists. Those states had indeed made things worse by allowing yet more of Palestine to fall under Israeli control. From 1967 the Palestinian revolution rapidly came to eclipse the Egyptian as the focus of progressive politics not only for Palestinians but for Egyptian intellectuals too. That the Palestinians were apparently fighting imperialism through Israel made the PLO the new vanguard for the Egyptian and broader Arab left and meant that Egyptian society, and not just the state, retained its role as agent of history.

The notion of people's war continued to inform PLO thinking after 1967, due to the conviction that the Arabs' greater numbers should be leveraged in order to prevail.[18] After 1967, Fatah's call for a 'popular liberation war' proved to be a popular rallying cry in Egypt, where, according to Fatah sources, '20,000 Egyptian students and former soldiers' sought to join it in this endeavour.[19] From 1969 Fatah's main rival, the Popular Front for the Liberation of Palestine (PFLP), also supported the 'people's war' option and, via its eloquent spokesman Ghassan Kanafani among others, won over many Egyptian students to this cause in the early 1970s. The PFLP took to hijacking planes in a bid to deal a 'blow to the US-Nasir conjunction' based on the conviction that liberation could be furthered through striking 'colonialism and Zionist centres outside the homeland.'[20]

Although sometimes calling for people's war to destroy 'all the military, political, economic, financial, and intellectual institutions of the Zionist occupation state', in a contradiction noted by Sayigh, Fatah also claimed to be for resolving 'Palestinian and Israeli problems [through] a popular democratic Palestinian state for Arabs and Jews alike in which there would be no discrimination and no room for class or national subjugation.'[21] The fact that this reading closely matched the traditional communist view was important in encouraging Egyptian leftists who may not have been keen on people's war to support the PLO as the new vanguard of revolution. Perhaps most decisive in solidifying the bond was the USSR's new endorsement of the PLO. In 1970, the Soviet

Union reversed its previous scorn for the 'mythical diversionary groups', as it dubbed the Palestinian guerrillas, and backed them as a 'progressive and patriotic liberation movement.'[22] Both the revolutionist and Palestinian solutions to Egypt's approach to Israel, therefore, remained salient, as they had since the mid-1950s.

The regime's own support for the PLO exposed inherent contradictions within its approach to Israel, and its essentially counter-revolutionary strategy at home. In accepting the Rogers Plan, and hence UNSCR 242 that affirmed the right of Israel to exist, Nasser indicated his willingness to come to terms with Israel. But in encouraging the PLO, which did not recognise any such right and rejected UNSCR 242, Egypt expressed its continued engagement in an existential struggle for Palestine, and not just for the restitution of Egyptian territory or redrawing of borders.[23] The contradiction reproduced itself in the fact that while Nasser sought to prioritise the interstate level of interaction in order to recover the lost territory, intellectuals of the left within Egyptian society saw their role as not only providing information on Israel but also supporting the PLO as the new vanguard of the broader Arab revolution.

Anwar Sadat perpetuated the dualism. In his inauguration speech, he identified three distinct threats to Egypt, reflecting the dualism of state and societal roles: 'we are required to define the enemies of our nation without equivocation, and our enemies are Israel, international Zionism and world imperialism,' and 'we are part of the great national liberation movement with its progressive socialist trend.'[24] In 1971, Sadat expressed to the UN Middle East envoy Gunner Jarring that he was willing to negotiate for a peace based on UNSCR 242, the first Arab leader to signal that peace with Israel was a prospect. This contradiction between dealing with Israel as a state and fighting Zionism/imperialism as a society would never be reconciled and continues to inform the dualistic approach to Israel of the Egyptian regime and intellectuals.

By the time Sadat consolidated his authority in May 1971, Egyptian communists were at the forefront of a growing discourse of criticism of the regime. For them, Nasser had not taken the revolution far enough and erred in ignoring the fact that a popular war of liberation was essential to defeating Israel, and hence imperialism. The backbone of this left-wing challenge was to be found amongst Egypt's university students. The student movement of 1972 called for:

> the rejection of any political solution to the conflict with Israel; withdrawal from the Egyptian acceptance of UN Resolution 242; the activation of full support to the PLO; the outright nationalisation of American firms operating in Egypt; the introduction of a war economy, including a more egalitarian salary system and the elimination of foreign tourism in the country; [and] the separating of Egypt's economy from 'the market of international capitalism.'[25]

The student movement lambasted Sadat's apparent reluctance to go to war with Israel. In Nasserist student circles, the call for war centred on Nasser's call to 'erase the traces of the aggression' via conventional warfare, rather than a popular liberation struggle to defeat Israel as a whole. The communist students, on the other hand, were calling for a 'popular struggle' to liberate the occupied lands, inspired largely by the Vietnamese and Algerian wars of liberation.

The Islamist challenge to the left

Although they would not prevail over Nasserists and communists until later in the decade, in the early 1970s Islamist groups were gaining some prominence in university politics thanks, in part, to encouragement from the regime. They too, organised through the *Jama'at Islamiyya* [Islamic groups], joined in the clarion call for war, and their discourse reflects the extent to which they used a conceptual framework that would resonate with students accustomed to leftist categories. Thus, the '"national liberation struggle against imperialism's policeman in the Arab world" became, for the *Jama'at* activists, "*jihad* to end the usurpation by the infidels of one of the lands of *Dar al-Islam {the Islamic world}*."'[26]

The Islamist student movement was supported at the regime level and received encouragement from the Muslim Brotherhood, to which part of it would affiliate. Soon after the magnitude of the June 1967 defeat grew apparent, Nasser had encouraged Egyptians to seek sol-ace in their religion and faith. Al-Azhar and other Islamic institutions helped the regime reformulate its position—namely that Egypt con-fronted a danger far greater than Israel itself—in religious terms. The Supreme Council for Islamic Affairs (SCIA), for example, published a book in 1969 by Mustafa al-Sa'dani entitled *'Adwa 'ala al-Sihyuniyya. {Focus on Zionism}'*[27] The book constitutes a lengthy exposition of the eternal Jewish threat not only to Islam, but to the entire world. Relying heavily on, and translating much of, the *Protocols of the Elders of Zion*, the book reveals the other side of the Nasser regime's approach to Israel, one which stressed its Jewish nature in ways similar to those of the Muslim Brotherhood.

Just as the Egyptian Islamist movement was affected by left-wing categories of analysis, following 1967 the writings of Islamist intellec-tuals like Yusuf al-Qaradawi, as well as the religious pronouncements of the regime, led many leftist intellectuals to islamicise their own discourse. Arab revolutionary thought was, Sadiq al-Azm lamented in 1968, becoming reactionary. As al-Azm noted, some 'so-called leftists', including writers for the Egyptian Marxist journal *al-Tali'a*, expounded upon elaborate new political formulae like *al-ishtirakiyya al-'arabiyya al-'ilmiyya al-islamiyya al-mu'mina* or 'Arab-Scientific-Islamic-Believing-Socialism'.[28] An example of this as applied to Israel is perhaps that of William Sulayman, who in the July 1967 issue of *al-Tali'a*, argued that although Judaism was not the same as Zionism, Israel was nothing more than a base for imperialism since during World War Two the Zionists 'conquered the United States'.[29]

Leftist exponents of 'third ways' between socialism and capitalism, between modernity and tradition, would help pave the way for the widespread acceptance of not only the Islamist prognosis for domestic social and political change, but also for an interpretation of regional identity that eliminated socialist revolution as a feature of the politi-cal landscape and emphasised, instead, 'authentic' cultural and reli-gious factors. The general political and intellectual retrenchment that took place after 1967 also contributed to the greater prominence given to religion in Egyptian political discourse, with liberal frame-works of analysis also contributing to this. As Sayyid Yasin wrote in reference to the relative merits of the Marxist and Islamist intellectual currents:

> If we may use the terms 'the authentic' and 'the modern', which have become popular in Arabic literature in the last years, we would say that the aim of the Muslim Brotherhood to create an Islamic state constituted a search for authenticity without sufficient attention to modernity. In contrast, the Marxist aim of establishing a socialist state signified a search for the modern without sufficient attention to the authentic.[30]

There was substantial continuity in the Islamist writings both before and after the 1967 war. Their views of history, the nature of the challenges Egypt faced and the source of societal strength were essentially those of Muhammad Husayn and others from earlier periods. Statements of the Islamist case after 1967 emerged throughout the Arab world, including in a conservative form in Saudi Arabia and Jordan, where such a position bolstered, rather than challenged, the prevailing orders in those states. In Egypt, Islamist intellectual responses to 1967 represented, directly or indirectly, criticisms of the Egyptian regime and a call for Islam, not socialism, to form the basis of societal strength.

The Brotherhood thinker Muhammad Galal Kishk laid the blame for the defeat squarely at the feet of regimes that had blindly followed Western political doctrines, including Marxism and liberal nationalism, while ignoring the basic driving force in all world conflicts, which was the 'clash of civilisations'. Kishk shared with liberal nationalists and the left the conviction that Egyptian society must be reformed, but for him reform—indeed revolution—could only grow out of the objective reality of Egyptian Muslim life, not through the application of foreign ideas to an Egyptian reality. Translators, he wrote, have never transformed societies.[31]

Kishk wrote two books in the 1960s that formed the basis for his views on the twin prongs of a Western 'intellectual invasion' in the 1967 defeat. Like Qutb, Kishk asserted the unity of interest between the communist East and the capitalist West, both of which targeted

Islam and helped establish Israel for this purpose.[32] In his own words, the conceptual framework of his books derived from the central assumption that Western civilisation represented one analytical category in terms of its 'enmity toward Islam.'

> This civilization divides into a number of states and systems, including communist, socialist, capitalist, republican and monarchist. But they all come from the same point: the split from the East and hostility towards Islamic civilisation. This is what supports the unity of interests (*wihdat al-masalih*) and unity of ambitions (*wihdat al-atmi'a*) they harbour toward our countries, invigorated today by the unity of Zionist activity that moves inside the communist and capitalist 'camps' for Israel's benefit (*li-hisab Isra'il*) ... [33]

It was this unity of interests between Russia and America that explained the defeat of June 1967, and it is in this context that Kishk emphasised the need to expose 'the role played by communists in the service of Zionism' and called on Arabs and Muslims to rely 'on our own efforts alone' to 'achieve victory over our historic enemy.'[34]

Kishk condemned the Arab communists as 'traitors to the Arab nation' for their stance on Palestine and for putting internationalism above national interests, arguing that 'it is not possible to accept the destruction (*ifna'*) of our *umma* for the interests of world progress.'[35] The Arab communists were mistaken in that they opposed Zionism in the beginning, but failed to understand the link between Zionism, Israel and the Jews, and in particular were unable to see the problem in the fact that '90 percent' of their leaders were Jewish while the Arabs were battling the Zionists.[36]

Kishk was concerned with highlighting the differences between Islamism and communism as components of the Egyptian national movement, vehemently impugning the authenticity and legitimacy of the latter. The Arab communists were, for Kishk, not only deluded, but were also a 'danger to national existence—a danger in our national struggle against Israel.'[37] It was world and Arab communism, working in the service of Israel, that wanted to force the Arabs to accept a peace settlement and make them 'accept the reality that is the existence of Israel and co-existence with it.'[38] Although Kishk acknowledged—in terms that suggest this was beyond doubt—the links between Israel and the United States, which supported 'all Israeli crimes against the Arabs', the real danger did not come from the United States, because the people were all too aware of its aggressive intentions. The threat of communism was far greater, because the USSR was believed to be a friend, while it and the Arab communist parties were, in reality, acting to destroy 'the Arab resistance to Israel.' Those who supported the USSR, he concluded, 'do not want to finish with Israel.'[39]

Kishk's order of priority was consistent with the historical Muslim Brotherhood position, which placed the liberation of Palestine ahead of Arab unity. The Syrian and Iraqi Ba'th also, for Kishk, were working in the service of Israel, since they focussed on internal revolution over the liberation of Palestine. He lambasted the Egyptian communist Mahmud Amin al-Alim who challenged progressives for focusing on development and internal political work instead of confronting Israel. Al-Alim had argued that such an approach deprived the progressive camp of any hope of mobilising support. But Kishk, in somewhat circular fashion, argued that the progressives did not actually want development, since their primary goal was preventing the liberation of Palestine, and 'whoever supported a progressive power that allowed the occupation of land while concentrating on development?'[40]

Interestingly, Kishk derided liberalism and Marxism as internationalist or cosmopolitan movements, even as he called for the unity of the *umma* and implied a universal Jewish solidarity. Although clear that a unified 'West' represented a cultural and intellectual threat to the Arabs and Islam, he also stressed the primacy of nationalism and national interests. Though following the Brotherhood line that Egyptian patriotism should serve the greater loyalty to Islam, Kishk devoted substantial space in his book on Marxism to a discussion of the Sino-Soviet rivalry to show that communism is nothing more than a front for national interests. Similarly, he argued that despite the Zionist influence on world communism, 'when Russian national interests are at stake, [Russia] does not hesitate to strike [the Jews].'[41] In realist terms, Kishk argued that internationalism was merely the ideology used by powerful nations to dominate weak ones, or by the weak to dissolve themselves into powerful nations.[42] Islam, apparently, was the mutual enemy of both communism and capitalism and as such would unite the West against it.

Kishk dismissed the communist position as expressed in *al-Tali'a* and *Ruz al-Yusuf* after the Six-Day War that Israel presented a danger because it was an imperialist base, rather than because Jews lived there. For Kishk the two were inseparable:

> We confront Israel fundamentally because of those Jewish citizens, not because they are Jews but because they occupied our land, destroyed its unity and expelled our people, and because they have limitless ambitions for our land. If they were English or German, or Gog and Magog (*ya'juj wa ma'juj*) then the danger of Israel would be embedded in the fact that the inhabitants were Gog and Magog, not just for their position in the global struggle.

He pointed out that Israel's establishment as an imperialist base could not be separated from the fact that its inhabitants were Jews, and this was the salient factor, not its political system: 'We are against 1.5 million Jews as individuals as long as they accept their presence on another people's land.'[43]

In light of this, Kishk viewed as preposterous the left's call for the liberation of the Israeli people and the alliance with progressive forces in Israel.[44] For Kishk, the difference between Israel and other imperialists like the US or Britain was that with the latter anti-colonial struggles aimed only at ending the occupation, and did not require hatred of British or Italian people. With Israel, such a rule could not apply—it was impossible to distinguish between the Israeli people and the Israeli government. Israel was an 'aggressive entity: people and army, worker and peasant and soldier.' When an 'Israeli' moves to Israel, Kishk pronounced, he loses the right to belong in the 'camp of the people' and becomes a violator of the rights of others, whether a peasant or a soldier. Rejecting a broader universalisation, Kishk concluded that this position—the Arab Islamic position—was just 'even if the whole world denies it' since 'we own this land.' The usurper must be evicted and returned to his original country.[45]

Yusuf Qaradawi was also at the forefront of the paradigm shift from Marxist to Islamist approaches to Israel. In *al-Hall al-Islami*, [The Islamic solution], Qaradawi excoriated both liberal nationalism and revolutionary socialism for their failings on all levels, including militarily. The military inadequacies were highlighted in Arab regimes' inability to defend the paramount Arab and Muslim cause, that of Palestine—the first of the *qiblas* and the third of Islam's Holy Places. The defeat of 1948 was testimony to the bankruptcy of liberal nationalism, while the 1967 defeat highlighted the failings of socialism. As with figures in the Arab New Left like Sadiq al-Azm, Qaradawi rejected the call to 'erase the traces of the aggression' since it legitimised the 5 June 1967 borders of Israel.

Just as Nasser chided the Egyptian revolutionaries of 1919 for not recognising the connection between the Egyptian revolution and a broader Arab world, Qaradawi lambasted the Free Officers for ignoring the 'organic link' between the Arab revolution and the Islamic *umma*. The post-1952 leaders thus got the 'Arab personality' wrong and were unable to see beyond the Arabian [i.e. Persian] Gulf. As the Arab nationalist Sati' al-Husri had accused the Egyptian nationalists of narrowness, so Qaradawi levelled the same accusation at Husri, suggesting that the title of the latter's famous work *Arabism First* should be *Islam First*. This narrow vision was particularly important in the struggle against Israel, since:

The Arabs entered the most dangerous stage of their struggle against world Judaism represented by Israel, and with the Western crusaders represented by Israel's supporters, without benefiting from the massive Islamic energy from the ocean to the ocean, or from Indonesia to Casablanca.[46]

'World Judaism', for Qaradawi, recognised this potential in the past and so destroyed the Caliphate, the last embodiment of Islamic unity. Qaradawi belittled Nasser's attempts to present himself as defender of Islam. The attempts of the Nasser regime to organise an international politics based on Islam were perfunctory and fake. Islam was only mentioned at the end of the UAR Charter, in the section on foreign policy, and the Islamic Congress established by Nasser was a hollow structure, in reality no more than a building.[47]

The failure of the Arab revolution was, for Qaradawi, due to the flaws inherent in revolutionary socialism. Following the 1967 defeat, which revealed its bankruptcy, Qaradawi saw two possible solutions to the decline of the Arabs. The first was the 'overt red communist solution' (al-hall al-shuyu'i al-ahmar al-sarih), while the second was Islam. Qaradawi devoted substantial attention to rubbishing the former possible solution. Communism denied Islam and all religion, it was materialist and against the shari'a, amoral, an affront to human nature in its call for violence and bloodshed, and antithetical to freedom and dignity. It also contravened national sovereignty because of its allegiance to the USSR, and constituted a new form of imperialism. On top of all of this, communism for Qaradawi was the child of World Judaism. Marx, Lenin and Trotsky were all Jews, and so too were the leaders of the communist movement in the Arab world.[48]

Qaradawi suggested that the world's 600 million Muslims—one-fifth of the population—could be a third bloc able to change the global balance of power. The Muslim countries occupied important strategic areas in the world and the numerical weight of Islamic states meant that, were they all to take a single stance, they would represent a strong international power. For Qaradawi, the Muslim world encompassed all countries settled by Muslims, where Islamic slogans are raised and the call to prayer is heard from the mosques. This was the Islamic watan (country) to be protected. Muslims living as minorities in other countries were also part of the umma (community) and should be defended. For Qaradawi, the unity of the umma, was a given, its actualisation prevented by inauthentic regimes in each of the states of the Islamic watan. The solution was to eradicate atheism and ignorance in the administration of Muslim states. Arab leaders following independence were khawagat bidun quba'at (foreigners without hats). Through them, Western imperialism (communist and capitalist) continued to exert moral, cultural and intellectual influence over Muslim societies. Thus, he called for enforcing moral and religious entry criteria for all public offices, including candidates in parliamentary elections, to ensure that Muslim states further Muslim interests.[49] The basic shortcoming of the Arab revolutions for Qaradawi lay in their failure to 'change souls' (*taghyir al-nafs*), which alone would constitute real revolutionary change, and which was possible only through faith.

Sadat's recourse to Islamist categories

The anti-communist/anti-Zionist link drawn by Brotherhood figures like Kishk and Qaradawi became increasingly salient after Sadat had decided to split from the USSR altogether. If Nasser's concessions to Islam either failed to convince or were only half-heartedly offered, Sadat more stridently sought to incorporate Islamic actors into the state, and enacted policies to that end. Sadat's dramatic expulsion in 1972 of some 15,000 Soviet experts was condemned by the left and applauded by Islamists. Sadat's bold move can be understood in terms of both foreign and domestic political calculations. On the foreign policy level, Sadat was keen to demonstrate to the United States that he was serious about building a new relationship with the West.[50] But Kissinger himself expressed his surprise that Sadat had gone this far. Perhaps as important, as with Nasser before him, Sadat's anti-communism reflected a concern with his domestic position. In his memoirs, Sadat described the ASU secretary general and 'centre of power' Ali Sabri, as Moscow's number one man in Egypt.[51] By expelling the Soviets, Sadat sought to undercut regime Nasserists. The expulsion of the Soviet advisors, the release of Muslim Brotherhood members and the growth of Islamism on the university campuses were related. With the dominant political movements in Egyptian universities, in the press, and within the regime broadly supportive of Egypt's relationship with the USSR and suspicious of an exclusive relationship with the West, Sadat needed voices in society that would support change. The Muslim Brotherhood and their supporters in the universities, while not natural advocates of rapprochement with the United States, could be relied upon to be critical of the Soviet Union and communism. Sadat also held that the communist movement in the university was sponsored and supported by the Soviets and, in his memoirs, justified expelling the advisors in these terms.[52]

Sadat relied heavily on religious language in his speeches in his attempt to Islamise Egyptian national identity. He described Egypt as *'dawlat al-'ilm wa-al-iman'* (state of science and faith) and became known as the *'ra'is mu'min'* (believing president). The Constitution of 1971 stipulated that the *shari'a* should be the main source of all legislation. Prior to 1973, Sadat expressed his position towards Israel in these terms as well, and the 1973 war was framed as a religious war. 'Faith is not enough on its own' he said in a 1971 speech, 'because the enemy has the most recent innovations of the age and will win battle after battle if we do not arm ourselves with that with which it is armed.'[53] But, he also said, 'true power is not the power of guns, but is only the power of faith, the power of the individual, and the power of the message, faith in doctrine (*'aqida*) and faith in principle (*mabda'*). The issue against the United States and Israel was not one of arms, Sadat explained, but an issue 'of the believing individual: we believe that God is with us, we believe that right is with us, we believe, as God said, that we are the best nation offered to mankind (*khayr umma akhrajat li al-nas*).'[54]

In September 1972, Sadat drew on Islamic reasoning to explain his reluctance to negotiate directly with the Jews:

> This is what our Prophet did ... We will never negotiate with them directly. We know our history, and we know their history: a people disposed to treachery. This year I promise you we will celebrate not just the liberation of our land, but also the conquering of this noisy Israeli invasion so they will return again as our book said to us: 'I have decreed for them ignominy and misery' and we will not relinquish that.[55]

The association of Zionism with imperialism was not abandoned, but Sadat also stressed the cultural element to the Zionist threat, suggesting that this assumption had become axiomatic: 'Today we must confront this evil invasion, the Zionist and imperialist invasion, because it is not aimed *just at our creed only*, but also at our land, our fate and the life of our descendents.'[56]

Sadat justified his policy of steadfastness (*sumud*) on 14 January 1971 by remaining faithful to Nasser's policy of portraying Egypt as the leader of the Arab world. But above serving Arabism or neutralism, Egypt was defending Islam and its Holy Places:

> Egypt is Egypt. It will preserve faith and spread faith, God willing, over this earth. Steadfastness was always to defend Islam and its holy places and this land will continue, with God's help, to be a citadel to defend the Holy Places of Islam and Islamic heritage, whatever the battles, whatever the evils.[57]

The liberal agenda

In addition to new left and Islamist resurgence after 1967, liberalism of the type common before the revolution of 1952 reappeared among intellectuals, though it was extremely weak among students and the broader intelligentsia.[58] The distinguishing feature of liberal discourse on Palestine was the conviction that the Arab-Zionist conflict could only be won if the Arabs modernised and democratised their societies and dealt with Israel as a state. It is important to note that although liberals were later associated with greater receptivity towards 'normalisation' with Israel, the liberal position is not necessarily any less critical of Israel.

Undoubtedly the most important (re)statement of the liberal position on Palestine after 1967 came not from an Egyptian but from the Syrian Arab nationalist, Constantine Zurayq, whose work would mark the first point of engagement for liberal Egyptians seeking to understand and react to the defeat.[59] A teacher at the American University in Beirut, Zurayq had written two important books, at either end of the Nasser experiment, attempting to explain the Arabs' inability to defeat Zionism. The first, *Ma'na al-Nakba*[60] (*The Meaning of the Catastrophe*), was written during the first Arab-Israeli war in 1948. The second appeared after the 1967 defeat, entitled, *Ma'na al-Nakba Mujaddidan*[61] (*The Meaning of the Catastrophe Revisited*). Zurayq's post-1967 work did not represent a dramatic intellectual reorientation, but a restatement of earlier views. A central problematique for Zurayq after June 1967 was that Arab nationalism, whose greatest achievement was the ending of Egyptian isolation, had failed to defeat Israel.[62] Zurayq's work represented a model for liberal-minded Egyptians seeking to engage with the Palestine issue. He was explicit about the necessity for democracy and strategic behaviour to regain Palestine and located the secret of success against a 'modern' adversary like Israel in society, in the spirit and scientific advancement, as well as empowerment, of the people.

The Arabs, for Zurayq, had suffered two crushing defeats at the hands of Israel because Israeli society was modern and united, whereas the Arabs were backward and divided: they belonged to different civilisations.[63] The conflict with Israel was, he concluded in his 1967 book, essentially civilisational. But this was no 'clash of civilisations' thesis that posited the primordial animosity between Muslims and Christians or Jews, or East and West. Instead, Zurayq viewed civilisation as a relational and relative concept. It was not evenly spread around the world. Thus, even in the advanced countries, not all of society was civilised. But, relatively speaking, the developed world—to which Israel belonged—was more civilised than the Arabs, who must, as a first priority, strive to rectify this imbalance and thus stand a chance of defeating Israel.[64]

Whereas leftists like Sadiq al-Azm argued for deeper socialist transformations, Zurayq was in favour of modernisation along the lines of the French, rather than October, revolution. Zurayq stressed that communists did not have the monopoly on progressive ideas about social reform. He saw ending feudalism, tribalism and sectarianism as prerequisites for nationalism, but was against divisive class conflict.[65] Arab unity depended on the deepening of bourgeois revolutions throughout the Arab world, with the attendant embrace of modern science and learning, democracy and the separation of church and state. Zurayq criticised the socialist movements for sowing disunity and class conflict in the Arab world, diverting energies from the real problem that faced the Arabs—Zionism. Though the language was different, this was essentially the view also being put forward by the Muslim Brotherhood.

Zurayq considered it axiomatic that the defeat of Zionism was the Arabs' paramount interest. With his view of Arabs and Jews as 'peoples', Zurayq complained that even though Arab leaders proclaimed that Palestine was their primary cause, they had been divided and pursued more marginal or vested interests at the expense of the paramount goal.[66] Zurayq also saw the Arab world oppressed and Israel ascendant not because of global imperialism, but because the Arabs had not yet learned the rules of international politics. United and modernised, the Arabs would be able to achieve their primary objective—the liberation of Palestine—by exchanging other, less central, interests. Also, socialism had clouded the issue by splitting the *umma* into 'progressives' and 'reactionaries', when the real enemy was Israel. Related to this was the fact that the Arabs did not yet exhibit 'fighting spirit' (*ruh nidali*), which should be based on an attachment to the land and the nation. The struggle for Palestine must thus emanate from the Palestinian Arabs, with other Arabs playing a supporting role, as the Jews did for Israelis. But this support could only be realised through a scientific revolution (*inqilab 'ilmi*) in the Arab world. While communism may have suited the Soviet Union, it was premature or inappropriate for the Arabs since the USSR was only successful because it had people with the focus and knowledge (*ilm*) to industrialise.[67] Like Sadiq al-Azm, Zurayq saw North Vietnam also as able to confront the United States because it had *ilm* and a fighting spirit. The Arab world, however, lacked these things.[68]

Zurayq argued that increased mutual understanding was a central prerequisite to solving the Arab-Israeli conflict. The Arabs must apply themselves to the detailed study of their primary international adversary. Only by learning about all aspects of Israeli and Jewish culture, society and politics could the Arabs hope to understand Israel's interests and political positions. The United States supported Israel because it deemed it in its interests to do so, and those interests too must be studied and understood. On the other hand, Zurayq blamed US one-sidedness in the conflict on the failure of the Arabs to adequately publicise their position in international forums. He thus advocated strengthening Arab public diplomacy in the United States and Europe such that their citizens, and hence governments, would see that the Arab cause was valid and genuine and, crucially, corresponded to Western ideals of fairness, justice and self-determination. This public relations campaign must, he argued, form an indispensable part of the Arab strategy for securing the main Arab objective of liberating Palestine. Zurayq's view of the conflict had remained consistent through the years since the *nakba*. In 1948 he had argued that the struggle for Palestine was the fight of 'all humanity', since it concerned the safeguarding of universal values of justice and freedom, the rights of every people. It was these 'shared values' that would, in the end, present the solution to the problem.[69]

In discussing Israel's interests, Zurayq assumed that the Zionist state represented, and was bolstered by, the Jews of the world. To a great extent, Zurayq accepted the founding myths of the Israeli state, as well as the prevailing Islamist narrative: the Jews were a unified national community, with a common history and sophisticated strategy for achieving their political objectives. Israel was thus not the Arabs' only opponent, since it was the embodiment of world Zionism and Judaism, which counted on allies in the United States, Germany, Britain and elsewhere, and had managed to win over Western public opinion to its side.[70] This ethno-religious conception of Israel has its counterpart in Zurayq's Arab nationalism. In the Diaspora, the Jews succeeded in sustaining and intensifying national feeling, which, with their simultaneously wholehearted embrace of modernity, was sufficient to enable them to establish their state on firm foundations, creating an Arab diaspora in their place. In order to turn the tables, the Arabs must adopt the methods of the Jews. Despite obvious differences, there were thus clear overlaps between the liberal and Islamist perspectives on Israel.

Shortly after the Six-Day War, Ahmad Baha al-Din wrote an article in the journal *al-Musawwar* that shared many of the assumptions evident in the work of Zurayq, particularly a preoccupation with modernity and 'stateness'. The paper published a series of Arab responses to Baha al-Din's article in the following issue, which, along with Baha al-Din's subsequent rejoinder, were published as book in January 1968. In a significant departure from the established Arab orthodoxy of the 1960s, the author proposed that the solution to the Palestine problem was the creation of a Palestinian state in the Gaza Strip as well as the West Bank and parts of Jordan east of the Jordan River. Baha al-Din echoed Nasser's call to 'erase the traces of the aggression', but insisted that reclaiming the Arab land occupied in June 1967 could not constitute a return to the status quo ante.

Like Zurayq, Baha al-Din noted that the Arabs' approach to Palestine differed dramatically, and to their detriment, from the approach of the Jews to Israel. Whereas Jews had emigrated to Israel in large numbers following 1948, thus creating not only a mass of population but also a progressive and skilled society, the Palestinians had become refugees, leaving not only the land that became Israel, but also those parts of historic Palestine that fell under Arab control. Palestinians either languished in refugee camps or, as was the case with most educated 'progressive' elements of Palestinian society, emigrated to other Arab countries and the rest of the world. As such, there was no 'Palestine' to challenge Israel, but rather a group of Arab states challenging one Jewish state, a factor that led to widespread misunderstanding of the balance of power and interests in the region around the world.[71]

Baha al-Din drew a sharp distinction between the nature and capacity of the Jewish Agency and that of the PLO. Echoing al-Azm as well as Zurayq, Baha al-Din pointed out that the 'Jewish Agency, like the Zionist movement itself, was only effective insofar as it was attached to the land.'[72] Although Zionism was a global political movement there was a concrete entity, Israel, around which this global campaign was focussed. The PLO, on the other hand, was not rooted in the land but instead operated out of Arab capitals. The Palestinian commitment to returning to the land, then, must equal or exceed that of the Jews. But, crucially for Baha al-Din, the Palestinian desire to return to homes lost in 1948 would not be fulfilled unless Palestinians first 'returned' to that land that had not been absorbed into Israel, land that 'is still Palestine.' Baha al-Din's proposed slogan was 'Palestinians for Palestine, and after that Palestine for the Palestinians.'[73]

The Palestinian state, once established, would absorb the Palestinians from the refugee camps and constitute a modern productive society, with a functioning economy, educational system and military. Baha al-Din pointed out other international examples, such as Korea and

Vietnam, where conflict had existed over land and national identity, but where each opposing side at least had a state from which to operate. The Palestinians were denied this luxury, their cause becoming subsumed under the general Arab cause. The role of the Arabs should be to provide support and 'strategic depth' to the struggle for Palestine, in which the Palestinians themselves would be the vanguard. Thinking strategically, Baha al-Din pointed out that creating a state with the name 'Palestine' on land historically known as such would alert the world to the justice of the Palestinian case, as well as highlight the flaws in Israel's claim to be the underdog.[74]

Also, reflecting a commitment to downgrading the primacy of socialist revolution, Baha al-Din suggested that the political system established in the new Palestinian state was of secondary importance to establishing some kind of state, since while peoples differ in the type of political system under which they live, they do not differ in the desire to be organised in a state. For representatives of the new left, like Sadiq al-Azm, the idea that a 'reactionary' Palestine would prevail, or even engage, in battle with a Zionist Israel when both were organically a part of Western imperialism was preposterous.

Among the reactions to Baha al-Din's 'proposal' published in the book was that of Clovis Maksud, who, while tentatively accepting Baha al-Din's ideas, stressed that the Arabs must maintain their 'rejection' of Israel's legitimacy and cautioned that 'Palestine the state' must remain 'Palestine the cause,' since Zionism was not only aimed at Palestine, but at obstructing Arab unity, for which Palestine must remain the focus. As Maksud's interjection clarifies, Baha al-Din's proposal was in reality a restatement of the 'Egypt as state; Egypt as revolution' formula that Nasser's intellectuals had been employing before 1967. This blending of Arabism and sovereignty was not particularly new, although Baha al-Din spelled out its full implications for the Arab-Israeli conflict more clearly than before.

Baha al-Din's intervention made explicit the conclusion to which Egyptian foreign policy discourse was ambiguously pointing all along: that the Palestinians—the lynchpin of Arabism—should have a state. Why should the Palestinians have to wait in refugee camps or in exile until Arab unification, Baha al-Din asked, when it was not even clear how that interim goal would be reached? Although Baha al-Din's proposal was couched as a 'first step' towards the liberation of Palestine, his level of analysis entailed a decisive shift from a view of the Middle Eastern dynamic as a battle between imperialism and revolution towards one between states with divergent interests and claims to sovereignty.

Following Nasser's death, some Egyptian intellectuals experimented with far more dramatic suggestions. Encouraged by Heikal who had earlier called for caution in the drive for war, some began to voice doubts about the path of confrontation. In April 1972 *al-Ahram* organised a symposium on the conflict with Israel, at which were present the intellectuals Tawfiq al-Hakim and Nagib Mahfuz, as well as Husayn Fawzi, who would later gain some notoriety by visiting Israel. These thinkers, for perhaps the first time in an Egyptian semi-official forum, argued for negotiations and the renunciation of war with Israel. Mahfuz was later accused of 'submissiveness' to Sadat, although he claimed in the early 1980s that 'The reverse is true. In fact, it was Sadat who supported me … When I announced that we must initiate talks, I did anticipate being bitterly denounced. Yet I never wavered from my position because I believed that first and foremost it was in Egypt's and the Arabs' interest to achieve peace …'.[75]

Mahfuz's sentiments were shared by Tawfiq al-Hakim, who later that year published the first major critique of Nasser's rule in *Awdat al-Wa'i (Return of Consciousness)*. Hakim even described Egypt and Israel as 'linked as islands of civilisation in a sea of barbarism.'[76] The main problem facing Egypt was the economic situation, which, if it deteriorated further, would have a retarding effect on Egyptian culture and society as a whole. Thus Mahfuz insisted that he was against Nasser's War of Attrition because 'prolonged military confrontation … will impoverish our resources and strength, while retarding our march to civilization by at least a hundred years. Why in the world should we not seek peace?'[77] Describing the event later, Mahfuz recalled his statement:

> … war is not an option [I said]. We must choose a different path, the path of negotiations. We find ourselves in a no-war-no-peace

situation that has no parallel in history, and its consequences
may be far more disastrous for us.[78]

Mahfuz's statement reveals the dualism within the liberal position.
On one level, it stressed the necessity for compromise and dialogue
to achieve more immediate national goals. On another, there was a
grander objective at stake: the march to civilisation. The two were
reconcilable, as achieving the more limited objectives involved playing
the modern game of international politics which would, in conjunction with developing the economy, liberalising the political system and
reforming social mores, make Egypt, and the Arabs, 'civilised.' What
Egypt needed was peace and stability in order to focus on the greater
goal of achieving civilisation and democracy. Sadat would later justify
the peace process with Israel with reference to Egypt's need for stability in order to develop and achieve democracy.

The six years from 1967 to 1973, then, marked a period of transition
from the previous decade, when Israel had been represented as primarily an appendage of imperialism and thus the target of a broad-based
societal movement, to one in which the reality of Israel as a state in its
own right was recognised. This had much to do with the fact that in
1967 Egypt lost part of its own territory and could not rely on blus-
ter and rhetoric to recover it. Egypt's intellectual traditions emerged
more confidently to conduct the post-mortem of defeat as the Nasserist
formula, which had relied on the left as an ally of convenience, was
shattered by the 1967 war, and the protestations of al-Khuli and other
'domesticated' Marxist intellectuals that the Arab revolution was alive
and well rang increasingly hollow.

This period was one of many contradictions in the political ideas
of both regime and societal groups. The regime's support for UNSCR
242 and desire to 'erase the traces of the aggression' contradicted
giving full support to the PLO, which rejected these goals. Islamist
critiques of the left for focussing on development and espousing proletarian internationalism rather than the war with Israel contradicted
the Muslim Brotherhood's own programme of reviving Islam in the
souls of the Egyptian people and working for Islamic unity. The New
Left, which called for revolution and people's war against Israel was

perhaps the most intellectually consistent. But it was crushed in 1972 and its vision of a societal revolutionary war upstaged by Sadat's statist triumph in October 1973. Sadat consolidated his power in May 1971, but—like Nasser, whose position was secured in 1954—would wait two years for the military 'victory' that would allow a change in ideology, the restructuring of the political arena and an attempt to find a new formula for Egypt's relations with Israel that would unite state and society towards a common purpose.

CHAPTER 5

PEACE PROCESS (1973-1979)

Conceptions of Israel, as we have seen, were closely related to the shifting political landscape in Egypt. The latter half of the 1970s represented a key transition from a political sphere dominated by the single-party Nasserist state to a, superficially at least, more pluralist system. The political transmission belt up until 1973 was the Arab Socialist Union and the language of official communication largely remained, for all the post-1967 rethinking, socialist-oriented Arab nationalism. Under a newly empowered Sadat politics divided into a superficial multiparty system wherein 'official' political pluralism was practiced and an unofficial public sphere dominated more and more by the Muslim Brotherhood and other Islamist actors. The ASU, as the imperfect vehicle for disseminating left-wing dogma, essentially became the even more ideologically dilute National Democratic Party (NDP), which inherited the ASU's network of party offices around the country. Within the narrower 'official' political sphere, secular, particularly liberal, ideas witnessed something of a resurgence, but were politically inconsequential unless grafted onto some component of the Islamic nationalist narrative.

The way in which Israel was represented during this period reflected the transition. Following the October 1973 war and the series of initiatives that led to the Camp David Accords, anti-imperialism diminished as an organising principle of foreign policy discourse. The threat to Egypt became less about imperialism *per se* and more about Zionism as an ideology and 'civilisational' challenge. Reflecting the rise of

Islamist frameworks after 1973, Zionism was increasingly portrayed as an intellectual or cultural threat to Arab society as a whole.

When Sadat ordered the Egyptian army across the Suez Canal, it was to win a limited victory with the international goal of energising the US-led political process in Egypt's favour and the domestic aim of boosting his popularity among the Egyptian masses. Irrespective of the military balance sheet at the end of the conflict, Sadat secured a resounding political victory. To those who had chided him over the past two years for his failure to confront Israel, the surprise attack showed the president not as indecisive or cowardly, but as a strategic genius patiently planning his masterstroke. For those who insisted on people's war, the scope for revolutionary mobilisation dropped to near zero as Sadat was feted across the country as 'Batal al-'Ubur' (hero of the crossing). The war was a propaganda boon for the president, permanently silencing serious calls from society for war against Israel. That scepticism about the 1973 triumph remains one of the biggest taboos in Egyptian political discourse is indicative of the importance of this juncture.

As with Nasser's similar 'victory' in 1956, the October War dramatically increased Sadat's freedom of action domestically and abroad. He could more stridently champion a vision of a new Middle East allied with the United States and open to foreign investment. In April 1974, the first statement of Sadat's new 'free-market' economic doctrine—*infitah*—appeared in the form of the October Paper. The threat that Israel posed was explicitly linked to Zionism, rather than imperialism, and the Paper affirmed that the October War halted Zionism's 'expansionist tide'.[1] The Paper, which is couched in the language of statism, foreshadowed many of the themes later taken up by intellectuals in their treatment of the Israel issue and thus highlights the interplay between state and societal perspectives.

The foreign investment given the most discussion in the Paper is Arab investment, which Sadat encouraged in the name of Arab nationalism. The ultimate commitment to Arab unity was restated, but the road to its achievement differed significantly to that prevalent even under the 'Arab solidarity' permutation of Nasserism. Unity, for Sadat, would occur by way of Arab economic integration, a process facilitated and encouraged by the October War. Thus the Paper thanks the Arab kings and heads of state for their support, referring to the use for the first time of the 'oil weapon', and notes that 'perhaps one of the most important results of the October War is that Arab nationalism has transcended the confines of being a mere slogan to become a palpable, well-defined action.'[2] It continues:

> The idea of Arab nationalism has ... matured, emerging from the framework of enthusiastic slogans which gave rise to much controversy, to a trend towards possible practical measures despite disagreement over many other issues. Egypt being the heart of the Arab nation has to bear its responsibility in preserving, consolidating and promoting that constructive tendency, particularly in the field of economic co-operation.[3]

Despite efforts to portray the new policies as a continuation of, rather than departure from, the July Revolution, the Paper is a far cry from the UAR Charter. The word 'imperialism' appears only a handful of times, and only in the context of the past. The concept of 'reaction' is completely absent. The Paper celebrates the fact that 'imperialism with its old forms has withdrawn; doctrinal rigidity has been removed while human progress is moving ahead with unprecedented speed.'[4] The October Paper exudes the spirit of détente. It describes a reformed system of international relations, with the world community emergent from the Cold War. In this new system, a multiplicity of power blocs existed, with global significance related to economic viability. Most importantly, East and West Europe were drawing together, and the Soviet Union was on friendly terms with the United States and opening up its economy. As such, 'We have to locate and define our position within these new international realities.'[5]

The October War marked another global watershed, according to the October Paper. But this time it was Egypt producing, not simply reacting to, global transformation. That change, specifically, was the termination of the expansionist Zionist project. The war, the Paper notes, 'has finally halted the expansionist Zionist tide which has been gaining more lands and victories almost once in every generation for nearly a century now, when the first waves of Zionist immigrants started to flow uninterrupted into Palestine.'[6] Whereas before the war 'all the official programmes of the Israeli parties were based on gaining more forms of expansion, annexing new territories and building cities and settlements,' after Egypt's victory, 'a comprehensive process for self-revision has started in Israel itself, to revise the future of those springboards on which the Zionist belief and the then predominant image of the country's future—until the eve of the war—was built.'[7]

Egypt acted not just in its own interests, but to defend 'the entire Arab nation', which was threatened by Zionist invasion. Echoing statements Sadat had made during the war, the October Paper extends the universalist analysis of Egypt's performance even further:

> I can even say that our struggle was for the sake of mankind which wants to live in peace based on justice, to put an end to the policy of expansion and annexation and to assert the right of peoples to self-determination. For this reason, we believe that the support we enjoyed during the battle will continue and gain further momentum as a mainstay in the stage of construction and reconstruction.[8]

Thus the intellectual door to normalisation with a non-Zionist Israel was opened and linked to the 'peace dividend' Egypt could claim from the West.

In the wake of the October Paper Sadat promoted a statist 'Egypt first' approach to foreign policy. Whereas Nasser had sought to depoliticise Egypt's relations with Israel, and lower the risk of war, by employing a societal revolutionary paradigm that downgraded interstate conflict, Sadat officially renounced the war option via the Sinai disengagement agreements of 1974 and 1975 and hence had no need for such justifications. The Sinai II agreement of 1975 stated that '[T]he conflict between [Egypt and Israel] and in the Middle East shall not be resolved by military force but by peaceful means.' From the mid-1970s official and intellectual society diverged: the state pursued an official policy of peace; society a policy of war, conceived—largely due to the rise of Islamism as a societal force—as one of culture, religion and ideas. This had its own dynamic and was not orchestrated by the regime. But at the same time it shifted responsibility for action away from the state, and thus served a regime purpose.

Israel, Islamism and *Infitah*

The structural changes initiated by Anwar Sadat flowed from the new 'open door' orientation and were to change the composition of the middle class as well as affect the ways in which the politically active of this class could extend or deepen their support bases or reach a mass constituency. In the mid-1970s Sadat set in train the deconstruction of the ASU and its replacement by a multi-party political system. Leftists within the ASU were deprived of this connection with the masses, particularly as represented in and via the intermediary of the student population, a development also encouraged by the establishment of the independent, non-ASU-affiliated, General Union of Egyptian Students (GUES). The ASU's influence in this regard depended on its links with communist and Nasserist activists in the universities, who were rapidly losing the initiative to Islamists.[9] The ASU as a whole was subdivided into *minabir* (pulpits, sing. *minbar*) in 1975, in a bid to give voice to 'minority' political forces. While Nasser had replaced the National Union with the Arab Socialist Union in 1962 in order to contain a perceived threat from the political right, Sadat embarked on his reorganisation of the ASU to restore the political participation of the bourgeoisie that Nasser had sought to undercut.[10]

But the apparent pluralism was somewhat illusory. Strict limits were set on the extent to which the parties could criticise state policy, with foreign and economic policy declared outside the boundaries of 'constructive' criticism. The parties represented a democratic veneer without a strong popular base. Although the new system allowed for a greater multiplicity of political views to be aired at the state level, the dismantling of ASU structures meant that political mobilisation remained minimal, and combined with the encouragement of independent student political life, de-linked Nasserist and Marxist intellectuals from students as potentially 'organic intellectuals'.

The launching of Sadat's 'Open Door' economic policy, *infitah,* in 1974 created opportunities for importers and a comprador bour-geoisie—the 'fat cats', as well as for rural capitalists—the so-called 'fat *fellahin*.' Many members of the rural middle class, *kibar al-ayan,* which somewhat passively facilitated the Nasser regime's control of the countryside, were elevated under Sadat, where they were strongly represented in a newly invigorated parliament. For Hala Mustafa, the increased representation of the rural middle class in parliament helps explain the conservative/traditional orientation of the regime under Sadat. In the 1970s, this parliamentary presence was instru-mental in keeping such issues as personal status and *shari'a* law on the agenda in a way that dovetailed neatly with the agenda of the Muslim Brotherhood.[11] The Muslim Brotherhood was also support-ive of Sadat's open door economic policy. Beattie argues that 'fat cat wealth' knew no specific ideological orientation, and it is true that the proponents of *infitah* were just as likely to be Islamist as liberal. The Muslim Brothers were part of the fabric of *infitah.* The fact of being given a stake in the regime, alongside their close links with conservative regimes in the Arab world, de-radicalised the Muslim Brotherhood (Kepel dubs them the 'neo-Muslim Brotherhood' to underscore this fact).[12]

The social and ideological change in Egypt was part of an evolv-ing regional political economy. Although official Arab aid to Egypt was discontinued after the 1975 Sinai II agreement, private invest-ment, in the context of *infitah,* rapidly took its place. Increased wealth fuelled the 'parallel Islamic sector' in the 1970s. New business rela-tionships were greatly facilitated by Egyptian entrepreneurs residing in the Gulf, many of whom happened to have been Muslim Brothers who fled there during Nasser's purges in the 1960s, or had been con-vinced by Islamist thought while there. Many Brotherhood members and sympathisers had, in the Gulf, amassed substantial fortunes in the 1960s. The experience of living and prospering in the rich Islamic oil states had convinced many Egyptians that there was no contradiction between wealth acquisition, particularly via free enterprise, and Islam, and even that the latter was a prerequisite for prosperity as the experi-ence of the Gulf states proved.

The commercial links thus had an ideological dimension, reinforced by another major corollary of *infitah*: in lieu of state-led industrialisation as a means of improving the lot of the landless and impoverished, the government encouraged the emigration of Egyptians as labourers abroad, particularly to the Gulf.[13] Almost every Egyptian family had or knew of someone who was working in the Gulf, returning home a little wealthier, and a little more convinced that religion, rather than socialism, was the way to a better life.[14] For Wickham, 'the intensive exposure of Egyptian citizens to the social mores of Saudi Arabia and other Gulf countries where Islamic law was strictly applied pushed their own religious beliefs and practices in a more conservative direction upon their return home.'[15]

In Gramscian terms, ideological linkage between the peasantry and the political classes is achieved via 'organic intellectuals'. The extent to which the organic intellectuals can reconcile the worldviews of different social strata is a function of common language, something the left and liberals have struggled with in Egypt. The most important category of organic intellectuals in Egypt were, as we have already seen, arguably the students. The student movement in the early 1970s was dominated by communist groups, but they were gradually being supplanted by Islamist groupings in a process that would be completed by the late 1970s,[16] although as late as 1977 the left were still able to mobilise support during the January bread riots. The Islamist groupings were not creations of the Egyptian regime and had, from 1968, sustained an autonomous existence and modest following, though with much greater success in the town of al-Mansoura.[17] But, by the admission of one of their leaders, the Islamists could not have taken control of the student movement without government support, chiefly via the appointment of the Islamist Uhtman Isma'il as ASU youth secretary, alongside government repression of the leftist activists.[18]

By the end of 1972, the Islamist groups, emboldened by their high-level support and the changing regime discourse, had begun to more clearly break with the left, largely through focussing on domestic, rather than international, issues. Their central demand was the institution of *shari'a* law in Egypt. They also promoted social reforms in the universities, such as the wearing of the veil for female students and the provision of (segregated) transport facilities. The Islamist student groups, like the Muslim Brotherhood to which they were linked, received substantial funding from the Gulf and Libya, and were able to supply cheap textbooks and Islamic clothing to poor students. Outside of the university, Islamic activists were also able to reach otherwise apolitical Egyptians through the provision of services otherwise unavailable.[19]

There was thus a common political language between the student body and the largest opposition force in the country, the Muslim Brotherhood, and Sadat's support base among the rural middle class. This synergy transformed the terms of political discourse in Egypt and made distinguishing between 'official' versus 'opposition' discourses difficult. The Islamic revival of the 1970s was all-encompassing and transcended any one group.[20]

The Egyptian press began to cover Islamist student activities in a favourable light, whereas before the 1973 war the regime had felt constrained to criticise leftist students only with the simultaneous condemnation of the 'reactionary right' in the student body. Reflecting Sadat's desire to reach out directly to the people, as well as differentiate it from the 'revolutionary' or 'anti-imperialist' wars of Nasser, the conflict was presented in religious terms, taking place as it did during the holy month of Ramadan, the operation was code-named Operation Badr, in a reference to the Prophet's war against infidels. Sadat attributed the victory to the 'religious zeal' of the Egyptian army.[21] The military officer S'ad al-Din Shazli wrote a small book of religious inspiration for soldiers to carry during the 1973 entitled, *Our Religious Creed is Our Path to Victory* [*Aqidatuna al-Diniyya Tariquna, ila al-Nasr*]. This book cast the war in the familiar Brotherhood terms of Islam versus the Jews.[22]

The October War bolstered Sadat's popularity at home and won him great praise from wide sections of the intelligentsia, including the Muslim Brotherhood and the Islamist student leaders who praised the *ra'is mu'min* for his great strike against the Jews and solidarity with the Islamic oil states. By 22 March 1975, the last of the imprisoned Muslim Brotherhood were released. Although Sadat did not grant the Society permission to reform, he allowed the publication of a Brotherhood monthly newspaper, *al-Da'wa* [*The Call*] in 1976. Edited by Supreme Guide Umar al-Talimisany and Salih Ashmawi and with Brotherhood veterans Muhammad al-Ghazzali and Yusuf al-Qaradawi on the editorial board, *al-Da'wa* also gave voice to the student-based *gama'at islamiyya* [Islamic Groups]. For Baker, 'A key element in laying the groundwork for the Brotherhood's early and formative cooperation with the state was the Sadat regime's effort to oppose Nasserism, which the Brothers saw as the strongest political force opposing their own movement, and thus as the greatest obstacle to the attainment of an Islamic society.'[23]

Islamist writers continued to instrumentalise the conflict with Zionism for domestic political purposes, which in the 1970s meant discrediting Nasserist and other leftist forces and building a properly Islamic society. Intellectually, this meant downgrading the 'anti-imperialist' elements of the left's discourse. And, in a refrain now familiar to all political trends, leftists criticised Islamists for ignoring the perils of imperialism and Israel and focussing instead on domestic issues, in this case the veil and *shari'a*.

The Islamist discourse on Nasserism was encouraged by Sadat's deliberate conflation of Nasserism and communism, made concrete by the establishment of the 'left' *minbar* and subsequent formation of the Tagammu' Party, which lumped together Nasserists and communists as a single political force. As such, Islamist condemnations of communism, including equating it with Zionism, should be seen in the context of the Brotherhood and regime's own campaign against Nasser and Nasserists as their main political rivals in Egyptian society. Such writings reiterated axioms of Islamist, and much general, discourse on Israel whose pedigree goes back to the 1940s. Thus, the ultimate Israeli goal of establishing a Greater Israel 'from the Nile to the Euphrates' was emphasised and traced back through Ben Gurion to Herzl. The Jews were blamed for the collapse of the Caliphate and the *Protocols of the Elders of Zion* invoked as an historical source on the nature of the Jews. Behind Israel and Zionism, as well as communism, lay Judaism and Jews as the central problem.

This culturist paradigm was repeated by one of Egypt's most popular female authors, Aisha Abd al-Rahman, more commonly known as Bint al-Shati. One of the first Egyptian women to receive a university education, known for her work on the wives of the Prophet and occa-sionally described as having some feminist characteristics,[24] Bint al-Shati came from a peasant background and much of her work dealt with Egyptian rural issues. As the title of her 1975 work, *al-Isra'iliyat fi-al-Ghazw al-Fikri*, [*The Isra'iliyat in the Intellectual Invasion*] sug-gests, Bint al-Shati adopted the same conceptual framework regarding Jews and Islam as that employed by Qutb, Kishk and other Islamist thinkers. In the introduction she wrote that the impetus for this book came from her attempts, in the wake of the 1967 defeat, to understand what went wrong.[25] Like many, she saw the reason not so much in the strength of the Israeli adversary, Soviet inaction or US support for Israel, but primarily in problems within the Arab socio-political formations, in the 'intellectual invasion.' In seeking to understand the problems, she wrote, the road sometimes seemed to lead to imperial-ism, or to crusadersim, or to atheism.

In analysis that mirrored in its essentials that of Sayyid Qutb in his *Ma'rakatuna ma'a al-Yahud*, [*Our Struggle with the Jews*] some 30 years earlier, Bint al-Shati linked early Jewish infiltration of Islam, via the '*Isra'iliyat'*, to the Jewish hand behind the fall of the Caliphate; to the 'Jewish orientalists' that study and hence distort Islam; to the activi-ties of Western imperialism, which is in the service of the Jews; and finally to the cultural, social, religious and political effacement that is occurring in the Arab-Islamic countries as a result of the ongoing machinations of *Banu Isra'il* (the Jews) and which explain the Arabs' defeat in 1967 and inability to effectively retaliate.

Such themes were expanded upon in the pages of the Muslim Brotherhood paper *al-Da'wa*, which began publishing in 1976. In line with the Islamist movement's generally domestic orientation at this time, priority was given to discussions of correct Islamic practice, the need to Islamicise education and the characteristics of an Islamic state, including the necessity for and elements of *shari'a* law and the features of an Islamic economic system. Each issue had a section on events in the Islamic world in general, and it was within this context that Palestine was addressed, most notably through the detailed record-ing of Israeli settlement practices and other activities in the Occupied Territories. The articles, initially at least, dealt only obliquely with

Egyptian policy towards Israel, but had clear foreign policy import, particularly in the frequent condemnations and ridiculing of the Arab and Egyptian left, who supposed that the Soviet Union could play a role in securing Arab interests or called for a negotiated solution to the conflict with Israel. The main themes in the *al-Da'wa* articles reviewed below are the control of the world's superpowers by Jews, the ongoing danger of Zionist expansionism, and the confluence of Jewish and Western interests in the destruction of Islam.

The *al-Da'wa* writers saw a Jewish hand behind the foreign policies of both the United States and the Soviet Union. Abd al-Mun'im Salim, for example, pointed out the Jewish domination of the American economy, media and political system (as well as indicating that many British MPs were Jews). But like Muhammad Jalal Kishk, Salim did not give this as much attention as Jewish influence over the Soviet Union, a factor related to the support that Egyptian communists and Nasserists lent to the USSR, as well as to the assumption that 'everybody knew' Jews controlled the United States. According to the Brotherhood thinker Ali Jarisha, writing in *al-Da'wa*, communist Russia gave Israel manpower and intellectuals, while the United States gave it military and technical power.[26]

In April 1977, another contributor, Fu'ad Kuhlah, penned an article entitled 'Marxism and Zionism and Their Shared Roots'. He noted that Marx's grandfather was a Rabbi, and that Lenin, Trotsky and other prominent communists were Jews. Both Zionism and Marxism were solutions to the Jewish problem. But he also showed how, doctrinally, Zionism and communism were two sides of the same coin. Each ideology was, he averred, a cover for the conviction that the Jews were 'God's chosen people.' In Marxism, the concept of the 'vanguard' was equivalent to the Zionist grouping of Jews in the 'promised land'. In each, the goal was to enable the Jews to dominate the world. A third group of Jews was not strictly speaking Zionist, though due to its social position was also opposed to Marxism. It was this category of 'rich Jews' in Europe and the Americas that acted as financiers for Zionism. As such, the Marxist Jews suffered from a lack of funds and this explains the relative success of Zionism as compared to Marxism in the Middle East.[27] Kuhlah was keen to stress that Zionists and

Marxists were in competition for this Jewish funding, rather than in any kind of ideological conflict, since they were both based on the same idea of the primacy of the Jews as God's chosen people.[28]

Rejecting Sadat's suggestion that expansionist Zionism had run its course, Abd al-Mun'im Salim cited continued Israeli expansion into the West Bank and Gaza via settlements from 1967 as confirmation that the project was alive and well. In his first *al-Da'wa* intervention, Salim criticised those who, after 1967 and again after 1973, called for peace with Israelis—'those who slaughtered us yesterday and try to finish us off [*ijhaz*] today and want to extend their settlements from the Nile to the Euphrates tomorrow—or even from the ocean to the ocean.' Israeli expansionism remained a living threat, supported by 'all Jewish [Israeli] parties', with the left no less expansionist than the Likud, as well as the United States, regardless of who happened to be in the White House. Salim quoted Begin as saying there will be 'no peace for the Israeli people and not for the land of Israel nor for the Arabs as long as we do not liberate all of our homeland, even if we sign the peace treaty.'[29] Israeli expansion was to be implemented incrementally. The first stage was to consolidate Jewish control of lands occupied between 1948 and 1967. Stage two was to expand into the land conquered in 1967 and stage three will involve the further expansion to fill the land between the Nile and the Euphrates. The language of UNSCR 242, particularly the reference to 'secure borders' was, for Salim, code for further Israeli expansion. The correct Muslim position should be to reject the taking of any Muslim lands or the surrender of any part of it. This applied as much to land taken in 1948 as in 1967, since one 'cannot solve the new at the expense of the old.'

The effectiveness of Jewish domination in Palestine was guaranteed, for Salim, first and foremost by 'world Zionism'. Westerners that helped Zionists 'did so not out of love for them, as nobody could love them, the question was only imperialist interests and connivance against Islam.' In support of this contention, he cited the US vice president Nelson Rockefeller's statement that God sent the Jews to the East to help revive it, and that the Arabs would benefit from Israeli knowledge and civilisation. He went on to explain that the unity between Israel and the United States was encapsulated in their joint interests in 'developing' (*tatwir*) Arab society. Development, for Salim, was code for erasing Islamic identity, destroying customs and stamping out values and traditions. Salim observed that this goal was well known to all Jews and the capitalist and communist West, but ignored by many Arabs and Muslims.[30] The only way to stop it was by turning more resolutely to Islam, a conviction for which Salim found unlikely support in the words of Shimon Peres, who warned a group of Jewish youth that Islam was the main impediment to achieving peace in the region.[31]

On this issue, as with others, Salim implicated Arab communists. Palestinian communists were complicit in the Israeli project to erase the Arab identity of those living in 1948 Israel. Communism in the region was introduced, according to Salim, by Jews in Palestine and spread from there throughout the Arab world. Zionism and communism were virtually identical in their goals 'despite what the 'treacherous trumpeters' [*al-abwaq al-jawfa*] in the Arab world do to hide [that fact]'.[32] The Egyptian left, too, in denying the responsibility of Israeli workers and calling for a policy towards Israel based on an alliance of working forces, were guilty of aiding the plan of Muslim intellectual 'cleansing' (*tasfiya*) and 'dissolution' (*tadhwib*), a project that was no less dangerous than physical annihilation.[33] In the section of *al-Da'wa* given over to the activities of the student *Jama'at* in January 1977, a letter appeared that, echoing Qutb, described contemporary debates on the role of women in Islamic society as an issue 'created by Jews',[34] mirroring Qutb's contention that the Jews aimed to culturally debase Islamic societies through their women. The goal of cultural and religious liquidation in the region was also furthered, Salim argued, by projects for a 'Middle Eastern group', as voiced by then Israeli foreign minister Abba Eban and president of the World Jewish Congress Nahum Goldmann after 1967. In such 'federalist' formulations the states of the region could be united through a peace settlement around an Israeli civilisational mission that would 'wipe out' the original identities of the Arab world.[35] Particularly regrettable for Salim was that since 1967 Israel had been considered as a fact, with the idea of destroying it essentially unthinkable.[36]

From April 1977 *al-Da'wa* also began to devote more space to articles about Jerusalem, specifically in the context of Israeli plans to rebuild Solomon's Temple on the Temple Mount, which would threaten the al-Aqsa mosque. The issue of Jerusalem effectively integrated the themes of Israeli expansionism and Jewish enmity towards Islam. Salih Ashmawi, *al-Da'wa*'s editor, wrote an article warning the Arab leaders that they would face dire consequences if they did not keep Jerusalem and al-Aqsa safe.[37] In August, Ala' Zaydan alerted *al-Da'wa*'s readers to the construction work that was taking place around the mosque, using the immediate issue to discuss the 'religious roots of the Jews' war against the Arabs.' Rebuilding the temple was, for the Jews, a symbol of victory, whereas its destruction had signified defeat. The destruction of al-Aqsa was to be interpreted as a step along the road to destroying Islam and establishing a Jewish state from the Nile to the Euphrates. After al-Aqsa, the Israelis would move to Medina. 'When', Zaydan implored in conclusion, tying the issue again to a domestic issue, 'will the Muslim *ulama* [legal scholars] move?' 'When will the silence end?'[38]

It is interesting to note here that the Brotherhood was not calling for the state to act, but preferred to frame the conflict as societal and, to the extent it concerned officialdom, involving the Islamic authorities. This may have stemmed from the group's reluctance to antagonise the regime given its benevolence towards the Brotherhood. But it may also have stemmed from the longstanding Islamist desire to keep the conflict with Israel societal in furtherance of the Brotherhood's own social and political aspirations.

Sadat's visit to Jerusalem in 1977 severely tested the rapprochement that had developed between the regime and Islamists. The division of labour that had underpinned Egyptian foreign policy became almost untenable as criticism rose to fever pitch and Sadat turned to censorship and increased oppression. Although Sadat had been moving in the direction of a separate peace since the October War, the Brotherhood had been able to avoid criticising this policy. The Jerusalem trip made this impossible and seemed, to many, to validate Qutb's prognosis. Muslim Brotherhood leader Umar Talimisany criticised the peace process vehemently, warning of the dangers it posed to Islamic culture in Egypt, as well as the threat to the economy. Israel continued to be perceived as a manifestation of a much broader

Jewish-led anti-Islamic threat. But it was in fact Islamic rulers that should be criticised: 'The greatest blame is to be laid on the rulers of the Islamic countries who know all this and do not condemn it, but rather encourage it ...'[39]

He went further, in Qutbist language, to add:

> Consider to what extent there may be a connection between [our] real enemies and [our] rulers; the latter whom we would always have considered the strength of the Muslims—and once they were—but who [now] defend the Muslims' enemies. Our rulers have become as poisoned arrows in the very hearts of the Muslims ...
>
> The Muslim rulers love their enemies—the enemies of their religion. This is something their subjects cannot accept.[40]

Faced with such unacceptable criticism of Sadat's policy after the Jerusalem visit, the president enacted two laws that 'explicitly forbade public criticism of the peace treaty with Israel.'[41] One of them, law 33 of 1978 required that political parties abide by the 'principles of the 1952 Revolution and of the corrective measures of 1971'. Of the many restrictions on expression that this implied, banning criticism of 'foreign policy agreements' constituted just one.[42]

Until Sadat banned its publications, shortly before his death in 1981, the Muslim Brotherhood maintained that 'war is the way to liberate Palestine' but that this should be a societal effort and linked to social and cultural change at home. Consistent with its historic position, *al-Da'wa* called for:

> ... strengthening the internal front through the institution of justice and eradication of social and moral ills; the formation of a broad Arab-Islamic front with plans for serious contribution to the battle with volunteers, arms, money, and diplomatic pressure; severing ties with, and terminating the interests of, those who support Israel with money, arms, and diplomacy; sustained military, economic, and spiritual mobilisation of Arab material and human resources for a protracted war until victory.[43]

Societal paradigms of the left

The left, now an opposition force, also pressed the societal angle. Writers in *al-Tali'a* warned that the Egypt-Israel conflict could have an adverse effect on the social struggle at home—an argument that closely mirrored that of the most militant Islamists, and was used by the Brotherhood in the 1940s. The reason was that it enhanced the military as a 'centre of power' against the left. 'For this reason,' Baker writes, 'the Vanguard [*al-Tali'a*] writers consistently argued that the battle against Israel should not be the monopoly of the armed forces and a justification for its privileged position,'[44] and that the Arab liberation struggle against world imperialism could be won only through popular resistance. This, as we have seen, was a longstanding position of the left and one that Nasser encouraged. It served an important purpose for the regime in shifting responsibility for the conflict onto society.

Within the universities, although not with the same intensity that had characterised the movement of 1971–72, Nasserist groups in 1974–75 protested the Sinai Agreements and continued to oppose 'any agreement which implied an acceptance of Israel.'[45] As Sadat's peace initiatives accumulated through the decade, and the optimism of 1973 faded, Nasserist opposition grew stronger. Intellectuals proceeded from the Israel imperialism link to draw conclusions about the true nature of Sadat's peace initiative, in a way that, in stark contrast to the function of anti-imperialist discourse before 1973, had distinctly 'counter-hegemonic' implications. First published in Arabic in 1979, Ghali Shukri's work on Sadat's Egypt is true to the classic anti-imperialism paradigm that prevailed during the Nasser years. An activist during the student movement of the early 1970s, Shukri's work is representative of the Arabism of the Egyptian communists. Whereas Sadat portrayed Egypt as riding the wave of détente and technological innovation, Shukri accused Sadat of being the instrument of an international counter-revolution, with religious extremist dimensions. For Shukri, the Sinai Agreements, Zionism and the Lebanese Civil War were different dimensions of a single international strategy that united Muslim (Sadat), Christian

(Maronites) and Jewish (Israel) 'fascists' against the Arab masses. He wrote:

> In reality, the strategic plan of Tel Aviv and Washington ever since the tripartite aggression of 1956, consisted in finding a new formula for the Israeli-Western alliance, in such a way as to give the Hebrew State the chance of expansion in the Arab Mashreq, and to enable the Shah's empire to extend to the Arab Gulf, and the new American colonialism to impose its hegemony over the entire region from the Maghreb to the Near East.[46]

For Shukri, the failure of this plan for Israeli expansion and US hegemony in the 1960s necessitated the Israeli attack of 1967, with UNSCR 242 and the Rogers Plan being fully planned extensions of the grand strategy.

Lutfi al-Khuli shared with Shukri the conviction that the Egyptian regime was part of a global counter-revolutionary trend. Al-Khuli had apparently concluded after Sinai II that Sadat was a CIA agent. *Al-Tali'a*, which al-Khuli edited, set itself staunchly against the Sinai II Agreement, claiming that it was impossible for the United States to play the role of impartial mediator between the Arabs and Israel. For him, the Arab right (in which he implicitly included the Egyptian regime), which claimed 1973 as their victory, was assisted by hidden ties with neo-colonialism.[47] As with Shukri, al-Khuli saw that it was in this nexus, between the leaderships of the Arab states, Zionism and imperialism, that the extension of ethnic and religious conflict throughout the Arab world could be understood. Al-Khuli viewed the Egyptian-Saudi alliance as bad for the progressive programme and believed that working with the Arab oil powers in areas beyond essential shared interests would be wrong due to their reactionary natures and because they were helping America sell itself as a new 'friendly face' in the region, one that would not openly side with Israel as it did in the 1950s and 1960s.[48] The sectarian nature of the Israeli-Arab conflict, which used to be an exceptional condition in the region, was now spreading and acting to create a new system of statelets with factional, religious characteristics.[49] Ultimately, for al-Khuli, the social basis of the regime must change. The petit bourgeois role in the revolution was finished and a new class coalition must take over.[50]

Al-Khuli called on the Arab progressive movement to keep demanding progress in the cultural, social and economic spheres of society. But the movement, he observed, had known ebbs and flows and must be attentive to international changes. After the mid-1960s the progressive struggle witnessed an ebb (*mawjat jazar*). The 1973 War sparked a new 'flow' (*mawjat madd*) in the movement, and in the mid-1970s it oscillated between negative and positive impulses, negatively combating the oil hegemony of the conservative states and the related growth of a 'capitalist, parasitic comprador class' in most Arab countries, while positively fighting the American policy of step-by-step diplomacy and supporting the Palestinian revolution. Palestine had become the new focus for the Arab revolution, replacing Egypt as the 'nucleus state'. Supporting it was, for al-Khuli, the most constructive path since the Palestinian resistance mobilised the entire Arab movement,[51] including progressive religious forces, represented in the Egyptian Tagammu' party and similar groupings in Lebanon, Algeria, Iraq, Syria and Yemen. It was important for him that this unified movement resist the attempts of big (US) and little (Israel) imperialisms to use religion against it. He saw an imperialist hand in the regeneration of *salafi* movements that distracted the population with mythical battles and excommunication campaigns (*hamalat takfir*).[52] A strong movement uniting progressive religious and secular forces could end this Zionist and imperialist manipulation of religious differences.[53]

Imperialism, for al-Khuli, hoped to transform states like Israel into technological-industrial economic bases for world capitalism to help inhibit the spread of socialism in their regions; to constitute loci of advancement and civilisation in their backward hinterlands, and as such guarantee the continuity of the Third World as a source of energy and raw materials for the capitalist West; and also to ensure the survival of these states that, as the Cold War ebbed, were on the decline. In the Arab world, global imperialism and its Israeli protégé were forced onto the defensive by the transformation in the balance of power wrought by the 1973 War. They thus used various nefarious strategies to regain the initiative, including the 'occupying of oil wells' by the International Energy Agency, fomenting internal divisions to spark inter-Arab conflicts (between the October allies, Egypt, Syria and the PLO), border disputes (between Egypt and Libya), separatist movements (such as the Western Saharans and the Iraqi Kurds) and civil wars (such as Lebanon). [54] Al-Khuli predicted that in the years to come, they would try also to spread instability in Somalia, Southern Sudan and the Arabian Peninsula. Al-Khuli described the 'Palestinisation' of the Gulf, which had become *'Filastin al-Batruliyya'* (Oil Palestine), with the Shah's Iran representing *'Isra'il al-Batruliya'* (Oil Israel). The goal was to destroy the democratic national movement, particularly the Palestinian resistance—now the focus for the Arab revolution—and its progressive allies in Lebanon.[55]

But al-Khuli introduced a crucial and telling caveat into what would otherwise have been a genuinely subversive narrative. Despite expressing counter-hegemonic ideas linking Israel to Arab, including Egyptian, 'reaction' from within the anti-imperialism paradigm, al-Khuli shared with Sadat, and the Soviet Union, a view of the Middle East as a global flashpoint that threatened the peace and stability of the world in an era of superpower détente. The 'principal contradiction' facing the Egyptian progressive movement was not that with Sadat, in other words, but between the Arabs and Israel. In this, al-Khuli's intervention also reflected the Soviet rationale that calming the Cold War was in the interests of the entire world, and a universalisation of the Arab-Israeli conflict to portray it as threatening global peace and security. In the era of détente (*al-infiraj al-dawali*), the Middle East remained a centre of 'Hot War' because of the Arab-Israeli conflict. Al-Khuli considered two main possible trajectories for the Middle East. The first was that the region would explode into violence due to the fact that the parties to the Cold War—particularly the United States—ignored the locus of instability that was the Palestine issue, as well as the fact that the Americans had the monopoly over deciding the type of peace realised, in concert with Israel. The less likely, but preferable, path was that of détente, in which the independence and sovereignty of the states in the region would be respected, along with the rights and freedoms of its people, including the Palestinians' right to build their own state.[56]

Al-Khuli drew a distinction between the United States, as the embodiment of world imperialism, and Israel, its partner and 'little imperialism' in the region. Only by weakening the control of both powers over the destiny of the region could a just, stable peace be achieved. He saw the solution in the strengthening of ties between Arab states in order to achieve the primary goal of liberating the land. Restating ideas he, and others such as Heikal, had developed during Nasser's experiment with Arab 'summitry', al-Khuli argued for 'national coexistence' (*al-ta'ayyush qawmi*) with conservative states but stressed that it should be limited to those areas that directly served essential shared interests, such as creating an independent Palestinian state, while the social struggle continued throughout the entire Middle East region. The historical situation, al-Khuli averred, was right in that there were shared Arab interests in a 'unified national economic entity,' which would transform Arab 'quantity', or population, into Arab 'quality', or economic and technical capability, while respecting the rights of all systems and classes in the Arab world.[57]

Al-Khuli, like Sadat, recognised that in this era of détente, new power blocs had emerged in the world: China, Japan, Europe and, following the October War, the Arab world as the 'sixth world power'. The OPEC decision to raise oil prices after the War marked the first time the developing world had by its own initiative influenced the world capitalist economy, thus giving the Arab world significant weight in the Third World. Al-Khuli argued that the Arabs should build on this by strengthening ties between the Arab and African countries on one hand and Europe on the other to counterbalance the United States. By joining with Europe in the spirit of Helsinki—that is, while retaining their independence—the Arabs could break the 'American and Israeli monopolies' and bring the Middle East out of the Cold War and into the world of détente. In such a world, for al-Khuli, 'racist-colonialist entities', such as South Africa, Rhodesia and Israel, would lose their significance.

Although arguing for a Palestinian state, ascribing some autonomy to Israel as representing 'little imperialism' and arguing for a Middle Eastern détente, al-Khuli's focus was on peaceful coexistence among the *Arab* states of the region, with Israel as the unifying 'other', and as such represents a direct continuation of the Nasserist Unity of Action doctrine that he and others helped elaborate in the early to mid-1960s. A more radical intellectual development, which moved beyond Unity of Action, was spearheaded by another Marxist in the 1970s. Although the work of Mohamed Sid Ahmed could be construed to provide ideological support for Sadat's moves towards peace with Israel, he did not simply mimic Sadat, and continued to view the conflict on a regional level in a way that differed from the regime's conception since 1967. The main feature that distinguished his intervention was his suggestion that the links binding the United States and Israel could be broken and a peaceful resolution of the Arab-Israeli conflict was possible absent defeating imperialism as a whole. Thus, the principal contradiction had become that between the Arabs and Israel, on the one hand, and US imperialism, on the other.

Sid Ahmed had been active in the communist movement in the 1940s, a member of Iskra and henceforth the Egyptian Communist Organisation, known by its Arabic acronym, MISHMISH, that had adopted a position that argued strongly for Israeli self-determination. Sid Ahmed, along with many communists, had come to terms with Nasser's regime after 1955. He joined Heikal on the *al-Ahram* newspaper and was, from the late 1960s, a regular contributor and editor of *al-Tali'a*. The 1974 book, *After the Guns Fall Silent*, was, as its forward explains, the result of discussions within the al-Ahram Centre for Political and Strategic Studies in the wake of the October 1973 War. In it, he suggested that a peaceful resolution to the Arab-Israeli conflict was not only a possible, but the only plausible, outcome if the interests of both Arabs and Israelis were to be secured. In 1974, before Sadat's trip to Jerusalem and the diplomatic *volt-face* that it embodied, this position, essentially that of Hakim and Mahfuz two years earlier, remained extremely provocative. At the time, Sid Ahmed was part of a genuine vanguard of Egyptian intellectuals that moved away from bellicosity and, in many ways, closer to the traditional position of the Egyptian communist movement, and that of the USSR, that saw two legitimate communities in historic Palestine, Arabs and Jews.

The solution identified in the 1940s was to unite Jewish and Arab workers in the struggle against global imperialism and capitalist exploitation. This position had been invalidated by Pan-Arabism, which the Egyptian communist movement as a whole embraced through the 1950s and 1960s. In *After the Guns Fall Silent*, Mohamed Sid Ahmed did not talk of Arab and Jewish workers as equally oppressed in a global capitalist system, but stressed that two national communities existed, the Arab and the Israeli, and that each had rights that should be safeguarded, both for moral reasons and for the pragmatic reason that the Arabs would never achieve their goals unless they joined the rest of the world, including the socialist countries, in recognising the rights of Israelis.[58]

Like the October Paper, Sid Ahmed's book established that the world of the 1970s had changed. The era of détente, symbolised by the Strategic Arms Limitation Treaty (SALT), imposed new constraints and opportunities on the parties to what, after 1967, became known as the Middle East crisis.[59] He insisted that the conflict between Israel and the Arabs was the single most dangerous issue in international relations, and that détente between the superpowers would stand or fall on the outcome of the conflict. Another resort to war in the Middle East would, he predicted, shake the foundations of détente and lead to nuclear war.

One of the more dangerous factors for Sid Ahmed was that of the Palestinians, whose prestige had grown after the October War, the UN Resolution on Zionism and Arafat's appearance before the General Assembly, such that 'The Palestinians' struggle is now an inspiration for the revolt of the dispossessed against the affluent, not only in ends, but also in means.' The resistance, for him, had become the banner of the 'Sixth International.'[60] The parties thus had a responsibility to resolve the conflict peacefully. What was needed was a Middle Eastern détente in which the strengths and interests of Arabs and Israelis would be recognised and respected, and, unlike in al-Khuli's conception, would include Israel. In line with peaceful coexistence, grander objectives (such as ending the Zionist project and establishing a secular multi-ethnic state in Palestine) could be postponed in favour of establishing a stable status quo and more immediate goals, such as the establishment of a Palestinian state in the West Bank and Gaza Strip. Sid Ahmed was under no illusions that this was a simple matter, but maintained that this should be the first order of business and that the 1973 War opened up opportunities for the Arabs to move in this direction.

The War, for Sid Ahmed, exploded the myth of Israeli invincibility and, while not the resounding victory that some Egyptian journalists saw, was not an Israeli victory either.[61] The Arabs' major achievement in the war was to introduce a degree of strategic parity to the conflict that would encourage Israel to seek a negotiated settlement. And for the first time, the Arab aim of a just peace could be realisable. This would necessitate, for Sid Ahmed, marginalising 'rejectionists' on both sides. For him, the 'dissident movement emerging from the Palestinian resistance illustrates the fact that in the Arab world there are still many who persist in rejecting adamantly any solution.'[62] On the Israeli side, the anti-Zionist forces—Rakah, Matzpen and the Communist Party—had no effect on official policy. In light of this, the best hope for the Arabs would be to engage the Zionist doves who believed that coexistence sooner or later was inevitable, rather than the hawks who would settle for nothing less than overwhelming military superiority. The fact of dealing with Zionists should not deter Arabs since just as in the context of superpower détente, contradictions can be 'frozen' enabling the USSR to deal with 'imperialist' America, so too can Arabs and Israelis reach an accommodation without necessarily abandoning their ultimate goals.[63] Sid Ahmed would maintain this conviction in the 1990s via his membership of the pro-normalisation Copenhagen Group (see Chapter 6).

A key element in Sid Ahmed's rationale was his distinction between vertical and horizontal contradictions in the Middle East. Vertical contradictions, those between states, were likely to provoke intense conflict, while horizontal contradictions, within Jewish and Arab society as a whole, would remain independent of whether individual states were reconciled. Thus, accepting a settlement with Israel, like rapprochement with the conservative Arab states, need not be a 'reactionary' solution, since the social (horizontal) struggle can continue regardless.[64] Even if Israel was a 'tool' of imperialism, this should not deter the left from supporting a settlement with it. The progressive Arab strategy would involve two distinct steps. First, in order to stand up to Western economic imperialism, the Arabs would have to reinvigorate indigenous capitalism. Then, having separated the Arab nation from the world imperialist system, it could break with capitalism altogether. As for Israel, released from its imperialist tethers it could, much like the crusader states of the Levant, fade into the Arab landscape to become a focus for Jewish culture in the region 'freed from manipulation and exploitation.'[65]

Sid Ahmed did not downplay the scale of the threat Israel presented to Arab aspirations. Although he warned against viewing Israel in purely colonial or racial terms, as he saw to be the prevalent Arab view, he insisted that Zionism was organically linked to colonialism and imperialism, quoting Herzl: 'We shall be a rampart against Asia, an outpost for civilisation against the barbarians.'[66] But he cautioned against equating it with traditional settler colonialism as its inhabitants arrived from a variety of different countries to escape persecution. Thus, despite its roots, Israel could not accurately be described as a 'bridgehead' for colonialism. World imperialism sought to use Israel in this way, but that was not to say that the 'bridgehead' could not be detached. Sid Ahmed's work provided a Marxist rationale for both peaceful negotiated settlement with Israel and unity of Arab states irrespective of social system. It represented a shift in Egyptian Marxist thought back to the traditional communist, and longstanding Soviet, view of Israel, and a rejection of the simple equation of Israel with imperialism. Although he identified problems in Israeli society, such as a racist hierarchy among Jews that would render unlikely any rights being granted to Palestinians, he viewed these problems as analogous to the social inequalities within Arab states. The confrontation with Israel was thus no longer to come out of a general anti-imperialist struggle, but could be averted altogether via détente. The ultimate victory over imperialism, rather than being a prerequisite for neutralising Israel, would follow an Arab-Israeli rapprochement.

Zionism in the crosshairs

Islamist and more 'liberal' approaches shared a focus on Israeli 'culture', typically juxtaposed to a correspondingly bounded Egyptian, Arab or Islamic culture. In an article in the liberal journal *al-Musawwar* shortly after the 1973 war, for example, the literary critic Raja al-Naqqash observed that Israeli scholars were studying Nagib Mahfuz and Tawfiq al-Hakim, in order to 'know thy enemy.' Naqqash argued that this was part of an Israeli 'culture war' against the Arabs and that the Arabs should, for their part, respond in the same way, by learning about Israeli culture and literature.[67] The idea of a culture war became more salient as Egypt renounced the war option in its relations with Israel, and many works positioned themselves largely in these terms.

Whereas the analyses of Sid Ahmed and al-Khuli promoted statism by modifying the Nasserist view of Israel as part of Western imperialism, and, in Sid Ahmed's case, calling for peaceful coexistence with Zionist Israel; and the *al-Da'wa* writers saw Jewish imperialism and a civilisational threat, from the mid-1970s some intellectuals were highlighting the problems posed by Israel's Zionist underpinnings. Many did not describe Israel as a military threat to Egypt but, in line with Sadat's assessment, focussed on Zionism's local effects, rather than its nature as an expansionist project linked to imperialism threatening the broader Arab world. Also in keeping with the regime's position, which was to portray Egypt's role as serving universal civilisation, this work portrayed Zionism as its antithesis. Internationally, this perspective was supported by the UN General Assembly resolution in 1975 designating Zionism as a form of racism. Although not treating the Arab-Israeli conflict as a religious war after the fashion of Islamist intellectuals, the prioritisation of the specific ideological—and to an extent cultural—content of Zionism, over Israel's imperialist links, meant that there were certain synergies between the statist perspective promoted in this work and the more essentialist writings of the Muslim Brotherhood.

In 1975 Sayyid Yasin, Mufid Shihab al-Din and Yunan Rizq published a short collaboration entitled *Zionism and Racism*, addressing the UN resolution mentioned above. The preface noted that despite a large volume of work on the Palestine cause, there was very little on the issue of Zionism. Shihab al-Din, in his contribution, noted that Zionism constituted one of three solutions to the Jewish problem, with the others being liberal and socialist revolutions. Zionism, he argued, stemmed directly from European colonialism and the desire to exploit economically the non-European world. He went so far as to assert, following Baha al-Din's argument a decade earlier, that Zionism was in fact a variant of Fascism, constituting as it did a form of nationalism based on racism. Under the influence of Zionism, Shihab al-Din suggested, Judaism itself underwent a transformation in the 20th century, from being a universalist religion to a racist form of national solidarity in which Jews were elevated to the status of 'God's chosen people.'[68] In 1948, Israeli racial discrimination (*al-tamyiz al-'unsuri al-Isra'ili*) became the other side and expression of Zionist discrimination (*al-tamyiz al-Sihyuni*), since Zionism was the intellectual and ideological underpinning of 'Israeli discriminatory practice'.[69]

Shihab al-Din divided the development of the State of Israel into three distinct periods. The years from 1948 to 1967 were, for him, the period of Israeli consolidation around Zionism and imperialism. The next period, from 1967 until 1973, represented the consolidation of Zionism around the State of Israel, and the post-1973 era the stage of return to Israeli consolidation around Zionism.[70] In other words, while the years from 1967 until 1973 were characterised by Israeli expansionism, the current period was defined by Zionism's turning inward as racism. Shihab al-Din pointed out that whether talking about Israeli or Zionist racism, it is the same story. He illustrated three effects of this linkage. (1) The expulsion of the Palestinian Arabs by force from their land and the creation of the state of Israel which prevented their return, despite UN resolutions, (2) the passage of land laws in 1948 enabling Israel to acquire as much land as it wanted and (3) the crushing of the revolution of the Arab people in the Occupied Territories after 1967 and the violation of the Geneva conventions in its practice there.

Shihab al-Din went on to outline various UN positions on racism, and those dealing with the question of Zionism in particular. He noted that although the UN was behind the creation of Israel, via the Partition Plan of 1947, it did not confer any legitimacy on the 'racist discriminatory policy of the Hebrew state.' Indeed the Partition Plan itself stipulated that certain rights and responsibilities be observed, particularly with regard to the Holy Places, as well as proscribing discrimination based on ethnicity, religion, language or nationality.[71]

Shihab al-Din's analysis was couched in the language of international law. He described Zionism and Israel as being out of step with the international community. Shihab al-Din saw the General Assembly resolution on Zionism as representing the fruits of non-alignment in general, and of the October War in particular. The resolution represented the culmination of efforts by the oil-producing, Non-Aligned and Third World states in the wake of the October War. The Arab world's struggle against Zionism was a dimension of the broader global struggle for a 'new economic order, built on justice and economic liberation, and the global call to expand the Non-Aligned bloc.'[72] In this regard, Shihab al-Din's analysis reflected the changing emphasis of the Non-Aligned Movement as a whole, from anti-imperialism to economic independence. In concluding, Shihab al-Din pointed out that in light of the interconnectedness of Zionism and Israel, the resolution not only constituted a condemnation of Zionism, but also called into question the legitimacy of Israel as a state—of the presence, and not just the practices, of Israel. It called into question the Partition Plan and Israel's membership in the United Nations. For Shihab al-Din, this should form the foundation of an intellectual effort to expose the racist essence of Zionism—and, by extension, Israel. In this way, not only Arab, but also world, public opinion could be convinced of Israel's true nature, and prepare the ground for 'the Arab liberation movement to enter into the fateful struggle against Zionism.'[73]

Work by Abdelwahhab Elmessiri[74], like that of Yasin and Shihab al-Din, examined the questions of Israel and Zionism using western social science frameworks and in terms of a war of ideas. Working from the al-Ahram Centre for Political and Strategic Studies, Elmessiri wrote a series of works on Zionism from 1973, most prominently his 1975 *Encyclopaedia* on Zionism, as well as the 1973 *Nihayat al-Tarikh: Muqaddama li-Dirasat Baniya 'al-Fikr al-Sihyuni [The End of History: Introduction to the Foundation of Zionist Thought}* and the 1977 *Land of Promise: a Critique of Political Zionism*, published in English. Like Saad Eddine Ibrahim, Elmessiri was a student in the United States during the Six-Day War and was active there in left-wing politics. The fact that Elmessiri published in English as well as Arabic is significant in that it reveals his conviction that the Arab-Israeli conflict was reproduced as a war of ideas not only in the Middle East but in the West as well, and that it behoved the Arabs to not only present their case as right and just, but to portray that of Israel as bogus, 'ideological' and running counter to the stream of modern civilisation, with a view to weakening Western support for Israel.

Israel, for Elmessiri, was organically linked to imperialism, but this factor was most important in that imperialism allowed, or encouraged, the persistence of 'fascist' Zionist ideology. The features and function of Zionism, in turn, could not be explained without reference to Judaism, and he saw the threat of Zionism to Egypt and the broader Arab world as primarily cultural. At the same time, Elmessiri allowed that were Israel able to 'de-Zionise' it could exist as a legitimate nation-state.[75] Elmessiri pointed out in the introduction to his encyclopaedia that all previous such compendia published since the outbreak of the Arab-Israeli conflict had been written by Zionist Jews, and that the result of this was that Arabs had to refer to Zionist sources in order to find out about Judaism and 'the enemy.'[76] Elmessiri's encyclopaedia purported to include all concepts related to Zionism and the Arab-Israeli conflict and sought to uncover the ideological nature of terms like 'the Jewish people' and 'Jewish history'.[77] Elmessiri argued that Jewish parties and organisations were named so as to disguise their true purpose: settlement and colonisation, and that it was the Arabs' task to expose this disguise.[78]

Like Saad Eddine Ibrahim, Elmessiri noted that there had been two main conceptions of Israel prevalent in Arab political thought: what he termed traditional (*taqlidiyya*) or conspiracy (*ta'amuriya*) theories and scientific (*'ilmiyya*) theories. The former viewed Israel and Zionism as part of an ancient Jewish conspiracy going back to the time of Moses, and encompassing the *Isra'iliyat*.[79] The conspiratorial view also took seriously the *Protocols of the Elders of Zion* and implicated social and political movements, such as freemasonry and communism, in the grand conspiracy. 'Zionism,' in this conception, 'is nothing but the latest round in this continuous conspiracy.' Elmessiri pointed out that, unfortunately, most Arab writings about Zionism had until recently fallen under this framework. Under the scientific approach, on the other hand, Zionism was inseparable from imperialism and was primarily the result of economic factors in European imperialist societies at the end of the 19th century. This approach saw no relation between the Jewish religion and other parts of Jewish civilisation and the Zionist project, but instead posited that Zionism and imperialism used the Jewish religion to hide the truth of their plans from the 'oppressed Jewish masses' (*al-jamahir al-yahudiyya al-makhdu'a*).

For Elmessiri, both approaches to Israel were useful in some ways but wanting in others. As far as the traditional interpretation is concerned, some conspiracies were real: the goal of a Greater Israel from 'the Nile to the Euphrates', for example, was not an anti-Semitic accusation, for Elmessiri, but a real statement made by Herzl, Jabotinsky and Begin. The traditional explanation also shed light on the precise form that Zionism assumed. The problem of 'who are the Jews', Elmessiri argued, occupied Israelis from the beginning and was not part of an imperialist design that could be explained by looking at economics in Europe in the 19th century: 'As such, the traditional (conspiratorial) conceptions can give us some explanations for this phenomenon that the scientific accounts obscure because these accounts focus on the superstructure and on Zionist myths and their assumptions about themselves.'[80] The traditional approach failed in other ways, however. It could not explain the timing of Zionism at the end of the 19th century. It also failed to explain why Zionism never really became convincing until the Balfour Declaration, and why Zionism's headquarters moved from Istanbul to Paris, to London and to Washington. Only the scientific view could answer such questions, such as how Zionism gained ground in 1917 because of the Bolshevik revolution and the Arab revolt and Britain's desire to stop the revolt and prevent Jews from joining communist parties.[81] There were problems with the scientific approach as well, for Elmessiri. It could not explain why social and economic problems of the Jews became the 'Jewish question', or why only Jews emigrated to Palestine and not Christians as well, as was the case in Algeria and Rhodesia. It did not explain why Zionism became 'settler colonialism' in particular, and why it was different from traditional settler colonialism in that it relied also on the transfer of the indigenous population.

The nub of the issue for Elmessiri was that the traditional approach looked at the Talmudic 'superstructure' separately from the European 'base', while the scientific approach did the opposite. Both approaches neglected the interrelationship of the superstructure and the base and the relationship between form and substance, ideas and reality. The ideational superstructure (*al-bina al-fikri*) had many contradictions and some things lay dormant and not realised. But the key was that when the superstructure was in balance with the base, transformative or revolutionary processes were 'activated.' Anti-Semitism constituted an example of such a process, and so too did the Zionist solution itself.[82] Elmessiri argued that in Israel—'like all fascist structures'—the superstructure predominated (even though ultimately it was the base that determined reality) because fascism was the victim of its own manufactured false consciousness, separate from all reality. Imperialist countries kept Israelis in this state of false consciousness, imprisoned in Talmudic myths, through their economic, military and moral support. It was this disconnect between base and superstructure that explained the socialist form, but fascist practices, of the kibbutzim.

The *Encyclopaedia* of Elmessiri represented a manifestation of the Arab-Israeli conflict as a war of ideas, perceptions and ultimately culture. Influenced as he was by Mannheim and the sociology of knowledge, Elmessiri denied that Zionist mythology was recognised as such by Israelis, or that myths were used in an insidious or devious way: that ideology constituted, in other words, 'lies'. Rather, Israelis subscribed willingly to these ideas as a result of the fusion between Judaism and the Zionist national project to form Israeli culture. The danger for the Arabs was two-fold. The first was that Zionist ideology would in turn permeate Arab consciousness and culture. As evidence of this process in action, he lamented the fact that Hebrew phrases and names of groups were transliterated directly into Arabic resulting in 'ugly' syntactic formulations. The second was that Zionism also infused Western culture and thus posed an indirect threat. The *Encyclopaedia* itself thus represented an act of resistance against the perceived intellectual threat of Zionism to the Arab consciousness.

Elmessiri's discussion of the different conceptions of the Palestine cause held by sympathisers in the region as well as the West, and his advocacy of a conception that combined these varied perspectives, indicated his conviction that groups within the West could and should be mobilised against Zionism. Also, since he argued that Zionism itself persisted as a result of imperialist support for Israel, he also believed that without this support Israeli culture could change, and 'de-Zionise'. This presentation of the issue, although couched in historical materialist terms, differed sharply from that of Sadiq al-Azm and other Marxists who argued that it was not Zionism or Jews that drove US policy in the region, but capitalism. Elmessiri's combining of both leftist and Islamist societal models in a 'scientific' way was novel, as was, for the Islamist camp towards which Elmessiri intellectually 'migrated', his differentiation between Zionists and Jews and his criticism of the use of dubious Western anti-Semitic sources, such as the *Protocols of the Elders of Zion*. Despite the fact that Elmessiri, who was in the United States at the time of Camp David, apparently found it impossible to gain a public audience (or even physically access the al-Ahram building) on his return to Egypt in 1979,[83] Elmessiri became the doyen of Egyptian intellectuals on the subject of Zionism, Israel and Jews. His work, perhaps more directly than any other, has helped underpin the principle of societal agency in the Arab-Israeli conflict.

The al-Ahram Centre for Political and Strategic Studies continued to see as its mandate the production of social scientific, dispassionate and rigorous analyses of Zionism and Israel. In addition to 'big picture' studies such as that of Elmessiri on the roots and character of Zionism, the Centre analysed the more quotidian elements of Israeli policy and strategy—something that was still relatively rare. A good example of this was a book by Usama al-Ghazzali Harb, who would go on to be a prominent liberal politician closely associated with the ruling establishment, published in November 1977—the month of Sadat's visit to Jerusalem. The book, completed under the supervision of Ali al-Din Hilal, another future thinker of the NDP, analysed Israel's political and military strategy in the Occupied Territories, and in particular the Palestinian resistance therein. Harb also examined the Palestinian strategies and the prerequisites for the resistance's success. The author wrote squarely within the narrative of Palestinian self-determination and nationalism, and although he clearly equated Palestinian resistance with revolution (comparing it, as others had, with revolutionary struggles in Vietnam, Algeria and China) and argued that the Israeli strategy towards the Palestinians was just one part of its broader approach to the Arab-Israeli conflict, he confined the responsibilities of the Arab states to supporting the Palestinian people in their struggle.

Harb's interpretation of the conflict between Israel and the Palestinians closely resembled Ahmad Baha al-Din's *Proposal for a Palestinian State* in the wake of the 1967 war. What was important was that the Palestinians continued to exist and that they remain on the land as the agents of resistance. Despite its overwhelming military superiority and draconian tactics in the West Bank, Israel, Harb concluded, has not been successful in crushing Palestinian resistance because it has not 'crushed the Palestinian existence or terminated (*al-qada ala*) Palestinian identity as a consequence of its partial successes against the resistance in the occupied territories.'[84] The conclusion is singled out in the book's forward, under the name of the Centre, as the study's major finding:

> Israel may have realised temporary and prominent successes, here and there, in the occupied territories against the resistance, or against the Arabs, and in the military, political and economic spheres or in the area of psychological warfare. But these successes will remain temporary and ephemeral because they rest on the historical fallacy on which the Zionists established their state: that there is 'no existence, and there must be no existence, of a thing called the Palestinian people.'[85]

Harb's analysis, and that of his publisher, also reapplied to the Palestinian domestic context the argument of the Nasserist left, which argued after 1967 that in failing to topple the Egyptian revolution Israel had not defeated the Arabs. With the locus of societal agency transferred to Palestine, the fact that Israel had not obliterated Palestinian national identity meant the battle was ongoing. Now it was Palestinian society, supported by Arab states, which must shoulder the burden of confronting Israel, with the—distinctly minimalist—benchmark for success being the mere survival of the Palestinian people.

Liberal nationalism resurgent

If Marxist intellectuals like Mohamed Sid Ahmed departed from the anti-imperialist conception of Israel, subtly reverting to a pre-Nasser analysis, many other intellectuals explicitly criticised Nasser and both his foreign and domestic policies. The anti-Nasserism that characterised much intellectual work had begun prior to October 1973, probably with Tawfiq al-Hakim's *Return of Consciousness* in 1972, but after the war had enabled Sadat to consolidate his own position domestically, attacks on Nasser became more explicit, widespread and permissible. For secular critics, this tended to involve a critique of Nasser's 'adventurism' overseas. Nasser, in the UAR Charter and elsewhere, had criticised the beneficiaries of the 1919 revolution for failing to recognise the 'Arab' dimension that revolution would need to acquire. Many of those that attacked Nasser in the 1970s argued in favour of re-evaluating the pre-1952 period in a way that encouraged a reversion to a more 'Egypt-first' posture and, inevitably, statist conception of the region as a whole.

For many liberals the Egyptian revolution that began in 1919 was never completed. The Nasser years may have advanced it incrementally, but Egypt's democratic and social transformation was yet to occur. As such, Nasser was wrong to try to export an incomplete revolution.[86] For Nagib Mahfuz, writing in the mid-1970s, the way to export revolution was to set an example, rather than intervene militarily or defame 'reactionary' leaders via the media.[87] Whether intentional or not, the critical discourse on Nasser served not only Sadat's purpose of stepping out of Nasser's shadow, but also the regime's desire to focus on internal economic development rather than Egyptian leadership in the Arab revolutionary movement. This was, indeed, what Sadat promised the peace with Israel would achieve—an opportunity for Egypt to develop without the costly drain of maintaining a state of war.

While there was widespread disaffection amongst Egypt's political and intellectual classes in the wake of Sadat's visit to Jerusalem, on a wider popular level the move may have been less objectionable. For one thing, censorship laws and media control meant that objectors from both leftist and Islamist perspectives were swamped in the media. For Saad Eddine Ibrahim, 'Egyptian public opinion was to undergo an intense and sustained media campaign to prepare it for the change. Egyptians were told that they had done all that was humanly possible in their fight against Israel'[88] and that peace with Israel would bring the country much-needed prosperity. Ibrahim sees this public relations campaign as contributing to the steady erosion of 'the thirty-year national consensus on armed struggle against Israeli usurpation of Arab Palestine' and majority public support for Sadat's initiative.[89] The promise of prosperity was not an empty one. It was underwritten by a massive economic undertaking on the part of the United States— 'one of the most huge commitments of foreign economic assistance since the Marshall plan'—intended among other things to 'underwrite Sadat's pledge to the Egyptian people that peace would be accompanied by a new era of prosperity.'[90]

By the end of the 1970s, some beneficiaries of Sadat's economic initiative, *infitah*, took this reasoning so far as to argue in favour of strengthening Egypt's ties with Israel as an economic partner and gateway to the West. Perhaps the most audacious was the construction magnate and close Sadat ally Osman Ahmed Osman, who 'consistently opposed efforts to focus on Israel's expulsion of the Arabs of Palestine and its potential threat to Egypt' in favour of building economic links with 'an economically and technologically superior country that could aid Egypt.'[91] Osman also charged, according to Baker, that 'Nasserist foreign policy … exaggerated Israel's role as an expansionist state that threatened the Arab world; instead of seeking accommodation, Egypt was dragged unnecessarily into the devastating wars with Israel.'[92]

On 3 March 1978 Tawfiq al-Hakim published an article entitled 'al-Hiyad' (Neutralism) in *al-Ahram*. The article argued that Egypt as a state should follow the Swiss model of neutrality. Hakim couched his argument in favour of neutralism in terms of Egypt's significance as a museum of the world—Pharaonic, Greek, Roman, Christian and Islamic—which would be threatened if Egypt continued to shoulder military risks. On the other hand, though, he stressed that Egypt was the cultural centre of the Arab world and that the Arab states should do more to preserve this culture by assuming some of the military and political burden. In a subsequent article, Hakim questioned the existence of an Arab nation with a single cause, but conceded that 'only when profits from the oil wealth were distributed equally among all Arabs would the Arab states begin to enjoy the commonality of a single cause.' As such, neutralism represented strategically the best option for Egypt. In another intervention, Hakim expressed bitter resentment at the wars Egypt had fought on behalf of the Arabs, while leadership had fallen to those with wealth. Hakim's argument, further developed by the editor of *al-Ahram*, Ali Hamdi al-Jammal, also contributed to a growing current of resentment in official circles towards the PLO specifically. The attack on the PLO was significant since it was seen as the model of the secular revolutionary current in Arab politics at that time. Although the Islamist current had long used Palestine as a mobilising issue in Egyptian politics, the left argued in favour of solidarity with the PLO in its revolutionary course.[93]

The veteran journalist and novelist Ihsan Abd al-Quddus represents a good example of a synthesis of the various elements of the intellectual and official discourse on Israel as it evolved under Sadat, as well as an explicit statement of the dualism that underpinned Egyptian foreign policy towards Israel. Abd al-Quddus, a long-time personal friend of Sadat was chairman of the board of *al-Akhbar* in the early 1970s and of *al-Ahram* from 1976, when, following the second Sinai Agreement, Sadat reshuffled editorships and press publishers to encourage more sympathetic coverage. Abd al-Quddus wrote a series of articles in 1978 commenting on Egypt's dramatic foreign policy shift. His perspective reflected the prioritisation of Israeli interests over those of 'imperialism', as well as his support for Sadat's strategy of 'taking the battle to the United States' by trying to weaken Israel's supporters there. He frequently asserted that 'the Jews' are in control of United States policy.

For Abd al-Quddus, America's number one interest in the region was oil, and the Arabs should use this to their advantage in moving the conflict to the United States. But he acknowledged that there were 'complications' caused by 'Jewish dominance over the main US centres: production, financial services, and over US public opinion.' Jewish dominance in America was too strong and governed all that state's behaviour towards Israel.[94] He exclaimed that 'America does not govern in Israel, but Israel governs in America.'[95]

Abd al-Quddus noted in August 1978 that Israel preferred the continuation of the Cold War, since the 'Zionist centres' in the United States and Russia depended on crises to sustain US support for Israel and sought to transform the Cold War into a 'Hot War' in Africa and Asia. He cited such issues as the question of Jewish rights in Russia as one aimed at stirring up American public animosity towards Russia. The problem was that the Arabs were split between supporters of the United States and those that backed the USSR, and he argued that they should instead unite around confronting Israel and pressuring each superpower to support them in this endeavour.[96] For Abd al-Quddus, Sadat's stance towards the United States should provide the model for this. Before the Camp David Accords, he expressed his confidence that Sadat would never abandon the Sinai, the West Bank or the Golan. Israel, he did not doubt, was inherently expansionist, and Begin represented not an extremist, but the mainstream Israeli, will.[97] The only way to curb Israeli expansionism was to leverage the power of the United States, a task that Egypt was now well-equipped to carry out due to the 'global power' that Sadat achieved through his visit to Jerusalem. The trip to Jerusalem was not, as Sadat and others argued at the time, to break the 'psychological complex'[98] that existed between Israel and the Arabs, but to score a political victory over Israel in the United States.[99]

Abd al-Quddus hoped that Sadat would reject Israeli proposals at Camp David, thus inducing the United States to apply more pressure on Israel to offer more.[100] He shared with Sadat and the Islamists an anti-Soviet posture and celebrated the fact that Camp David was more powerful than any of the other summits because the USSR was absent, and it was to Sadat's great credit that he was able to get the United States to hold a conference.[101] The United States was the only power able to influence Israel and the Soviet Union would not be able to scotch the deal. Even if an agreement were reached, Abd al-Quddus warned, the threat of Israeli economic expansionism (its real reason for wanting peace) would remain. The region would, he predicted, drift once more into war, unless US force was brought to bear to prevent it.[102] Although firmly within the nation-state paradigm, viewing Israel, rather than Western imperialism, as the salient factor in the Arab-Israeli conflict, and optimistic about the potential for a positive US role in the conflict, Abd al-Quddus viewed Israel itself as imperialist and expansionist, mirroring al-Khuli's distinction between 'big' and 'little' imperialisms in the region. He wrote that 'I am accustomed to viewing Israel as an imperialist power and to comparing the events that happen between us and Israel with those between Egypt and Britain during the age of English imperialism.'[103] Thus, the Camp David Accords were a perfectly valid way of tackling an imperialist threat. Nasser, he pointed out, had accepted the Suez agreement in 1954, even with the right of automatic troop return, but had two years later liberated Egypt from the conditions of that agreement. Similarly Camp David should be viewed as such a first step, as a truce (*hudna*).[104]

This perspective was in accordance with Abd al-Quddus' theory of historical change, and an implicit acceptance of the division of labour principle that had in fact underpinned Egyptian foreign policy for decades. A national movement, he argued, required both moderate and extremist tendencies. The moderates enabled incremental gains to be consolidated, while the extremists moved the process of national liberation forward. Egypt had, in the 1970s, succeeded in combining the two tendencies, much as it did in the early 20th century. Abd al-Quddus also compared Egypt's policy towards Israel with the revolution of 1919 and the long Wafd-led process that led to Egyptian independence under Nasser. The October 1973 War was, for him, an example of Egyptian extremism, while the advances made then were consolidated through the moderation of Camp David. Abd al-Quddus argued that the moderates dealt in interests, the extremists in ideals. Sadat, in realising that Israel 'lived in America' took the 'moderate' step of taking the battle there and focusing on American interests towards Israel and Egypt. Israel too was driven by moderate and extremist impulses towards expansion, Abd al-Quddus argued.[105] The dream of a Greater Israel from the Nile to the Euphrates was, he argued, one that nobody in Israel denied. Although this remained a dream, some dreams had become reality, such as the Jordan River as a border or Jerusalem as Israel's capital. These had become, for Abd al-Quddus, reality from which Israel was not going to back down easily. America, then, held the key to forcing Israeli withdrawal from the West Bank and Gaza.[106]

Both statism and society-based paradigms for dealing with Israel developed in tandem following the 1973 war. The international context of détente encouraged some on the left to apply the principal of peaceful coexistence to the Middle East in a way that prioritised the strengths and interests of *states*. Statism was also directly related to a domestic context that encouraged a liberal nationalist discourse against Nasser and his foreign 'adventures' and in favour of 'Egypt-first', rather than an Arab nation. Arabism, as a framework for societal agency, evolved in an Islamist direction. The Islamist equation of communism and Zionism supported Sadat's battle with the left domestically, as well as his desire to distance Egypt from its erstwhile Soviet patron. For some, like Elmessiri, imperialism remained the issue to the extent that it allowed, or encouraged, Israel to remain Zionist. The idea of Israel as a 'nation-state' with which Egypt could make peace, thus existed along-side a conception that viewed Israel as the manifestation of a Jewish conspiracy against Islam and the conflict as inherently cultural.

Whereas after 1967 the threat of imperialism had contracted to the threat of Zionism, after 1973 Sadat signalled that the threat of expansionist Zionism had diminished. In the context of Egypt's hav-ing proven its military prowess in 1973, and then renounced the war option in the Sinai Agreements, Zionism remained an issue primarily as 'racism' directed at the Palestinians and a cultural or intellectual threat to Egyptian and Arab societies in general. As the Arab-Israeli conflict took on the contours of a war of ideas, many intellectuals focussed more closely on the ideological underpinnings of the Israeli state and Zionism's regressive, anachronistic, nature.

After the Sinai Agreements, some intellectual analyses of Israel became domestically subversive. For many on the left, the 'principal contradiction' shifted from being between Egypt and other progres-sive Arab forces, on the one hand; and Israel, imperialism and Arab 'reaction' on the other; to the Palestinian revolution and its support-ers in the progressive camp, on the one hand; and the Egyptian and other 'reactionary' Arab regimes, Israel and imperialism on the other. Similarly, the Muslim Brotherhood after Sadat's visit to Jerusalem saw a similar polarisation between Muslim societies, on the one hand; and 'so-called' Muslim leaders, Israel and the crusading West (and athe-ist East) on the other. In instrumentalising the conflict with Israel to attack the regime, they shared a focus on Palestine as the Arab cause *par excellence*, and an agreement that ramping up their own social and political agendas would be required to solve the problem. In the Mubarak era, which the next chapter explores, such approaches would be restricted to the most militant of jihadists. The mainstream, however, would cleave to the consensus that state and society had different and legitimate roles to play.

CHAPTER 6

THE CAMP DAVID CONSENSUS (1979–2009)

The Camp David Accords and the subsequent Egypt-Israel Peace Treaty have constituted the formal framework under which Egypt has conducted its relations with Israel during the Mubarak presidency. Under the terms of the Peace Treaty of 1979, following Israeli interim withdrawal from the Sinai, the parties 'will establish normal and friendly relations' including 'full recognition, diplomatic, economic and cultural relations.' While Israel and the Egyptian state are thus formally committed to 'normalisation', however, the first Camp David Accord of September 1978 stipulated that a 'self-governing authority' be established for Palestinians. Israel's continued occupation of the West Bank and Gaza, as well as the still only partial sovereignty Egypt enjoys over Sinai, have led many to accuse Israel of not keeping its side of the bargain and to argue that, as such, Egypt is not obliged to work towards normalisation. While for many the Treaty is thus unworkable and in need of adjustment or cancellation, there exists a strong societal norm of opposition to normalisation alongside an acceptance of the Camp David Accords as the instrument that ended the state of war between the two countries. Opposition to normalisation is reflected in the tone of the independent press, as well as institutionalized in the basic laws of syndicates, such as the journalists', that forbid contacts with Israelis. This was recently illustrated in the furore surrounding the editor of the state-owned *al-Ahram*'s *Democracy* magazine, Hala

Mustafa, who faced sanction from the journalists' syndicate for meeting Israeli ambassador Shalom Cohen.[1]

Under Mubarak, intellectuals have been relatively free to express their views on Israel and the nature of the Arab-Israeli conflict. Sadat was adamant that the peace agreement with Israel should not be derailed by any public protests within Egypt. The issue of Israel thus became depoliticised as intellectuals were forbidden to voice any objections to the Treaty. Anwar Sadat's assassination was preceded by a harsh campaign of arrests in Egyptian civil society, including not only the increasingly vociferous Islamist critics of his regime, such as Brotherhood leader Omar Tilimisani, but also secular intellectuals like Mohamed Sid Ahmed, Mohamed Hassanein Heikal and the feminist Nawwal al-Sa'dawi. When Mubarak took over as president in 1981 he dealt harshly with those found responsible for Sadat's killing but released those that had been rounded up without charge in Sadat's increasingly paranoid purges. Mubarak thus allowed the question of Israel to become once again an issue upon which intellectuals and groups could campaign, write and mobilise.

Israel, Iran and Islamic revolution

Mubarak adopted a conciliatory posture towards the USSR, which opened space for Nasserists and other leftist voices that continued to view Israel through the lens of the Cold War. But with the virtual neutralisation of the left through the 1970s, symbolised by the semi-domesticated Tagammu' party, the most politically salient would-be revolutionaries in Egypt were, through the 1980s and 1990s, Islamist. On a regional level, Iran was now the country seeking to export revolution, and with a street in Tehran named after Sadat's assassin Khalid Islambouli, relations between Egypt and Iran were destined to be frosty. Mubarak promoted Egypt as a 'moderate' Arab country that could, along with Saudi Arabia and Jordan, form a bulwark of stability in the face of revolutionary forces in the region.

The Iranian Revolution is often credited with unleashing Islamic radicalism across the Middle East. This is an overstatement. In the

Egyptian case, the Islamic 'revival' has, as we have seen, deep roots in the country's 20th century history. But the Islamic revolution was nonetheless of huge importance not only in increasing the confidence of Egyptian Islamist groups, but also in providing a concrete example of the revolutionary potential of Islam, which encouraged the further synchronisation of leftist and Islamist political trends in Egypt. For Islamists, the revolution of 1978–79 placed the idea of their seizing power within the realms of credibility.[2] The institution of al-Azhar was initially nervous about, and then overtly hostile towards, the revolution. The Muslim Brotherhood, on the other hand, saw the revolution as evidence of a global trend towards Islam and was, at least until the outbreak of the Iran-Iraq War in September 1980, highly positive about Khomeini. After this point, the regime's support for Iraq made outright praise difficult. The Brotherhood, at least as represented by supreme guide Umar al-Talimisany, argued that the Iran-Iraq War was instigated by Zionists to divide Muslims.[3]

The revolution in Iran engendered a paradigm shift in that country's foreign policy towards Israel and the West and seemed to lend credence to the 'near enemy' version of Islamist political action; or the idea that the regime at home had to be overthrown before the 'far enemy', meaning Israel and the West, could be confronted.[4] Khomeini approached Israel in globalist terms as a tool of US imperialism and enemy of revolution, universalising the threat in terms similar to those Nasser used to use, but this time casting Egypt on the enemy side:

> Today Israel and its close friend Egypt are thinking up ways of creating a united front to destroy the Muslims and their lofty ideals. Recently Iraq, along with some of the heads of the other regional countries, approved of this plan. For nearly twenty years now, I have been informing people of the danger of international Zionism. Today, I feel the danger for all the freedom-bestowing revolutions of the world, including the recent Islamic revolution in Iran, is no less than it was in the past, for at the present time these world-devouring bloodsuckers using various techniques to defeat the oppressed and weak of the earth have risen up and

are active. Our nation and the free nations of the world should bravely and vigilantly resist these dangerous plots.[5]

Clearly interested in the revolution's effects in Egypt, Khomeini combined anti-imperialist with Islamic symbolism in defending arrested Muslim Brotherhood members:

> Today, with the widespread arrests of the Muslim Brothers in Egypt, Sadat has completed his service to Israel. His alliance with America and Israel has shamed the Arab people. [He has formed] an alliance with an Israel which at this time, in addition to the crimes it carries out in the region, has committed another great crime, that is excavation work at the site of the al-Aqsa mosque, the first *qibla* of the Muslims; and with the weakening of the foundations of this mosque ... will, God forbid, be destroyed and Israel will achieve its vile wish.[6]

Khomeini's demand that Zionism be uprooted from Palestine was, unsurprisingly, praised by Islamists in Egypt and contrasted with 'the increasing trend among Arab states to limit their goal to Israeli withdrawal from the territories occupied in June 1967 and granting the Palestinian people their national rights.'[7]

Members of the so-called 'Islamic left', such as Hasan al-Hanafi, praised the revolution as 'a reinvigoration of the Nasserite ideals of anti-Zionism and a progressive anti-imperialist revolution,'[8] and celebrated the fact that 'Islam is capable of serving as an umbrella for all political trends in [Egypt]: liberation, Marxism, and Arab nationalism. The Iranian revolution did it and succeeded.'[9] Hanafi's appraisal was supported by Abd al-Sattar al-Tawilah, who in October 1979 wrote in the leftist *Ruz al-Yusuf,* '[w]e support every struggle against colonialism ... we supported the Iranian revolution because one of its affirmed objectives was to remove Iran from the American ascendancy.'[10] The example of an anti-imperialist, anti-Zionist and Islamic revolution in the region was one that clearly convinced some erstwhile leftists to entertain Islamist political programmes.

Mubarak's approach

Mubarak sought to position Egypt as the indispensible mediator between the United States, Israel and the Palestinians. His priority was, and has remained, to prevent other Middle Eastern powers replacing or competing with Egypt for this role and to seek to maximise its own interests bilaterally with the United States. At the same time, the Egyptian regime has presented itself as the main champion of Palestinian rights and as a sovereign entity capable of protecting the Egyptian people from neo-imperialism in its various forms. Mubarak sought to moderate Egypt's foreign policy by slowing significantly the march towards normalisation and seeking to rebuild bridges with the Arab states. The Camp David consensus, which crystalised during this period, helped reconcile these apparently contradictory dynamics.

Mubarak viewed Egypt's pioneering foreign policy towards Israel as indicative of its unique strength and centrality in the region, much of which was created—or at least demonstrated—by the 1973 October War. Egypt's prowess in that war has become central to Egyptian national mythology and is rarely—from any quarter—criticised. Even at times when the rapprochement with Israel has seemed the least tenable, such as in late 1982 when Israel invaded Lebanon and following the Sabra and Shatilla massacres, the Egyptian regime reaffirmed its commitment to peace irrespective of changing circumstances on the ground. Mubarak stressed Egypt's independence as a strong state and continued, like his predecessors, to justify Egypt's foreign policy stance with reference to the country's eternal role as a bulwark against imperialism:

> Our position must always be one of solidarity, because eternal Egypt (*misr al-khalida*) bears a special responsibility for the defence of security and peace in the region. And this is the basic factor in ensuring stability and balance and the best defence against the dangers of foreign intervention and the attempts to establish spheres of influence to dominate the people. Because of this, successive imperial powers attempted to subjugate the region by

working to neutralise and curtail the Egyptian role, even though we are fearlessly on the lookout for such attempts, because we embrace this role with firm will and determination.[11]

Mubarak affirmed that Egypt would remain the party most committed to peace:

With faith in the inevitable triumph of the people's will, and commitment to the agreements and treaties because peace for us is a firm strategic choice [*ikhtiyar istratiji thabit*] and not a luxury which we retain or abandon on a whim.[12]

But the 1982 Israeli invasion of Lebanon, and the Sabra and Chatilla massacres, almost completely destroyed what intellectual appetite there was for 'normalisation' with Israel. Even Tawfiq al-Hakim, throughout the 1970s an outspoken advocate of the peace process and Egyptian neutrality turned, after the 1982 invasion, against both of these things.[13] And one of Sadat's staunchest allies, who accompanied the president on his trip to Jerusalem, wrote in al-Ahram on 17 July:

There is not a single pen in Egypt which has not cursed Israel. There is not a single voice in Egypt that has not disavowed its previous faith in the possibility of total peace with Israel ... We had reconciled with Israel, looking forward to a comprehensive peace ... It turned out to be a mistake ... The most optimistic among us knows now that it will take another 34 years to correct that mistake.[14]

Such anger has not, however, translated into any concerted efforts to destabilise the regime as Egypt settled into its 'inclusive authoritarian' system.[15] The Mubarak era has seen the continuation, or institutionalisation, of the procedural democratic life instituted by Sadat. With the exception of the 1990 elections, which were boycotted by the opposition because of a new law allowing only individuals, not parties, to participate, Egypt's political forces enjoyed an apparent renaissance. The Muslim Brotherhood also made an important strategic choice to work within the system and not challenge it, since 'election campaigns allow the Brethren to spread the word of God.'[16]

Saad Eddine Ibrahim has helpfully discussed the positions of the legal political parties on Camp David and the peace treaty during the 1980s. The Socialist Labour Party, which called for the outright repudiation of the treaty in 1981, was for 'freezing' it during the 1984 elections. This, Ibrahim attributes to the party's desire to 'go easy' on Mubarak. In 1987, as the Islamic Alliance alongside the Muslim Brotherhood, the party called for 'freezing of Camp David in preparation for its abrogation' since 'Zionism is our most dangerous enemy.' The New Wafd Party (NWP) in 1984 argued in favour of Egypt building its deterrent military power, based on 'legality and justice' to counter Israeli expansionist policies but did not demand the nullification of the treaty. Instead, the NWP 'absolved Egypt from observing it.' As leader of the opposition until 1987, the Wafd supported the government's positions towards Israel. The leftist Tagammu' platform was in favour of terminating the treaty through a series of escalating steps, including opposition to normalisation. But the party was split between those for and against talking to the Israeli left.

The important point here is that whereas some politicians and intellectuals supported freezing normalisation and the application of diplomatic pressure on Israel to force its compliance with the Treaty, and rejectionists 'called for the abrogation of the peace treaty and sending Egyptian volunteers to fight alongside the PLO in Lebanon'[17] there was no expectation, or desire, that the Egyptian state would, could or should return to a war footing. Responsibility for 'Palestine the cause', as Clovis Maksoud put it in 1968, resided definitively with society and not the state. This, in essence, is the Camp David consensus.

Israel, the regime and Egypt's Islamist insurrection

Although the 1980s and 1990s witnessed, on one level, the 'moderating' influence of parliamentary life in Egypt, this was also the time when militant Islamist groups overtly challenged the legitimacy not merely of foreign policy, but of the Egyptian regime itself. The rise of militant Islam involved—though is certainly not solely explicable in terms of—the most radical instrumentalisation of Egyptian foreign policy towards Israel by a societal group. Sadat's visit to Jerusalem, as we saw in the last chapter, was taken by some Islamist thinkers to be proof that Qutb was right, that the Egyptian leadership was in bed with the Jews. Anti-Israeli sentiment in society, as we have seen, served the Sadat regime's broader purpose of eradicating the left as a societal force in Egypt. The Islamist violence that led up to Sadat's assassination (ostensibly because of Camp David) began as attacks on communists in Egyptian universities.[18]

Clearly 'jihadists' from the late 1970s, whose primary theoretician was Muhammad Abd al-Salam Faraj, did not accept the Camp David consensus that Egypt-Israel relations should be conducted through diplomatic channels, but like the left and the Brotherhood they were also against inter-state war between the two countries. For Faraj war between Israel and the current Egyptian state would only strengthen the latter. The leader of the Society of Muslims (also known as *al-takfir wa-al-hijra*), Shukri Mustafa, declared that were Israel to invade Egypt the appropriate Muslim response would be to flee and allow the current regime to fall. For this camp the primary enemy was the 'near' one, the Egyptian regime, and not Israel.[19]

The anti-systemic opposition in Egypt, although 'extremist' in the sense that its means and goals do not reflect those of the mainstream political forces, exploited the longstanding social text of animus and resentment towards Israel for its legitimation. Events also seemed to sharpen the resonance of militant propaganda. The second half of the 1980s hardened general public opposition to the peace with Israel. The fall in oil prices deepened, rather than improved, Egypt's economic crisis, thus removing one of the only crumbs of comfort supposedly coming out of the peace. Three years after evicting the PLO from Beirut, Israel bombed the Organisation's headquarters in Tunis. Days later, Palestinian militants hijacked the Achille Lauro cruise ship in the Mediterranean. The hijackers agreed to release the liner in return for safe passage, in an Egyptian jet, but American jets subsequently forced the Egyptian plane to land and arrested the militants. A humiliated Mubarak demanded an apology from President Reagan. On 5 October 1985 Suleiman Khater, a border guard, murdered seven Israeli tourists at Ras Burqa in the Sinai. In the context of general disillusionment with Israel, the murders were celebrated in much of the Egyptian press. And the Palestinian *intifada*, which began in 1987, only served to further energise general opposition to Israel.

Societal indignation towards Israel, which was to some degree tempered by the moderating domestic influence of parliamentary politics in the mid-1980s,[20] assumed a new form with the outbreak of the *intifada*. During the *intifada*, the Muslim Brotherhood, which came to lead the protests of solidarity, rose to prominence as a street presence. The Islamist profile, and its association with Palestine, was encouraged by the rise of the Brotherhood's Palestinian branch, which would become Hamas, to prominence. The *intifada* brought the issue of Israel-Palestine once more to the level of popular, as opposed to diplomatic, politics. In solidarity demonstrations in 1988, the Brotherhood demanded the 'rejection of Camp David and the treaty,' called for *jihad* to liberate Palestine and 'demand[ed] that Arab governments open their borders for the *"mujahideen"* from other countries to fight alongside their Palestinian brothers.'[21]

Those Islamists that directed their *jihad* against the regime rather than the Zionists took pains to intellectually rationalise their strategy with reference to an established discourse on Israel. As the authors of the radical *Jama'a Islamiyya*'s [Islamic Group] 1984 Charter saw it, the land that used to be governed by the Islamic Caliphate was in a state of 'submissiveness and disgrace,' comprising 'statelets' carved out by Christians, Jews, atheists and idol worshipers.[22] The Charter repeated Qutb's conclusion that an 'intellectual invasion' had succeeded in 'brainwashing' Muslims. The enemies of Islam used cultural, media and educational weapons to wage this war, in the form of 'organisations headed by Jews and Christians protected by states and armies.' Whereas the military dimension of the war on Islam targeted and toppled the Caliphate as a 'political system uniting the Muslims', the intellectual front 'aimed at Islam in people's hearts, and it succeeded to a great extent in brainwashing them.'[23] It was this intellectual invasion that was ongoing and must be repelled.

Similarly, one of the *Jama'a*'s other texts, *Hatmiyat al-Muwajiha* (*The Inevitability of Confrontation*), invoked the familiar conspiracy theory that

Dönmeh, or Crypto-Jews, were behind the Young Turk revolution of 1908 that toppled the 'last Caliph with effective authority', Abdul Hamid before leading Turkey into the disaster of World War One, which culminated in the ascent of Ataturk and the de-Islamisation of the country. The book quotes the influential Islamic nationalist Muhammad Muhammad Husayn, discussed in Chapter 3, here to substantiate this.[24] In this text, the *Jama'a* also decry the secularising and nefarious influence of the military that, supported by the occupying powers, led the 1952 coup (as with the 1949 one in Syria) and carried out the 'worst forms of oppression and abuse' against Islam and Muslims.[25]

It was, for the *Jama'a*, the penetration of Egypt and other nominally Muslim countries by Jewish and crusader interests that meant their governments could, and would, not declare or permit *jihad* to liberate usurped Muslim territories or avenge the atrocities visited on Muslims not only in Palestine, but in Afghanistan, the Philippines, Thailand, Burma, Assam, Ethiopia, Tanzania, Somalia and Eritrea:

> These sacred duties incumbent upon the Muslims, the liberation of usurped Islamic lands, rescuing prisoners, *jihad* to spread the religion – what is stopping the Muslims from carrying them out? Is it possible that the Egyptian regime will carry them out? ... Is it possible that Egypt will prepare an army to return the usurped Islamic countries, which the occupying unbelievers (*al-kuffar al-muhtillun*) have polluted, starting with Palestine and Lebanon and passing through India, Afghanistan until the Philippines? Is it possible that the Egyptian government will rescue Muslim prisoners or devote money and lives to them? Will the current ruler ever lead an army abroad, raising the banner of monotheism (*tawhid*) in the name of God and in the path of God, to spread truth and justice and discharge the duty of *jihad*?
> No sane person could answer yes to this question.[26]

In Islamic terms, the jihadists elaborated on the old anti-imperialist slogan of the Arab left that the road to Jerusalem passed through Cairo. Given that the secular regime in Egypt did not merely fail to wage *jihad*, but actively obstructed it—and has made peace with the Jews—the legitimate and legal (*shari'*), as well as logical, solution was to remove that regime:

> How can Egypt fight the enemies of God—the Jews—when it has signed with them treaties of peace and opened to them the country, and committed terrible treason against the suffering Muslims of Palestine? ... The road begins with Egypt. There is nothing for it but to liberate Egypt from the domination of the immoral secularists and nothing for it but to liberate Egypt from subservience to the Jews and the Christians. We must return Egypt to the Muslims and reinvoke the embrace of Amr Ibn al-As and the citidel of Salah al-Din al-Ayyubi [Saladin].[27]

Until at least 1996, the operational, and ideological, focus of Egyptian jihadist groups was the regime itself. Although the evils of Zionism and the end-goal of restoring the Caliphate and expansionist dynamism of Islam were ever-present in their literature, it was also clear that this was contingent on establishing an authentic Islamic state in Egypt. As late as 1995, the leader in exile of *Tanzim al-Jihad* [the Jihad Group], Ayman al-Zawahiri, was arguing that 'Jerusalem will not be conquered until the battles in Egypt and Algeria have been won and until Cairo has been conquered.'[28] But the Egyptian security forces were exacting a massive toll on operatives and enclaves in Upper Egypt and Cairo. For this, and other, reasons the *Jama'a* declared a ceasefire in 1997.[29]

'Fight those of the unbelievers that are close to you', the Qur'anic edict that had underpinned local *jihadi* activism, was perhaps no longer capable of winning support, particularly as the souring of hopes in the Oslo peace process once again brought the issue of Palestine to the heart of domestic politics. In calling for a one-year ceasefire in 1996, the *Jama'a* lawyer Montasser al-Zayyat said leaders counted the 'heightened interest in the question of Palestine' as a primary rationale.[30] And the revisions documents that justified this were produced under state auspices, and with al-Azhar's blessing: the regime was likewise happy with the new focus.

In very different ways, Egypt's militant groups returned to enemies that had, over many years, proven far more likely to gain acceptance among intellecuals: Israel, Zionism and, to a lesser extent, the United States. Following the *Jama'a*'s ceasefire initiative of 1997, many Egyptian jihadists, like Ayman Zawahiri, decided to join Usama bin Laden's International *Islamic Front for Jihad on the Jews and Crusaders.* As Zayyat recounts, 'it was after this collaboration that a new Zawahiri emerged: one more interested in the liberation of Palestine, urging Muslims to launch armed operations against the United States and Israel.' Zawahiri's instrumentalisation is clear. He was eager to claim credit for the embassy bombings in Nairobi and Dar al-Salam because

> ... he wanted to gain popular support from Arabs and Muslims by combating the American aggression. He needed this popularity after the failure of his operations in Egypt, in which he did not target Jews or Americans, but rather ended up killing Egyptian civilians such as Sayyid Yehia and the child Shayma.[31]

Within Egypt, imprisoned jihadists were also attempting to use Israel as a way of justifying, and to an extent disclaiming responsibility for, their actions. Thus, Muhammad Nasr al-Din al-Ghazlani, the Jihad Group leader in Giza addressed the court in 1998:

> [A]lthough the Jews are officially at peace with Egypt, their enmity towards the country has never died. The Jews want to ruin Egypt's present and future by targeting its young people because they are the secret of its strength, and because young people are the core of any civilisation and advancement.

He continued:

> The Jews will benefit from civil strife in Egypt because this will ensure that Egyptian officials are too busy with their internal affairs to notice the Jews' conspiracies and expansionist schemes. The Jews also exaggerated what happened to tourists to give the impression that Egypt is not a safe tourist destination, thus

turning thousands of dollars away to other countries, and weakening the Egyptian economy. They want a Mediterranean market in which Zionism controls the markets of the whole region.[32]

Ghazlani's demonisation of Israel and Jewish conspiracies reveals a distinctly mainstream concern for Egyptian society, and familiarity with a widespread, largely uncontroversial, reading of the Israeli and Zionist threat among Egyptian intellectuals. It conforms, in other words, to the Camp David consensus.

The Jihad Group, in merging with al-Qa'ida, was in a perverse way also moving closer to the Camp David consensus. Zawahiri was quite open about the instrumentality of using the Palestine cause to gain support for the broader jihadist movement against local regimes. In his 2001 call to arms *Knights under the Prophet's Banner*, Zawahiri insisted that the '*jihad* against Israel' was the one issue that Muslims around the world, and Arabs regardless of their beliefs, would rally around.[33] His goal remained regime change in Egypt, but was hardly short term since he cautioned that 'this is a goal that could take several generations to achieve.' Zawahiri was clear that he was not preoccupied with Egypt just because he happened to be an Egyptian, but because 'the base for *jihad* is Egypt and the Arab region, the heart of the Islamic world, where the basic battle of Islam was being fought.'[34]

The demonstration effect of Hizbullah

If some, like Zawahiri, reversed the old slogan of the left that 'the road to Jerusalem leads through Cairo' due in large part to their failure to defeat the 'near enemy', others took inspiration from a non-state actor that had demonstrated its success in vanquishing Israel. Much as the Iranian Revolution had appeared to vindicate the revolutionary potential of Islam, Iran's well-organised non-state ally, Hizbullah, showed the efficacy of non-state action. Adel Husayn had argued in favour of a united Arab-Iranian front against the American-Zionist alliance before Hizbullah's massive propaganda boon in 2000.[35] The youngest brother of Young Egypt founder Ahmed Husayn, he was one of a number of intellectuals to transition from Marxist to Islamist thought and politics, stewarding the Labour Party that he led until his death in 2001 through a similar migration. In an essay written after Hizbullah's eviction of Israel from South Lebanon in 2000, Husayn insisted that war against Israel was both possible and necessary. Husayn's work in some ways resembles that of Sadiq al-Azm in 1968 and constitutes a protest against the defeatist attitude of some that view the threat of Zionism as mainly cultural, religious and economic; and that adopt a passive or reactive approach to resistance.

For Husayn, Zionism was indeed a threat in these terms. Power was not just military and such factors as population, religion and ownership of oil resources were also valuable. The ideological or informational component of this war was evident in the American-Zionist attempt to discredit or 'marginalise the role of Islam (as a religion and civilisation) inside our societies and states.'[36] In addition, the American-Zionist alliance had ceaselessly sought to spread discord among the Arab states, and between them and Iran, and to engineer coups against radical regimes. But these facts did not mean that the military option could be allowed to wither away. 'Without military power,' Husayn wrote, 'security crumbles.' Reestablishing a military balance in the Middle East was paramount and not a fanciful idea. He identified three instances when the Arab-Iranian front achieved military parity with the US-Zionist alliance: during the 1973 Ramadan War; after the victory of the Iranian Revolution; and after Iraq emerged from the First Gulf War (against Iran) with huge military power.

Peaceful diplomacy was, for Husayn, a strategic dead-end. The decade of negotiations since the Madrid Conference had clearly ended in failure. Military action, therefore, was the only alternative way forward. But Husayn was adamant that this action should not be carried out as inter-state, or regular, warfare (*harb nizamiyya*). This, he accepted, was not feasible due to the technological gulf that had opened up between the Arabs and Israel since 1973. A superior model was the irregular warfare exemplified by Hizbullah. The group had proved the effectiveness of this model in its confrontation with Israel in southern Lebanon. Husayn was convinced that the Lebanese experience could be repeated in the Occupied Palestinian Territories, and rehearsed the usual examples of successful 'peoples' wars': China, Vietnam, Algeria.

But he allowed that people's war had so far failed as a model for the liberation of Palestine because the regimes in Egypt and Syria did not trust popular resistance not to threaten the stability of their regimes, and that they feared such threats more than they did Israel. Related to this, the regimes have insisted that state armies assume the principal role in any war against Israel.

The main problem for irregular warfare, for Husayn, was the absence of an external base to support the guerrillas. Arab states had been reluctant to provide such support because of the fear of Israeli reprisals on them, as Israel had demonstrated against Egypt and Syria in the past. But Husayn saw that the Arab-Zionist conflict had come to resemble the Cold War in microcosm. The Arab-Iranian front now possessed the advantage that both Iran and Iraq held Weapons of Mass Destruction sufficient to deter any Israeli or American attack. This was the 'revolution in military thought' which the Arab—particularly Egyptian and Syrian—regimes had yet to internalise, but which ultimately held the keys to defeating Israel. The Afghan struggle against Soviet occupation perhaps also shaped Husayn's analysis and in this sense he was not so far from Zawahiri and other theorists of *jihad*. Husayn insisted that with the support of well-armed regimes millions of Arab *mujahidin*, including suicide bombers, could liberate Palestine.

Just over two years prior to the US invasion of Iraq, Husayn was arguing that the Arab-Iranian front possessed a military deterrent that would allow irregular warfare to take place without exposing the Arab 'bases' to revenge attacks. Husayn's preferred strategy was close to the spectre frequently invoked by George W. Bush and his allies to justify the invasion. But it also represents another demonstration of the Camp David consensus that state and society had separate roles to play. Husayn's approach constituted a familiar attempt to reconcile the persistent heterogeneity of the Egyptian political context, or to concoct a positive division of labour between state and society. The idea of a military deterrent that would encourage Arab states to support mass guerrilla action against Israel even though they feared and opposed revolutionary people's war was as contradictory as Nasser's acceptance of UNSCR 242 while simultaneously lending the PLO his full support.

The second half of the 2000s strained the Camp David consensus as the Egyptian regime's complicity in Israeli atrocities seemed to grow more blatant. Mubarak blamed Hizbullah, and not Israel, for the 2006 Israel-Hizbullah war and met with foreign minister Tzipi Livni two days before Israel began bombing Lebanon. The regime was also seen to be acting on Israel's behalf in sustaining the blockade of Gaza by keeping the Rafah border closed and reinforcing it with a steel wall. 'In Egypt and across the Arab world, Iran and Turkey, protesters vilified the Israeli government and Mubarak in one breath.' As news emerged that one of Mubarak's friends held a majority share in an Egyptian-Israeli gas consortium, whereby the latter was supplied gas at cut prices, 'opposition voices drew a triangle between state-business crony ties, the national resources sold to Israel and the lack of basic public services.'[37]

Despite the fact that official parliamentary politics continued to represent a democratic veneer that, in many ways, allowed the Egyptian regime to remain authoritarian, and no legal party could claim any kind of popular base, elections were nonetheless important features of the political landscape, not least for their role in encouraging political views to be aired. Some see elections as a way for the regime to neutralise the more radical voices of criticism, as 'a time of building alliances within the ranks of the opposition, alliances which marginalized some radical elements and helped bring some moderate ones into the parliamentary institutions.'[38] But, increasingly, Egypt's political forces assumed a more prominent 'street' presence outside of election time. Following the outbreak of the al-Aqsa Intifada in 2000, leftist forces sought closer cooperation with Islamists, particularly the Muslim Brotherhood, in order to put forward anti-imperialist goals. Opposition to Zionism and US imperialism in the region formed a fulcrum of cooperation between the two.[39] At the same time, it would be premature to judge all such flowerings of political consciousness as evidence of a resurgent Egyptian civil society. In a vivid demonstration of civil society's interpenetration with the state, and the Camp David consensus at work, the Muslim Brothers and the ruling NDP held joint demonstrations against the US invasion of Iraq in 2003.[40]

Throughout the Mubarak era, left-wing and liberal activists realised that substantive political power—as an opposition—could only
come through alliance with the Muslim Brotherhood. This was clear
in the Wafd's 1984 electoral alliance with the movement, which
made the New Wafd Party leader of the opposition. Following that
election, the Brotherhood terminated its alliance with the Wafd in
favour of the Socialist Labour Party. In consequence, the Wafd fared
poorly in the following elections in 1987. [41] The left has, as in the
past, exerted an intellectual influence on the political sphere through
its liaison with Islamists. The Islamist slogan 'Khaibar, Khaibar, Oh
Jews, Mohammad's army will be back' was, for example, abandoned
at demonstrations involving leftist groups.[42] The most influential and
widespread analyses of Israel are perhaps now the product of a fusion
between leftist and Islamist assumptions.

Israel's civilisational challenge

The most prominent, and politically relevant, intellectual current in
Egypt today is undoubtedly Islamist, and it would be disingenuous to
speak of any kind of consensus without giving Islamist views centre
stage. Although there are numerous strands of the 'Islamic condition',
and even the Muslim Brotherhood cannot be considered as a unitary
actor, a view of Israel as representing some combination of imperialism, Judaism and unjustly wielded state power, can perhaps be posited as the 'mainstream' Islamist position. Society's oppositional role,
according to this view, is based on a conception of Zionism as economic
and cultural imperialism that should be resisted; as well as primarily
religious solidarity with the Palestinians. The celebrated leftist, turned
Islamist, judge Tariq al-Bishri, perhaps most explicit in putting the
Camp David consensus into words, argued that the Egyptian government had to deal with Israel via accepted diplomatic channels, while
Egyptian and other Arab and Muslim societies should campaign on a
social level against Zionism.[43]

But it has not just been 'card carrying' Islamists that saw things
this way. A similar dualistic framework was put forward by Sayyid
Yasin of the al-Ahram Centre for Political and Strategic Studies.

Sayyid Yasin has written at some length, and over a considerable time-span, of the 'civilisational' conflict between the Arabs and Israel. Yasin placed the conflict with Israel at the very heart of the Arab intellectual project. The central tension within Arab thought between 'origins' and 'modernity' must, Yasin argued, be resolved if the Arabs were to stand any chance of success in the conflict.

Yasin decried the fact that the various peace processes between the Arabs and Israel had enshrined the principle that the conflict was over borders (*sira' al-hudud*) when in reality it continued to be one of existence (*sira' al-wujud*). The Madrid peace conference was particularly damaging in this regard as it introduced the principle of land for peace. But for Yasin the conflict was only superficially over land. In a deeper sense, the Arab-Israeli conflict was a struggle for existence and 'in the long term it will be solved by the Arab popular forces, not the Arab regimes that are complicit with the West.'[44] Yasin was under no illusions that this interpretation rendered the Arab programme for action ambiguous in the extreme, since it did not answer the main question:

> What will the Palestinian people do in the short and medium terms? The most dangerous thing in this orientation is the arbitrary division between the contemporary Arab states and the masses, on the basis that these states, under dictatorial rule, are hopeless, and that there is no hope except in the rise of popular forces taking their historical role and finding the solution to the conflict—at its root by way of breaking up the existing Israeli state and establishing a democratic state on the land of Palestine where Arabs and Israelis can live in peace.[45]

Through his columns in *al-Ahram*, later collected into a book, Yasin provided his interpretation of the al-Aqsa Intifada and the way in which the Arabs should confront Israel. His prognosis was essentially that of al-Bishri: Arab governments should pursue firm but realistic diplomatic action, particularly within the United Nations, while civil society and other popular Arab forces should support the Palestinian struggle in all its forms.

Yasin elaborated in these articles on his conviction that the Arab strategy should combine a diplomatic process with confrontation and resistance. Diplomacy, moreover, should involve the freezing of the normalisation process—particularly on the economic level—but without cancelling negotiations. This would be to show the United States and Israel that the Arabs are capable of moving from talk to action. In this regard, Yasin excoriated those Arab leaders, intellectuals and pundits that call for war or the declaration of '*jihad*' against Israel. Such uninformed folly was what led to the debacle of 1967 and should never be repeated.

Pivotal in Yasin's thinking was—unlike Adel Husayn—his conviction that confrontation involved more than just military confrontation. On the contrary, the Arabs needed a 'civilisational strategy' over the long term to stand up to Israel. Here Yasin echoed the classic liberal ideas of Constantine Zurayq and others. The Arab, particularly Egyptian, cultural and civilisational development strategy meant first and foremost the establishment of a genuine democratic system in the Arab world, built on pluralism, respect for human rights and the removal of authoritarianism. This 'preparation' would enable the Arab world to become self-sufficient and independent enough to confront Israel. Yasin notably used the language of Islamists in quoting the Qur'anic verse to that effect, 'Against them make ready your strength to the utmost of your power' (Surat al-Anfal verse 60) noting that this preparation was now an 'individual obligation', *fard 'ayn,* for Arab societies.[46] In one of the most significant jihadist manifestos, written by the Jihad Group leader Sayyid Imam, this verse is frequently invoked to underscore Muslims' duty to wage violent *jihad*.[47]

Peace was a strategic choice for the Arabs and should never preclude continued resistance. The examples of Vietnam and Algeria were, for Yasin, sufficient to show that negotiations combined with resistance can yield positive results. The Palestinian people, then, have the right and obligation to resist occupation, and the Arab states and peoples 'from the Ocean to the Gulf' must wholeheartedly support them in this. Yasin departed from the liberalism of Zurayq or Baha al-Din, and the internationalism of Mohamed Sid Ahmed, in his conception of civilisational struggle; and it is in this that his affinity with

Elmessiri and other 'cultural Islamist' thinkers is most evident, and that is emblematic of the development of Egyptian political thought as a whole. Consistent with his own writings from the 1970s Sayyid Yasin insisted that Israel was really a backward, regressive and barbaric society based on racism and the principle of continual expansion. There was no question that Egypt or the Arab world should 'catch up' with Israel, which offered no model that should be emulated. To the extent that Israel was a 'democracy' it was the 'democracy of a gang of thieves.' That Israel enjoyed military supremacy did not indicate that it is 'civilised.'

Yasin's interventions in *al-Ahram* were rehersed some five years earlier in a more substantial essay entitled 'The civilisational struggle between Egypt and Israel.' In this Yasin restated, albeit in more 'scientific' terms, the longstanding Islamist argument about the existence of an Israeli and Western 'cultural invasion' aimed at diluting or 'taming' the Arabs' national feeling and character. In the information age the cultural invasion became ever sharper. Understandings of the Arab-Israeli conflict promoted by supposedly neutral 'conflict resolution' specialists in the West were but one facet of the intellectual invasion since they denied the existence of genuinely contrary interests. The Arabs needed to draw on the positive aspects of their own heritage to reinvigorate their own civilisation which was, in its heyday, world-leading. This in turn required a comprehensive civilisational strategy based on self-criticism and scientific thought. It was not the extent of civilisation that mattered, for Yasin, but the *type* of civilisation, and here he departs from liberals like Zurayq and Baha al-Din.

Yasin's approach was vigorously societal: in order to discern what parts of the Arab heritage to resurrect and which to abandon, society must become democratic and the gap between elites and masses narrowed. 'Organic intellectuals' must be allowed to propagate their thought among the masses; the gap between city and village narrowed.

Abdelwahab Elmessiri has also written—to an almost excessive degree—on the civilisational essence of Israel and the correspondingly holistic form resistance to it must assume. His *Encyclopedia of Zionist Concepts and Terms* was completed in 1999 and published as an eight-volume set, and his views on Israel, Zionism and Jews were expressed in other publications as well. Elmessiri saw the Jews as a 'functional group' in pre-renaissance Europe, in Marxist terms. They were demonised by the Catholic Church and the aristocracy as scapegoats to jusify the latters' exploitation of the masses. With the coming of the Enlightenment, Protestants used the Jews as an instrument of imperialism, and so encouraged the return to the promised land and Zionism. This, for Elmessiri as with Muslim Brotherhood authors, should be seen as beginning with Napoleon's invasion of Egypt in 1798, and not with Herzl in the late 19th century. The process of racism and dispossession embarked upon by Zionism was, for Elmessiri, no more than a varient of European humanism and modernity—a child of Darwin, Nietzsche and sibling of Nazism. Humanism became imperialism and instrumentalism, and then racism.[48]

Elmessiri's Marxist intellectual formation meant that he insisted Israel was more than simply a manifestation of Judaism and, indeed, in the Islamised intellectual milieu of modern Egypt his contributions have been celebrated as a valuable and original corrective to previous anti-Jewish writings. But although Elmessiri wrote of Israel's roots as a 'functional group' in the service of Western imperialism, his 'civilisational' frame of reference moved away from the internationalist sensibilities of Marxists. Just as Islam formed, or should form, the foundation of every Muslim's worldview, for Elmessiri, so too did Judaism every Jew and Catholicism every Catholic. Secularism, by contrast, emptied the world of meaning. The civilisational angle in Elmessiri's work, despite its 'scientific' pretentions, leads back to old essentialisms and a fundamental support for the Islamist programme of resistance to cultural infiltration.

The economist Galal Amin shares with Yasin and Elmessiri the notion of civilisational conflict and the intellectual invasion. [49] His interpretation has tended strongly towards the conspiratorial and holistic. A prodigious writer, a picture of Amin's somewhat inconsistent yet decidedly synthetic views on Israel can be gained from the enticingly (though misleadingly) titled *Arab Intellectuals and Israel*. Israel, for Amin in this book, was not a just a state, but a 'project', which aimed at further expansion to form Greater Israel. The 'Middle East market' that was much vaunted in the wake of the Oslo peace process was, in reality, a part of Israeli imperialism and should be opposed as such. The project was supposed to be a celebration of 'Middle Easternism', *al-sharq awsatiyya,* which Amin considered 'an ugly term because the project itself is ugly'. Like Elmessiri, Amin strenuously opposed the absorption of such lexical aberrations into the Arabic language. It was part of an Israeli, not an Arab, agenda, and its true purpose, to which the Arab supporters were blind, was to allow Israel access to the vast Arab market.

This was something the Arabs should oppose for the simple reason that Israel would benefit.[50] Instead, inter-Arab integration should be strengthened. Because Israel was not a state but a 'project', it would be suicidal for the Arabs to support any Israeli gains, no matter how much Arabs also stood to gain. This distinguished opening Arab economies to Israel from any other kind of economic opening. The Israelis were working to 'brainwash' the Arabs into thinking that this is a good idea and Amin feared the erasure of Arab identity by Middle Easternism. The project would introduce progressive changes to the educational system so that Arab children could be taught they are Middle Easterners and not Arabs.

Amin was less ready to engage in the self-criticism for which Sadiq al-Azm or Sayyid Yasin called. He objected to the deluge of anti-Nasserist publications and writers such as Fu'ad Zakariyya who pointed to lack of democratic participation as the cause of the June 1967 defeat. For Amin, Nasser's failings helped explain the defeat's scale and speed, but not its occurrence in the first place. The real reason was to be found in the international conspiracy against Nasser. The great powers conspired against Egypt and ensured its defeat due to Nasser's ability to ignite Arab nationalist feeling against imperialism and Israel.

The self-flagellation about 1967 should end, according to Amin, since it absolved the imperialists of all responsibility. Sadat worked as an American agent to bring about the surrender of Egypt to Zionist and imperialist objectives. But the other Arab states were also completely dependent on the United States and the much vaunted Egyptian return to the 'Arab fold' was, in reality, Egyptian surrender becoming Arab surrender. Amin went so far as to argue that the Iraqi invasion of Kuwait was orchestrated by the United States to allow the

Americans to re-enter the Gulf. Amin described Israel as the 'devilish child sitting on the shoulder of the powerful giant.' But, like Heikal and numerous liberal thinkers, Amin asked, 'Why has the child succeeded in dominating the giant and not us?' Why, in other words, has Israeli pressure with the United States succeeded where Arab pressure either failed or was absent?

The nub of the issue for Amin was that Arab societies are 'old', slow-moving and infatuated with the past. Somewhat contradicting his earlier scepticism about self-flagellation Amin enumerated the failings of Arab societies. Arab economists and ministers were like old men, crumpling in the face of any challenge and afraid of resistance. They have always ran away from independent economic development for this reason. Amin's proposed solution, like that of Lutfi al-Khuli in the 1970s, was to work towards the unification of progressive forces within the religious and secular camps.

Although conspiracy theories remain common, some self-awareness among Islamist intellectuals about the 'Jewish conspiracy' has crept in, although this occasionally smacks more of political correctness than radical rethinking. The changes reflect the influence of liberal and left-wing categories espoused by such thinkers as Amin, Yasin and Elmessiri. For many Islamist thinkers now, Israel does not so much represent the embodiment of an age-old Jewish conspiracy for world domination—the so-called 'traditional' thesis—as it does the spearhead of a broader Western agenda to subjugate the Arab world by, among other things, subverting its Arab-Islamic values and identity. The anti-Israeli sentiments espoused by the Muslim Brotherhood reveal a particular reading of modernity and its effects in the Middle East rather than anti-Jewish sentiment *per se*, although their historical analysis still tends towards the conspiratorial.

On more than one recent occasion 'Isam al-Aryan, the Brotherhood's 'modernising' political chief, has set out his interpretation of the birth of the modern Middle East, in which the role of Zionism has been both deleterious and central: Prior to the beginning of Zionist settlement in the 19th century the Muslims and Christians of the Middle East had good relations with Jews. It was the Ottoman sultan Abdul Hamid II's refusal to grant the Zionists a national home that led them into the arms of Western imperialists. The Caliphate itself was the number one victim of this unholy conspiracy, and the modern 'Western' states—not least Turkey—were set up to protect Israel, separate Muslims from their religion and prevent the unification of the Arabs. It is no coincidence, for Aryan, that Anwar Sadat had a picture of Ataturk in his office. But simplistic and conspiratorial though Aryan's reading of history may appear, it is a far cry from the age-old Jewish quest for world domination narrative the Brotherhood used to promote. For Aryan, the religious dimension of this history lies in the symbols the Zionist movement employed to attract non-Zionist Jews to the promised land.[51]

Aryan links Israel to the paramount political concern of the Muslim Brotherhood and other societal actors in the late-Mubarak era: the persistence of authoritarian rule—which again reveals the continuing instrumentalisation of the Israel factor by societal movements. It was primarily the regimes' suppression of democracy that allowed Zionism to flourish and Israel to survive in the region, and al-Aryan argues that realising democracy in Egypt would signal the beginning of the end for Israel. This is not because he believes a democratically accountable Brotherhood government would declare war on Israel, but because 'freedom' would allow Islam, the key societal bulwark against Zionism, to flourish. Rather vaguely, he concludes:

> Everyone is aware that the establishment of democracy in our country would hasten the abolition of the Zionist presence in Palestine, not because immediate wars would be launched, as some might imagine ... but because the real renaissance will begin when freedoms are unleashed.[52]

It is fascinating to compare these sentiments to an earlier comment al-Aryan made regarding the future foreign policy of a Muslim Brotherhood-controlled Egypt. Aryan affirmed that such a government would:

> Recognise Israel and respect the treaties, although the Camp David treaty would have to be modified in accordance with our

preferences. This does not mean that we will declare war, but we will revise some of the treaties and agreements to better suit Egyptian interests.[53]

Aryan was sharply rebuked and forced to retract this statement, in which he argued he was misquoted, by the then Supreme Guide of the Brotherhood Mahdi Akef, who stated that the Brotherhood did not and will never recognise Israel, and that 'Israel is not in the Brotherhood's dictionary.'[54] But Akef stopped short of explicitly promising to annul the treaty. He expressed the Muslim Brotherhood's position as being that 'our position will never be separated from the people's in their rejection of the treaty,' and that the 'Egyptian people will decide with their votes whether to accept or reject the treaty.'[55] The row illustrates the extent to which prominent intellectuals continue to reserve a distinct foreign policy role for society. As a social movement, the Muslim Brotherhood will continue to fight Zionism, but as a government, it would deal with Israel state-to-state. It also seems that Aryan's main crime was to make the Brotherhood's acceptance of the Camp David consensus explicit, whereas Akef and others would rather it were kept secret. The Brotherhood's stance is notably not so far from that of the liberal cause célèbre, Ayman Nur, who has argued that greater democracy, transparency and accountability are the priority in determining Egypt's policy towards Israel, and that it is those values that have been sacrificed in the name of 'no sound louder than the battle'.[56]

A similar perspective is expressed in a recent article by prominent Islamist thinker Fahmi Huwaydi. The article appeared against the backdrop of the Hala Mustafa affair described above. Huwaydi's analysis is McCarthyist in tone: Israel is trying to dominate Egyptian society by penetrating its political and media, as well as business, establishment. Names are revealed. Huwaydi bemoans the weakness of an Egyptian national movement that cannot even sustain a boycott of Israel, despite the fact that even European countries can. He too argues that the main reason for society's weakness in the face of Israel, which represents an existential security threat to Egypt, is the lack of democratic freedom and the regime's progressive eradication of independent civil institutions.[57] Again, there is an implicit assumption that it is Egyptian society that should, and will—sufficiently empowered— play the decisive foreign policy role.

To reiterate, the view of Zionism as part of a much broader Western cultural, political and economic edifice has emerged and the 'intellectual invasion' motif is accepted not only by Islamists. Thinkers like Elmessiri have successfully linked Zionism with Western civilisation as a whole, which has broadened the Israeli threat to include Christian Zionism in the United States and allowed the instruments by which Zionism is spread around the world to multiply. For the journalist Salah al-Din Hafez, to cite one recent example, the Zionist lobby in the United States plays two roles. First, it influences American policy makers to continue their support for Israel. Second, it generates anti-Arab and anti-Muslim feeling in American society.[58] Christian Zionism supports it in this. For Hafez, the fact that Zionism resonated with America's Christian majority meant that Jews ascended to powerful positions in the United States government and financial institutions.[59] Hafez painstakingly lists the 'Jews' in the Clinton administration, down to ambassador level, as if being Jewish is self-evidently indicative of support for Israel. In his enthusiasm, Hafez also lists the Greek Orthdox former CIA director George Tenet as a Jew, and hence participant in the 'Zionist invasion' of the Clinton administration. For Hafez, Arab relations with America are hindered primarily by Israel's supporters there. In a perspective that echoes that of Heikal in the 1960s, he implies that under 'normal' conditions the US would support the Arabs.

The perseverance of the traditional thesis

Despite the rise of the Islamic left, the contributions of liberal thinkers and the various fusions between Nasserist or Marxist conceptions of Israel and those based on more 'traditional' Islamist conceptions, there remains a strong populist trend that views the conflict in primarily religious terms. The issue here is not so much one of 'moderates' versus 'extremists', but rather of divergent epistemology. A good example of this may be found in the contemporary writings of so-called 'moderate' jurists like Yusuf al-Qaradawi or Muhammad Imara. Qaradawi, probably the most respected Sunni legal authority, published a mammoth two-volume work on the *Jurisprudence of Jihad* in 2009. The book has been hailed as a major intervention in the debate on *jihad* that has pitted the mainstream Muslim world against 'globalists' like Usama bin Laden. Its main thrust is to declare that the al-Qa'ida style of *jihad* against any and all deemed to be non-Muslim is illegitimate. Revealing a consistent Brotherhood position (see the discussion of Kishk in Chapter 4) Qaradawi excludes the suicide attacks against Israelis, within and outside of Israel, from this prohibition since:

> Due to its settler occupying racist usurping colonial composition [Israel] is a military society flesh and blood. It is a society completely militarised, in that everyone exceeding the age of childhood in it, man and woman, is recruited in the Israeli army ... Those known as 'civilians' are really soldiers in the army of the tribe of Zion.[60]

Of the legitimate *jihad*s, that for Palestine looms large and Qaradawi devotes a chapter of his book to discussing it.

Qaradawi realises that the Islamist camp is often accused of anti-Semitism and that Israel uses this to win favour in the West. But the ways in which he goes about debunking this accusation speak volumes about his worldview. He rehearses the old, and largely irrelevant, argument that Arabs cannot be anti-Semitic because they themselves are Semites. He points out further that Islam is a humanist religion that does not discriminate on the basis of race. Pushing his point further, Qaradawi insists that Judaism is in fact closer to the nation of Abraham than the Christians and that from a religious point of view the Jews are closer to Islam than the Christians. In support of this assertion, Qaradawi points out the similarities between halal and kosher food and the absence of the trinity or deification in Islam and Judaism.

But Qaradawi cannot move away from a religious view of the conflict in his basic terms of reference. Why, he asks, do the Muslims hate the Jews more than they hate the Christians? The reason for the

Muslims' 'battle with the Jews' (the use of the title of Qutb's book here is surely not coincidental) is as follows:

> The truth is that the battle began between us and the Jews for one reason alone: they took our land—the land of Islam, the land of Palestine, and expelled our people, the people of the land of our ancestors. The imposed their intruding presence with iron, fire and blood.[61]

The conflict, therefore, is one between two religious communities, and all members of each community should feel the pain, and share the interests, of the whole.

Practically, Qaradawi accepts that a truce is possible and even necessary, 'where the sides abstain from violence and stem the blood,' but insists that 'nobody [has the right] to give up Islamic land.' In line with Sayyid Yasin, he rejects the principle of land for peace as a reflection of uneven power configuration (between Muslims and Jews). The land is unequivocally Muslim land, no matter what.

But Qaradawi remains, even where talking about land, keen to stress the essential religious character of the conflict: 'every battle that a Muslim enters to defend truth, or resist wrong, or establish justice, or revolt against oppression, is a religious battle because it is a battle in God's path.' *Jihad* is an individual obligation (*fard 'ayn*) 'and if its people cannot defend it, those neighbouring it must do so, until eventually it involves all the Muslims.' Qaradawi provides a rhythmically revealing statement of his conception of the conflict:

> If its usurpers fight us with religious motives and religious dreams, it is incumbent upon us to fight them with that with which they fought us. If they fight us with the Torah, we fight them with the Qur'an, if they return to the teachings of the Talmud, we return to Bokhari and Muslim. If they glorify Saturday, we glorify Friday. If they say the temple, we say al-Aqsa. In sum, if they fight under the banner of Judaism, we fight under the banner of Islam. If they recruit their soldiers in

the name of Moses, we recruit in the name of Moses and Jesus and Muhammad. We are closer to Moses than them.[62]

Another prominent Egyptian Islamist thinker, Muhammad Imara, has also written from much the same perspective about the legitimacy of *jihad* for the sake of Palestine. He too proceeds to recount the long history of Jewish hostility towards Islam from the birth of Islam before focussing on the modern Palestinian context. His stated goal is to raise awareness of the identity (*hawiya*) of the conflict and debunk the Western-promoted myth that it began with the Balfour declaration or the first Zionist congress in Basle.[63] *Jihad*, he shows, has been the dominant theme in Islamic history and continues to be the only way to liberate Palestine from the Jews.

Imara also focuses on the 'treacherous' behaviour of the Eastern—particularly Egyptian— Jews, 'most of whom' ungratefully forgot the tolerance of Islam and supported the Zionists in the early part of the 20th century.[64] Liberal and secular intellectuals are also demonised in Imara's short book. Secularism in particular is to blame for obscuring the religious dimensions of conflicts in general, which 'played a role in the "cultural coldness" [*al-barud al-thaqafi*] that afflicted these liberals in the face of Zionist dangers that were creeping toward Jerusalem and Palestine.'[65]

The only intellectuals to recognise the Zionist threat for what it was were Islamic intellectuals, particularly Rashid Rida, to a review of whose views Imara devotes considerable space. In a discussion of Rashid Rida's approach to Zionism, Imara repeats the now well-worn theory about the role of Jews in the fall of the Caliphate. He also recounts Rida's unceasing attempts to 'persuade the Jews to break their link with the Western colonialist project and agree with the Arabs to live—in the Arab countries, including Palestine—free, safe and enjoying all the civil and personal rights that all their people (*ahl-uha*) enjoy.'[66] Instead, though, the Zionists spurned Islam's hand of friendship and collaborated with imperialism to usurp the land. Rida also, according to Imara, recognised that the Zionist-Crusader alliance would not be satisfied with Palestine alone, but coveted the 'entire Ottoman state'.[67]

It was Palestinians themselves who, in the final analysis, took the initiative and launched a *jihad* against the Zionists. Imara eulogises Izz al-Din al-Qassam, the Islamic leader who rose to prominence during the Palestinian revolt of 1936, and reserves a particularly long section for a discussion of the life of assassinated Hamas spiritual leader, Ahmad Yasin. Yasin, was born 'six months after the martyrdom of Izz al-Din al-Qassam' and is to be viewed as his successor in the *jihad* for the liberation of Jerusalem and Palestine. Imara, like Qaradawi and other Islamist or Brotherhood-aligned figures, not only accepts but vigorously promotes a religious view of the conflict and its history, which dates back to the founding of Islam. Imara's religious view of the conflict, as one essentially between all Jews and all Muslims, confirms the familiar societal—and Palestinian—approach to its solution, with *jihad* against Israel constituting the 'only way to restore the stolen right in Jerusalem and Palestine.'[68]

The mainstream of Egyptian Islamism, which Qaradawi and Imara epitomise, in a way that is not inconsistent with their approach to the *jihad* for Palestine, nevertheless accepts statism. The aftermath of the 2006 Israel-Hizbullah war exposed this. The war was deeply embarrassing for the Egyptian regime as Egypt, initially at least, blamed Hizbullah for the hostilities. Two years later the arrest of individuals accused of belonging to a Hizbullah 'cell' in Egypt provided an opportunity for further public discussion about Egypt's role regionally and its responsibilities towards the Palestinian resistance in particular. The regime for its part, as well as regime intellectuals like Ali al-Din Hilal complained that Hizbullah's actions were illegal, a threat to Egyptian sovereignty and even, most stridently, part of a Syrian-Iranian plot to overthrow the Egyptian regime. The Muslim Brotherhood and other intellectuals, such as Diyaa Rashwan, Muhammad Salim al-Awa and the lawyer defending the arrested men, Muntasir Zayyat, dismissed the case as politically motivated arguing that Hizbullah was not challenging Egyptian security. For the Brotherhood, as with Hizbullah itself, the Palestinians had a right to resist Israel militarily and Egypt had a moral obligation (especially as Mubarak had, like his predecessors, recognised the existence of this right) to at least allow this resistance to take place.

What is interesting about these exchanges is that the Brotherhood, al-Awa and others were arguing that the presence of a Hizbullah cell was not a threat to Egyptian security or an attempt to destabilise the regime. Their demand was essentially that the regime allow the Camp David consensus—that the regime allows Egyptian and Arab forces to exercise their right to confront Israel while those popular forces in return refrain from challenging the role of the state—to continue. It is telling that the state-run *al-Ahram* newspaper ran a rather hysterical story warning of an impending coup attempt in Egypt—clearly calculating that if loyal readers believed this to be the case they would stop supporting Hizbullah, Iran and Hamas.[69] And it is also significant that the version of *jihad* elaborated by Imara and Qaradawi is entirely consistent with the Camp David consensus: the Palestinian *jihad* is legitimate, as is the *jihad* of any private Muslim who chooses to join that *jihad*; but the obligation of the state is to support, facilitate or at least not obstruct this *jihad*.

The exception that proves the rule?

Although this chapter has focussed on those who oppose normalisation, by far the most widespread position, not all of Egyptian civil society falls into this category. As such, and unsurprisingly, the Camp David consensus is not absolute. For some, Israel exists as a legitimate nation-state with the right to pursue 'normal' relations with its neighbours. Thinkers and analysts like Saad Eddine Ibrahim, Tarek Heggy, Imad Gad or Abd al-Mun'im Sa'id have rejected the idea that Israel represents an imperialist or cultural threat to the Arab world, in the context of embracing Western liberal values and advocating the deeper integration of Egypt and the region as a whole into the global economy. Some have seen a greater threat in Egypt's own Islamist movement than in the encroachment of Zionism, or seen the barrier to increased normalisation as, in large part, problems with the 'Arab mindset' or psychological or mental 'blocks' about accepting Israel, as well as Palestinian blunders and miscalculations.[70] Not all Egyptian intellectuals are part of the 'culture of war.'

The most prominent example of an attempt to institutionalize progress towards cultural, or societal, normalisation is perhaps the so-called 'Copenhagen Group' that was formed during the right-wing Netanyahu premiership in 1997.[71] Linked to the Israeli 'Peace Now' movement, the Cairo branch of the International Alliance for Arab-Israeli Peace included Lutfi al-Khuli and Mohamed Sid Ahmed. The group brought together Israeli, Egyptian, Jordanian and Palestinian intellectuals to campaign for peace. 'Peace is too important to be left only to governments', announced the Copenhagen Declaration that inaugurated the movement. This group and its members were pilloried by many who opposed 'normalisation', as, for example, 'a poison dagger splitting our movement'.[72] Galal Amin sharply criticised Lutfi al-Khuli, who argued in favour of building links with the Israeli left, which he saw as evidence of his cooptation by Mubarak.[73]

Those supportive of normalisation often view themselves as 'liberals'.[74] And Sadat indeed appealed to liberal ideas of interests and state sovereignty to justify his foreign policy shift towards Israel. But not all agree that this position is in Egypt's interests. In an interesting series of articles in the popular independent Egyptian daily, *al-Masry al-Youm* (*The Egyptian Today*), Ahmad Muslimani accuses the 'normalisation liberals' of hijacking Egyptian liberalism and contributing to the misunderstanding that only the left and Islamists oppose normalisation. Muslimani complains that many see Islamist and leftist positions as 'ideological' but not liberal ones. For Muslimani, on the contrary, the 'normalisation liberals' support normalisation on principle, rather than based on a pragmatic assessment of 'interest' as true liberals should. Supporters of normalisation do so no matter what happens; they do not adapt to change:

'If Sharon comes to power, no change ... ; if Gaza is pounded, no change; if Egypt is cornered in international and global forums, no change; if foreign alliances and the American military umbrella ... threaten our independence and national security – no change.'[75]

Normalisation, for Muslimani, is not in Egypt's interest and supporters of it should be exposed for the 'ideologists' that they are. They are not sincere either as patriots or as liberals. Muslimani's analysis is perhaps typical of the Camp David consensus: 'there is a big difference, in my interpretation, between the Egyptian-Israeli peace agreement and normalisation … I am one of those that support Camp David and reject normalisation.' For Muslimani, the Camp David Accords ended a state of war between Israel and Egypt such that politics could take over from armed conflict: this is normal where war has not yielded sufficient results but it is not possible to continue fighting. Both the military and political approaches are valid national positions,

> But I do not see any valid patriotic justification for the normal-isation process, by which I mean normalisation of journalists, intellectuals, artists and technocrats, who see in Camp David the beginning of love, and not a kind of politics. Camp David was an effort at national liberation after an unprecedentedly glori-ous war. But normalisation is an exercise in national regression, wasting the efforts of war and peace alike.[76]

Opposition to normalisation with Israel has become one of the main hallmarks of intellectual legitimacy in Egypt and a central refrain of resurgent civil society in the country. But this seemingly vibrant civil society, including the rise of the Muslim Brotherhood as a quasi-legit-imate political actor, apparently freer elections, active syndicates and a vibrant independent press has constituted what Eberhard Kienle has called a 'grand delusion.' Intellectuals and civil society actors, includ-ing former radicals, have accepted that they are not going to change the system of rule in Egypt and that the regime, in one form or another, is there to stay for the foreseeable future. The fact that political parties, and the Muslim Brotherhood, continued to contest elections in the sure knowledge that they would never win a parliamentary majority is indicative of this. This acceptance—not to say malaise—is epitomised by the Camp David consensus whereby intellectuals accept the reality of the state and its foreign policy stance but seek to exploit the long-standing tradition of anti-Zionism for their own ends.

CHAPTER 7

CONCLUSION

As a result of its centrality to the evolution of various types of Egyptian nationalism, Israel has been 'instrumentalised' by regimes and social movements in Egypt to the extent that, in ideational terms, the relationship with Israel has been *about* significantly more than itself. While the instrumentalisation of foreign policy, particularly in the Middle East, has been adduced to serve the purpose of legitimating the suspension of democracy or political violence and oppression domestically, the nature of instrumentalisation can be further unpacked and 'deepened' to include the ways in which social movements instrumentalise foreign policy. Israel, or the Arab-Israeli conflict, has been instrumentalised in complex ways, which can be roughly schematised as follows:

Since the 1930s Egyptian intellectuals have approached Zionism and Israel in statist, religious and political economic terms. 'Arabism' combines the latter two perspectives, which are often set erroneously in opposition to the former statist views. The extent to which culture and religion feature in analyses of Israel is related to the popularisation of Zionism and the Palestine issue from the 1930s. This in turn owes much to the rise of the popular nationalist movement, and the Islamic trend within it, which from that time saw the rejuvenation of Islam in society as the sine qua non for tackling Christian and Jewish encroachment on the land of Islam. The religious perspective came gradually to pervade elite circles as well, including those which had tended to view the Zionist issue dispassionately as a strategic or moral and humanitarian issue. More importantly, and lastingly, the religious frame blended with the anti-imperialist theories developed by intellectuals of the Egyptian left, which following the war was increasingly dominated by Arabic-speaking 'native' Egyptians and new middle classes. It is in this nexus that the 'Arabist' version of anti-Zionism cohered. But these paradigms never fully excluded statism, or the idea that Egypt and Israel were in the final analysis states that would have to interact as such, due to the dynamic and contradictory processes of nationalism and state-formation.

Many of the dynamics that underpin the Camp David consensus can be traced back to the formative period in Egypt's modern ideological development, the 1930s and 1940s. During this period, and particularly after World War Two, the political sphere expanded dramatically and politics ceased to be the concern of a narrow bourgeois elite. The expanded public sphere essentially comprised Egypt's 'Islamic public'.[1] For this public, the Caliphate had formed the emotional centre of gravity for generations. Until the penetration of modern systems of thought and production into this society, there was no contradiction between a set of loyalties Egyptians perceived, whether to tribe or clan or to religion or *umma*, or to Egypt. But with modernity came the exclusivity of the nation-state as focus for political identification, a fact that emerging universalist social movements in the end merely disguised.

During this time, social movements like the Muslim Brotherhood and communists evolved theories of political action in which society took centre stage. The rise of societal militancy, in opposition to a monarchy perceived to be in league with the British occupier, adopted a supra-Egyptian worldview and came to view events beyond Egypt (especially Palestine) as essential Egyptian political issues. The intertwined questions of Palestine and Zionism were thus politicised and linked to the national and revolutionary struggle in Egypt as a whole. Although clearly bitter rivals, the left and religious right were competing for the same supporters in society and united over their desire to deny the existing regime any opportunities to distinguish, expand or enrich itself. The Muslim Brothers and communists alike were, from an early date, in favour of *popular* action in support of the Palestinian Arabs and against Zionism, with the left in particular opposing Faruq's intervention in 1948 as a diversionary tactic aimed at self-aggrandisement. Such arguments would return in the 1970s and continue, implicitly, to underpin Egyptian intellectuals' approach to Israel today.

During the heyday of Nasserism—the decade from 1956 to 1967—Israel was considered to be part and parcel of imperialism, part of the radical left's 'axis of evil' that linked Zionism, imperialism and Arab reaction. This allowed Egypt's policy towards Israel to be instrumentalised to justify not going to war with Israel while extending Egyptian hegemony. If Israel was not more than a creation, manifestation and extension of imperialism, the argument went, it could not be defeated other than through popular revolution. This would have to be accomplished by the Arab progressive forces through their unity and through the export of the Egyptian revolution. Interstate war against Israel, opposed by the left and Islamists on strategic and ideological grounds, was thus also discouraged by the ruling regime itself, which had inherited the 'statist' penchant for sovereignty and moderation that had also characterised the prerevolutionary regime. The focus on Israel *per se*, rather than the more amorphous and intangible imperialism had historically been regarded as a rightist, distracting and reactionary position.

This picture of the Nasser period is of course a simplification and there were significant shifts in emphasis throughout the period, as Chapter 3 detailed. In particular, the short period of Arab summitry, from 1963, involved a scaling back of anti-imperialist, anti-conservative rhetoric and the foregrounding instead of a more specific anti-Israeli discourse. The establishment of the PLO at this stage helped remove some of the onus on the regime to attack Israel, but the appearance of a discourse whereby Arab sovereign states, reactionary or otherwise, would join together to destroy Israel would have serious implications that would be revealed in 1967. This discourse was not just the result of inter-Arab state dialogues. It reflected the fear of popular grievances against economic hardship becoming political and the related shift in the political balance of power within Egypt, in particular towards the political and religious right, as well as changes on the global level from the late 1950s that saw Nasser move away from the Soviet Union and seek rapprochement with the United States.

With the Muslim Brotherhood decimated in 1954 and the communist movement throwing its lot in with the regime, the only social movement in Nasser's Egypt was the revolution itself, as manifested in the series of mass parties the regime created to either neutralise or mobilise mass sentiment. But the apparent unity of the revolution concealed the diverse strands of the pre-revolutionary national movement. The communists and Muslim Brothers had evolved their own views on Israel, in distinctly instrumentalist terms, and it was into these that Nasser tapped. Part of the trouble with the anti-imperialist paradigm he pursued after 1956 was that it granted too much prestige and risked relinquishing power to the left as a political and intellectual force in Egyptian society. As such it was not surprising that in moving rightwards Nasser turned to the other, more powerful, social movement, the Muslim Brotherhood. 'Imperialism is the same whether it is from the left or the right', declared Nasser. He equated Zionism with communism, which was a technique employed by the Brotherhood in its battle against the left before the revolution.

Nasser's brutal treatment of Muslim Brotherhood activists, combined with the faltering of Egyptian economic development, meant, however, that by the 1960s it was impossible to rely on the Brotherhood as an ally—defending the authenticity of Arab socialism and the revolution against the subversions of fifth column communists. The Brotherhood split and the tendency around Qutb itself instrumentalised Israel to attack the regime. Nasser, for Qutb, was nothing but a Zionist and Israel could never be defeated unless the regime at home (the 'near enemy') was overthrown. The regime and Israel were, in other words, in the same camp.

The period between the two wars of 1967 and 1973 marked a major conceptual shift away from the idea of negating Israel either as the vanguard of Arab revolution or as a sovereign state allied with other Arab states. Rather, the goalposts shifted and the regime's goal became the recovery of the lost territory, and much needed prestige. 'Erasing the traces of the aggression' became Nasser's watchword. Israel was still asserted to be 'merely' part of the firmament of imperialism, which helped explain the ferocity of the defeat, but the regime's new goal and responsibility was now to be regaining the Sinai. For Sayyid Yasin, the war over Israel's presence (*harb al-wujud*) became a war over borders (*harb al-hudud*).

This period also saw the unravelling of the chimerical unity between state and society that had characterised the Nasser years. The 1967 defeat ushered in a period of long-dormant criticism of the regime, primarily from students and the youth. Dominated by the left, this force intersected with a broader Arab—and indeed global—New Left, which shot to prominence in 1968. The New Left criticised Nasser and Nasserism for not taking the revolution further and argued that deepening the revolution was essential to defeat Israel—as imperialism. Israel, then, was instrumentalised as an axis around which a resurgent left could build a popular following.

After 1973 Sadat began to move squarely towards burying the war option as an instrument of foreign policy towards Israel. Sadat also tried to repress opposition to Israel from civil society, although this proved irreconcilable with his policy of resurrecting the Islamists as a counterweight to the left. From 1977 bellicosity towards Israel became an oppositional position. At the same time, there was a general consensus—responding to and echoing the regime's pronouncements—that Egypt's priority was to develop its political and economic system. The peace process with Israel was supposed to allow for this, freeing Egypt of the crippling economic burden of maintaining the war footing. On the political front, liberals called for expanding democracy while Islamists agitated for the institution of *shari'a* and the Islamic state. On the left and for Islamists growing disquiet with Sadat's policy of conciliation with Israel was tempered by their reluctance to allow the regime to further strengthen itself by waging a successful war against Israel or to risk squandering the freedom of action and expression Sadat had allowed them. This contributed to the elevation of Zionism as the main threat and the casting of the conflict as essentially societal. Opposing Israel thus came to be in seeking to gird Arab and Muslim society against Zionist influence and supporting the PLO agenda to liberate Palestine.

Since the death of Anwar Sadat in 1981, Egypt has settled comfortably into the 'cold peace', or a situation of 'no war, no peace', with Israel. With a few exceptions intellectuals broadly accept that the regime must deal correctly with Israel as a state, while society confronts Zionism and supports Palestinian resistance. Egypt's social movements have, since the pre-revolutionary period, seen the state's role as allowing this resistance to take place. The 'cold peace' is to be explained not so much in terms of the regime's abiding by the letter of the peace treaty and withholding normalisation until the Palestinian issue is addressed, but more in terms of a societal role in, and instrumentalisation of, foreign policy that Egyptian social movements have defended vigourously for decades. This in turn confirms the view of the Egyptian state propounded by many scholars, as discussed in Chapter 1. It is important that the structural heterogeneity of the Egyptian state be factored into an analysis of the country's foreign policy, in particular as concerns the role of ideas, norms and ideology.

NOTES

Chapter 1

1. Mohamed Hassanein Heikal, 'Egyptian foreign policy,' *Foreign Affairs* (July 1978): 716.
2. Michael Barnett, *Dialogues in Arab Politics: Negotiations in Regional Order* (New York: Columbia University Press, 1998).
3. Steven Heydemann, *War, Institutions, and Social Change in the Middle East* (Berkeley: University of California Press, 2000); Avraham Sela, *The Decline of the Arab-Israeli Conflict: Middle East Politics and the Quest for Regional Order* (New York: State Univeristy of New York Press, 1998).
4. Sela, *The Decline of the Arab-Israeli Conflict*, 298–299.
5. For a good example of how intellectual labour in Egypt cannot be disentangled from political and social factors see Anthony Gorman, *Historians, State and Politics in Twentieth Century Egypt: Contesting the Nation* (London: Routledge, 2003).
6. Karl Mannheim, *Ideology and Utopia: An Introduction to the Sociology of Knowledge* (London: Routledge and Kegan Paul, 1960).
7. Ibid., 31.
8. Antonio Gramsci, *Selections from the Prison Notebooks of Antonio Gramsci* (New York; London: Lawrence and Wishart, 1971), 7.
9. Ibid., 5.
10. Michael Mann, *The Sources of Social Power* (Cambridge: Cambridge University Press, 1993), 7.
11. Asef Bayat, 'Revolution without movement, movement without revolution: comparing Islamic activism in Iran and Egypt,' *Comparative Studies in Society and History* 40, no. 1 (1998): 136–169.
12. Robert Bianchi, *Unruly Corporatism: Associational Life in Twentieth-Century Egypt* (New York; Oxford: Oxford University Press, 1989), 23.

13. Nazih N. Ayubi, *Over-stating the Arab State: Politics and Society in the Middle East* (London: I.B.Tauris, 1995), 100.

14. Maxime Rodinson, *Islam and Capitalism* (London: Allen Lane, 1974).

15. Hamied Ansari, *Egypt, the Stalled Society* (Albany: State University of New York Press, 1986); Leonard Binder, *In a Moment of Enthusiasm: Political Power and the Second Stratum in Egypt* (Chicago; London: University of Chicago Press, 1978).

16. Iliya Harik, *The Political Mobilization of Peasants: A Study of an Egyptian Community* (Bloomington; London: Indiana University Press, 1974).

17. Carrie Rosefsky Wickham, *Mobilizing Islam: Religion, Activism, and Political Change in Egypt* (New York: Columbia University Press, 2002); Diane Singerman, *Avenues of Participation: Family, Politics, and Networks in Urban Quarters of Cairo* (Englewood Cliffs, NJ: 1996).

18. Maye Kassem, *Egyptian Politics: The Dynamics of Authoritarian Rule* (Boulder, CO: Lynne Rienner Publishers, 2004); Eberhard Kienle, *A Grand Delusion: Democracy and Economic Reform in Egypt* (London: I.B.Tauris, 2001).

19. Mann, *The Sources of Social Power.*

20. Clement M. Henry and Robert Springborg, *Globalization and the Politics of Development in the Middle East* (Cambridge: Cambridge University Press, 2001).

21. Holger Albrecht, 'How can opposition support authoritarianism? Lessons from Egypt,' *Democratization* 12, no. 3 (June 2005): 378–397; See also, on this latter point, Noha El-Mikawy, *The Building of Consensus in Egypt's Transition Process* (Cairo: American University in Cairo Press, 1999).

22. Albrecht, 'How can opposition support authoritarianism? Lessons from Egypt,' 390.

23. Ervand Abrahamian, 'The causes of the constitutional revolution in Iran,' *International Journal of Middle East Studies* 10, no. 3 (August 1979): 386.

24. Tom Nairn, *The Break-up of Britain: Crisis and Neo-Nationalism* (London: NLB, 1977), 340.

25. For a discussion of the multi-valent nature of 'jihad' see Paul L. Heck, 'Jihad revisited,' *Journal of Religious Ethics* 32, no. 1 (3, 2004): 95–128; Sherman A. Jackson, 'Jihad and the modern word,' *Journal of Islamic Law and Culture* (Spring/Summer 2002); For reflections on Islam as a challenge, as well as support, to the socioplitical order see Joel Beinin, 'Political Islam and the new global economy: the political economy of an Egyptian social movement,' *CR: The New Centennial Review* 5, no. 1 (Spring 2005): 111–139.

26. Ghali Shukri, *Egypt: Portrait of a President, 1971–1981; the Counter-Revolution in Egypt; Sadat's Road to Jerusalem*, Middle East Series (London: Zed Books, 1981).

27. Jacques Berque, *Egypt, Imperialism and Revolution* (London: Faber, 1972).

28. Rudolph Peters, *Jihad in Classical and Modern Islam: A Reader* (Princeton, NJ: Markus Wiener Publishers, 2005), 59.

29. Albert H. Hourani, *Arabic Thought in the Liberal Age, 1798–1939* (London; New York: Oxford University Press, 1962).

30. Berque, *Egypt, Imperialism and Revolution*.

31. Hourani, *Arabic Thought in the Liberal Age, 1798–1939*, 202.

32. Muhammad Muhammad Husayn, *al-Ittijahat al-Wataniyya fi al-'dab al-Mu'asir: min al-Thawra al-'Urabiyya ila Qiyam al-Harb al-'Alamiyya al-Ula {Patriotic Tendencies in Contemporary Literature: From the Urabi Revolution until World War One}*, vol. 1, 2nd ed. (Cairo: Maktabat al-Adab, 1962).

33. Panaylotis J. Vatikiotis, *The History of Modern Egypt: From Muhammad Ali to Mubarak*, vol. 4 (London: Weidenfeld and Nicolson, 1991), 205.

34. Ibid.

35. Tariq al-Bishri *al-Haraka al-Siyasiyya fi Misr 1945–1953 {The Political Movement in Egypt, 1945–1953}*, 2nd ed. (Cairo: Dar al-Shuruq, 2002).

36. For a detailed examination of the early development of Arabism in the press, see James P. Jankowski and Israel Gershoni, *Redefining the Egyptian Nation, 1930–1945* (Cambridge: Cambridge University Press, 1995).

37. Abdallah Laroui, *The Crisis of the Arab Intellectual: Traditionalism or Historicism?* (Berkeley; London: University of California Press, 1976), 118.

38. This urban middle class was distinguished from the ruling elite, the *bashawiyya*. See James P. Jankowski and Israel Gershoni, *Egypt, Islam, and the Arabs: The Search for Egyptian Nationhood, 1900–1930* (New York: Oxford University Press, 1986); Michael Eppel, 'Note about the term effendiyya in the history of the Middle East,' *International Journal of Middle East Studies* 41 (2009): 535–539.

39. Adnan Musallam, *From Secularism to Jihad: Sayyid Qutb and the Foundations of Radical Islamism* (Wesport, CT; London: Praeger, 2005).

40. The Suez War secured for Nasser the allegiance of the masses and remaining political opposition (the left). The nationalisation of the Canal itself as well as the subsequent sequestrations of property concentrated decisive economic power in the regime's hands.

41. John Waterbury, *The Egypt of Nasser and Sadat: The Political Economy of Two Regimes* (Guildford, CT: Princeton University Press, 1983); Ghassan Salamé, *Democracy without Democrats?: The Renewal of Politics in the Muslim World* (London: I.B.Tauris, 1994).

42. Anouar Abdel-Malek, *Egypt: Military Society: The Army Regime, the Left, and Social Change under Nasser*, 1st ed. (New York: Random House, 1968).

43. For a discussion of the split see Barbara Zollner, *The Muslim Brotherhood: Hasan al-Hudaybi and Ideology*, 1st ed. (New York: Routledge, 2008).

44. Ellis Goldberg, 'Smashing idols and the state: The Protestant ethic and Egyptian Sunni radicalism,' *Comparative Studies in Society and History* 33, no. 1 (1991): 3–35.

45. Gilles Kepel, *The Prophet and Pharaoh: Muslim Extremism in Contemporary Egypt* (London: Al Saqi Books, 1985).

46. Husam Tammam, *Tahawulat al-Ikhwan al-Muslimun: Tafakkuk al-Idiyulujiya wa-Nihayat al-Tanzim {Transformations of the Muslim Brotherhood: Fragmentation of Ideology and the End of the Organisation}* (Cairo: Maktabat Madbuli, 2006).

47. Kepel, *The Prophet and Pharaoh.*

48. Khalil al-Anani, *al-Ikhwan al-Muslimun fi Misr: Shaykhukha Turasi' al-Zaman {The Muslim Brotherhood in Egypt: Gerontocracy against Time}* (Cairo: Dar al-Shuruq al-Dawaliya, 2007).

49. Ibid.

50. Ray Bush, 'Facing structural adjustment: Strategies of peasants, the state and the international financial institutions,' in *Directions of Change in Rural Egypt*, ed. Nicholas Hopkins and Kirsten Westergaard (Cairo: American University in Cairo Press, 1998); Nicholas Hopkins, 'Sufi organization in rural Asyut: The Rifa'iyya in Musha,' in *Upper Egypt: Identity and Change*, ed. Reem Saad and Nicholas Hopkins (Cairo; New York: American University in Cairo Press, 2004); Mamoun Fandy, 'Egypt's Islamic group: Regional revenge?,' *Middle East Journal* 48, no. 4 (Autumn 1994): 607–25.

51. See Ewan Stein, 'What does the Gama'a Islamiyya want now?' *Middle East Report* 254 (Spring 2010).

52. In an interview with the author in August 2009 Nagih Ibrahim, one of the leaders and chief ideologue of the Islamic Group remarked that, in his view, an Islamic party could never take power in Egypt as the United States, Israel and Europe would simply intervene to remove it. See Ibid.

53. Ann Mosely Lesch, 'Egyptian-Israeli relations: normalization or special ties?,' in *Israel, Egypt, and the Palestinians: From Camp David to Intifada*, ed. Ann Mosely Lesch and Mark Tessler (Bloomington, IN: Indiana University Press, 1989), 61.

Chapter 2

1. Edward Hallet Carr, *The Twenty Years' Crisis, 1919–1939: An Introduction to the Study of International Relations*, ed. Michael Cox, vol. 2 (Basingstoke: Palgrave, 2001), 67.

2. Abd al-Azim Ramadan, *al-'Alaqat al-Misriyya al-Isra'iliyya: 1948–1979 {Egyptian-Israeli Relations: 1948–1979}* (Cairo: al-Hay'a al-Misriya al-'Ama lil-Kitab, 1991), 17.

3. Patrick Seale, *The Struggle for Syria: A Study of Post-War Arab Politics, 1945–1958* (London; New York: Oxford University Press, 1965), 19.

4. Michael Doran, *Pan-Arabism before Nasser: Egyptian Power Politics and the Palestine Question* (New York; Oxford: Oxford University Press, 1999).

5. In the late 1920s, Harb visited numerous places in Syria with a view to establishing branches of the bank, including in Jaffa to pursue the establishment of a joint Egyptian-Palestinian bank. Awatif Abd al-Rahman, *Misr wa-Filistin {Egypt and Palestine}* (Kuwait: Alim al-Ma'rifa, 1980), 88.

6. Ramadan, *al-'Alaqat al-Misriyya al-Isra'iliyya: 1948–1979 {Egyptian-Israeli Relations: 1948–1979}*, 11.

7. Ibid.

8. Gudrun Krämer, *The Jews in Modern Egypt, 1914–1952* (London: I.B.Tauris, 1989); But for a discussion of earlier apprehensions about Zionism, including from Rashid Rida, see Hilmi Namnam, *al-Tarikh al-Majhul: al-Mufakkirin al-'Arab wa-al-Sihyuniyya wa Filastin {Unknown History: Arab Thinkers, Zionism and Palestine}* (Cairo: Ru'ya li-al-nashr wa-al-tawzi', 2007).

9. Although Jews were disproportionately represented among Egypt's business elite, Joel Beinin has pointed out, they remained a small minority among the bourgeoisie as a whole and were generally not Zionist. Their 'distorting' influence should thus not be overstated. *The Dispersion of Egyptian Jewry: Culture, Politics, and the Formation of a Modern Diaspora* (Cairo: American University in Cairo Press, 2005), chap. 9.

10. Bishri, *al-Haraka al-Siyasiyya fi Misr 1945–1953 {The Political Movement in Egypt, 1945–1953}*, 316.

11. Abd al-Rahman, *Misr wa-Filistin {Egypt and Palestine}*, 117.

12. For a relevant discussion of how popular concerns influenced the ideas of one elite intellectual, see Israel Gershoni, 'Haykal's recantation of positivism,' in *Middle Eastern Politics and Ideas: A History from Within*, ed. Moshe Maoz and Ilan Pappé (London: I.B.Tauris, 1997), 236.

13. Muhammad Hassanein Haykal, *Sphinx and Commissar: The Rise and Fall of Soviet Influence in the Arab World* (London: Collins, 1978); this interpretation was not unique to the Islamic movement and was elaborated in the West soon after the Russian revolution. Winston Churchill wrote in the early 1920s of the competition between communism and Zionism for the 'Jewish soul' and argued strongly in favour of Zionism as a way of discouraging Jews from becoming communists. Winston S. Churchill, 'Zionism versus Bolshevism: a struggle for the soul of the Jewish people,' *Illustrated Sunday Herald*, February 8, 1920.

14. Richard P. Mitchell, *The Society of the Muslim Brothers* (New York: Oxford University Press, 1993), 56.

15. Ramadan, *al-'Alaqat al-Misriyya al-Isra'iliyya: 1948–1979 {Egyptian-Israeli Relations: 1948–1979}*, 18.

16. Abd al-Fattah El-Awaisi, *The Muslim Brothers and the Palestine Question, 1928–1947* (London: I.B.Tauris, 1996), 242 (My emphasis).

17. Ibid., 243.

18. Mitchell, *The Society of the Muslim Brothers*, 221.

19. Suha Taji-Farouki, 'Thinking on the Jews,' in *Islamic Thought in the Twentieth Century* (London: I.B.Tauris, 2004), 324.

20. Isra'iliyat had long been considered of dubious reliability, even though 'early Muslims were not discouraged from turning to Jewish (and Christian) sources in order to learn their traditions and legends about the biblical motifs and stories found in the Qur'an.' By the ninth century though, 'disapproval ... was based on the view that the Israelite Tales were traditions that had been distorted by Jews because of their jealousy of the power and political hegemony of the Muslims.' Reuven Firestone, *Journeys in Holy Lands: The Evolution of the Abraham-Ishmael Legends in Islamic Exegesis* (Albany, NY: State University of New York Press, 1990), 13.

21. For a discussion of Rida's views on the deleterious role of Jews see Muhammad Imara, *Fi Fiqh al-Sira' 'ala al-Quds wa Filastin {On the Jurisprudence of the Conflict over Jerusalem and Palestine}* (Cairo: Dar al-Shuruq, 2005); Namnam, *al-Tarikh al-Majhul al-Mufakkirin al-'Arab wa-al-Sihyuniyya wa Filastin {Unknown History: Arab Thinkers, Zionism and Palestine}*; and Gilbert Achcar, *The Arabs and the Holocaust: The Arab-Israeli War of Narratives* (London: Saqi Books, 2010), 110–118.

22. Taji-Farouki, 'Thinking on the Jews,' 325.

23. Ronald L. Nettler, *Past Trials and Present Tribulations: A Muslim Fundamentalist's View of the Jews* (Oxford: Published for the Vidal Sassoon International Center for the Study of Antisemitism, the Hebrew University of Jerusalem by Pergamon, 1987), 49.

24. Ibid.

25. Abd al-Rahman, *Misr wa Filastin {Egypt and Palestine}*, 70.

26. Brynjar Lia, *The Society of the Muslim Brothers in Egypt: The Rise of an Islamic Mass Movement 1928–1942* (Reading: Garnet, 1998), 235.

27. Walid Mahmoud Abdelnasser, *The Islamic Movement in Egypt: Perceptions of International Relations, 1967–81* (London: Kegan Paul International, 1994), 41–42.

28. Ghada Hashem Talhami, *Palestine and Egyptian National Identity* (New York; London: Praeger, 1992), 14.

29. Beinin, *The Dispersion of Egyptian Jewry*.

30. Abdel-Malek, *Egypt: Military Society*, 35.

31. Lia, *The Society of the Muslim Brothers in Egypt: The Rise of an Islamic Mass Movement 1928–1942*, 244.

32. Ibid.

33. Carr, *The Twenty Years' Crisis, 1919–1939: An Introduction to the Study of International Relations*, 2:129.

34. Quoted in Guiseppe Fiori, *Antonio Gramsci: Life of a Revolutionary* (London: New Left Books, 1970), 105.

35. Abdelnasser, *The Islamic Movement in Egypt: Perceptions of International Relations, 1967–81*, 53.

36. El-Awaisi, *The Muslim Brothers and the Palestine Question, 1928–1947*, 243.

37. Bishri, *al-Haraka al-Siyasiyya fi Misr 1945–1953 {The Political Movement in Egypt, 1945–1953}*, 49.

38. Quoted in Fouad Ajami, *The Arab Predicament: Arab Political Thought and Practice since 1967* (Cambridge: Cambridge University Press, 1992), 61.

39. Eric Hobsbawm, *Age of Extremes: The Short Twentieth Century, 1914–91* (London: Abacus, 1995), 172.

40. Gilles Perrault, *A Man Apart: The Life of Henri Curiel* (London: Zed Books, 1987).

41. Ibid.

42. Gilles Perrault, 'Henri Curiel, citizen of the Third World,' *Le Monde Diplomatique*, April 1998.

43. Rifa'at El-Sa'id and Tareq Y. Ismael, *The Communist Movement in Egypt: 1920–1988* (Syracuse; London: Syracuse University Press, 1990), 43.

44. Roel Meijer, *The Quest for Modernity: Secular Liberal and Left-Wing Political Thought in Egypt, 1945–1958* (London: Routledge Curzon, 2002), 76.

45. Joel Beinin, *Was the Red Flag Flying There?: Marxist Politics and the Arab-Israeli Conflict in Egypt and Israel,1948–1965* (London: I.B.Tauris, 1990), 2.

46. Hana Batatu, *The Old Social Classes and the Revolutionary Movements of Iraq: A Study of Iraq's Old Landed and Commercial Classes and of Its Communists, Ba'thists and Free Officers*, Reprinted edition. (Princeton, NJ: Princeton University Press, 1992), 821.

47. El-Sa'id and Ismael Tareq, *The Communist Movement in Egypt: 1920–1988*, 98.

48. Ibid.

49. El-Sa'id and Ismael, *The Communist Movement in Egypt: 1920–1988*, 98.

50. Batatu, *The Old Social Classes and the Revolutionary Movements of Iraq*.

51. Haykal, *Sphinx and Commissar: The Rise and Fall of Soviet Influence in the Arab World*, 49.

52. Beinin, *Was the Red Flag Flying There?*, 24.

53. Selma Botman, *The Rise of Egyptian Communism, 1939–1970* (Syracuse, NY: Syracuse University Press, 1988), 89.

54. Shukri, *Egypt: Portrait of a President, 1971–1981; the Counter-Revolution in Egypt; Sadat's Road to Jerusalem*, 178.

55. Kepel, *The Prophet and Pharaoh*, 41.

56. Musallam, *From Secularism to Jihad*, 139.

57. Hala Mustafa, *al-Nizam al-Siyasi wa-al-Mu'arada al-Islamiyya fi Misr {The Political System and the Islamic Opposition in Egypt}* (Cairo: Markaz al-Mahrusah lil-Nashr wa-al-Khidmat al-Suhufiyah, 1995), 132.

58. Gamal Abdel Nasser, Speech 29 April 1954 (Nasser Institute and Bibliotheca Alexandrina, [accessed 10 October 2007]); available from http://nasser. bibalex.org/Data/GR09_1/Speeches/1954/540429_1.htm. [In Arabic]

59. Hassan Hanafi, *al-Din wa-al-Thawra fi Misr, 1952–1981 {Religion and Revolution in Egypt: 1952–1981}* (Cairo: Maktabat Madbuli, 1989).

60. Kirk Beattie, *Egypt during the Nasser Years: Ideology, Politics and Civil Society* (Boulder, C.O.; Oxford: Westview Press, 1994).

61. The US was also not above taking sides in the Nasser-Nagib power struggle, favouring Nasser over the more democratically-inclined Nagib as the least likely to allow communism to take hold in Egypt. Ibid., 58–59.

62. Fayez A. Sayegh, *The Dynamics of Neutralism in the Arab World: A Symposium* (San Francisco: Chandler, 1964), 195.

63. Eran Lerman, 'A revolution prefigured: foreign policy orientations in the postwar years,' in *Egypt from Monarchy to Republic: A Reassessment of Revolution and Change*, ed. Shimon Shamir (Boulder, CO; Oxford: Westview Press, 1995), 284.

64. Seale, *The Struggle for Syria*, 102.

65. Perrault, *A Man Apart*, 188.

66. Talhami, *Palestine and Egyptian National Identity*, 66.

67. Ibid., 105.

68. Perrault, *A Man Apart*, 118.

69. Panayiotis J. Vatikiotis, *Nasser and His Generation* (London: Croom Helm, 1978), 250.

70. Ibid.

71. Ibid., 249.

72. Laura M. James, *Nasser at War: Arab Images of the Enemy* (Basingstoke; New York: Palgrave Macmillan, 2006), 7.

73. Avi Shlaim, *The Iron Wall: Israel and the Arab World* (New York: W.W. Norton, 2000), 78.

74. Ibid., 111.

75. Ibid., 118.

76. Mitchell, *The Society of the Muslim Brothers*, 108.

77. Richard H. Dekmejian, *Egypt under Nasir; A Study in Political Dynamics* (Albany, NY: State University of New York Press, 1971), 38.

78. Kirk Beattie, *Egypt During the Sadat Years* (New York and Basingstoke: Palgrave, 2000), 104.

79. James, *Nasser at War*, 13.

80. Ibid., 14.

81. George M. Kahin, *The Asian-African Conference, Bandung, Indonesia* (Ithaca, NY: Cornell University Press, 1956), 82.

82. Beinin, *Was the Red Flag Flying There?*, 153.

83. For some discussion of this, see Fred Halliday, *The Middle East in International Relations: Power, Politics and Ideology* (Cambridge: Cambridge University Press, 2005).

Chapter 3

1. Gamal Abdel Nasser, *The Charter: Draft of the National Charter Presented...at the Inaugural Session of the National Congress of Popular Powers on the Evening of 21st May 1962* (Cairo, 1962), 41.

2. Harik, *The Political Mobilization of Peasants,* 68.

3. Hedley Bull, 'The emergence of a universal international society,' in *The Expansion of International Society*, ed. Hedley Bull and Adam Watson (Oxford: Oxford University Press, 1984), 224.

4. Gamal Abdel Nasser, 'Speech to the Popular Congress in Jumhuriyya Square' (Cairo, July 22, 1955).

5. Abdel-Malek, *Egypt: Military Society*, 230.

6. Sayegh, *The Dynamics of Neutralism in the Arab World*, 200.

7. El-Sa'id and Ismael, *The Communist Movement in Egypt*, 108.

8. The contradiction here is that after the 'thaw' the Soviets came to view Pan-Arabism as a constructive liberating force, despite the dubious class basis of that ideology too.

9. Karen Dawisha, *Soviet Foreign Policy towards Egypt* (New York: St. Martin's Press, 1979), 151.

10. Yitzhak Shichor, *The Middle East in China's Foreign Policy, 1949–1977* (Cambridge; New York: Cambridge University Press, 1979).

11. Dekmejian, *Egypt under Nasir*, 211.

12. El-Sa'id and Ismael, *The Communist Movement in Egypt*, 84.

13. Mahmud Amin al-Alim, *I'tirafat Shaykh al-Shuyu'iyin al-'Arab: Mahmud Amin al-'Alim {Confessions of the Shaykh of the Arab Communists: Mahmoud Amin al-Alim}* (Cairo: Maktabat Madbuli, 2006), 29.

14. Robert Tignor, 'Foreign capital, foreign communities, and the Egyptian Revolution of 1952,' in *Egypt from Monarchy to Republic: A Reassessment of Revolution and Change*, ed. Shimon Shamir (Boulder, CO; Oxford: Westview Press, 1995); Waterbury, *The Egypt of Nasser and Sadat: The Political Economy of Two Regimes*.

15. Beinin, *Was the Red Flag Flying There?*, 178.

16. Alim, *I'tirafat Shaykh al-Shuyu'iyin al-'Arab: Mahmud Amin al-'Alim {Confessions of the Shaykh of the Arab Communists: Mahmoud Amin al-Alim}*, 29.

17. Beinin, *Was the Red Flag Flying There?*, 170.

18. M. M. Badawi, 'Islam in modern Egyptian literature,' *Journal of Arabic Literature* 2 (1971): 154–177.

19. Fathi Radwan, *Hadha al-Sharq al-'Arabi {This Arab East}* (Cairo: Dar al-Ma'arif, 1957), 147.

20. Ibid., 151.

21. For a discussion of Tahtawi as a cosmopolitan thinker, see Hourani, *Arabic Thought in the Liberal Age, 1798–1939*.

22. el Kosheri Mahfouz, *Socialisme et Pouvoir en Égypte {Socialism and Power in Egypt}* (Paris: Librairie générale de droit et de jurisprudence, 1972), 87.

23. Muhammad Hassanein Haykal, *Nasser – the Cairo Documents* (London: New English Library, 1972), 187.

24. Rami Ginat, *Egypt's Incomplete Revolution: Lutfi Al-Khuli and Nasser's Socialism in the 1960s* (London: Frank Cass, 1997), 84. Also Malcolm H. Kerr, *The Arab Cold War, 1958–1964; a Study of Ideology in Politics* (London and New York: Oxford University Press, 1965), 38.

25. Nasser, *The Charter: Draft of the National Charter Presented... at the Inaugural Session of the National Congress of Popular Powers on the Evening of 21st May 1962*.

26. Ibid., 78.

27. Nasser, *The Charter: Draft of the National Charter Presented... at the Inaugural Session of the National Congress of Popular Powers on the Evening of 21st May 1962*, 136; See also Adeed Dawisha, *Egypt in the Arab World: The Elements of Foreign Policy* (London: Macmillan, 1976), 35.

28. Nasser, *The Charter: Draft of the National Charter Presented... at the Inaugural Session of the National Congress of Popular Powers on the Evening of 21st May 1962*, 114–115.

29. Yazid Sayigh, *Armed Struggle and the Search for State: The Palestinian National Movement, 1949–1993* (Oxford: Oxford University Press, 1999), 61.

30. Gamal Abdel Nasser, 'Speech During Visit to Gaza, 13 May 1956' (Nasser Institute and Bibliotheca Alexandrina, [accessed 10 October 2007]);

available from http://nasser.bibalex.org/Data/GR09_1/Speeches/1956/5605
13.htm.

31. Sayigh, *Armed Struggle and the Search for State*, 75.

32. Ibid., 73.

33. Ibid., 89.

34. Cited in Abd al-Fattah El-Awaisi, 'The conceptual approach of the Egyptian
Muslim brothers towards the Palestine question, 1928–1949,' *Journal of
Islamic Studies* 2, no. 2 (1991): 231.

35. Patrick Seale, *Asad of Syria: The Struggle for the Middle East* (Berkeley:
University of California Press, 1989), 65.

36. Leonard Binder, *The Ideological Revolution in the Middle East* (New York;
London: Wiley, 1964), 240.

37. Avraham Sela, 'Abd al-Nasser's regional politics: a reassessment,' in *Rethinking
Nasserism: Revolution and Historical Memory in Modern Egypt*, ed. Elie Podeh
and Onn Winckler (Gainesville, FL; London: University Press of Florida:
Eurospan, 2004), 185.

38. The Ba'th at this time were, contrary to many accounts, far more inclined
toward Marxism than fascism. For a penetrating discussion of this issue, see
Achcar, *The Arabs and the Holocaust*, 68–77.

39. Michel Aflaq, *Choice of Texts from the Ba'th Party Founder's Thought* (Florence:
Cooperativa Lavoratori (Arab Ba'th Socialist Party), 1977), 108.

40. Kepel, *The Prophet and Pharaoh*, 30.

41. Ali Ashmawi, *al-Tarikh al-Sirri li-Jama'at al-Ikhwan al-Muslimin:
Mudhakkirat 'Ali 'Ashmawi Akhir Qadat al-Tanzim al-Sirri {The Secret History
of the Muslim Brotherhood: Recollections of Ali Ashmawi, the Last Leader of the
Secret Organisation}* (Cairo: Dar al-Hilal, 1993).

42. Volume one was first published in 1954, with a second volume in 1956. A
second edition of volume one appeared in 1963. Volume two was reissued in
2004.

43. Safar Hawali, 'Ba'd al-Kutub alati Taruddu 'ala al-Afkar al-Hadima' [Some
books that refute destructive ideas],' http://www.alhawali.com/index.
cfm?method=home.SubContent&ContentID=2128#Alam1001131. (accessed
24 June 2010).

44. Muhammad Muhammad Husayn, *al-Ittijahat al-Wataniyya fi al-'Adab al-
Mu'asir: min al-Thawra al-'Urabiyya ila Qiyam al-Harb al-'Alamiyya al-Ula
ila Qiyam al-Jami'a al-'Arabiyya {Patriotic Tendencies in Contemporary Literature:
From WW1 until the Arab League}*, vol. 2, 2nd ed. (Cairo: Maktabat al-Adab,
1956), 133.

45. Alim, *I'tirafat Shaykh al-Shuyuyi'yin al-Arab: Mahmud Amin al-Alim
{Confessions of the Shaykh of the Arab Communists: Mahmoud Amin al-Alim}*.

46. Hanafi, *al-Din wa-al-Thawra fi Misr, 1952–1981 {Religion and Revolution in Egypt: 1952–1981}*, 104.

47. Muhammad Hasanayn Haykal, 'bi al-saraha [To be frank],' *al-Ahram* (Cairo, September 10, 1959).

48. Beattie, *Egypt during the Nasser Years*.

49. Dekmejian, *Egypt under Nasir*, 233.

50. Mustafa, *al-Nizam al-Siyasi wa-al-Mu'aradah al-Islamiyah fi Misr {The Political System and the Islamic Opposition in Egypt}*.

51. Mahfouz, *Socialisme et Pouvoir en Égypte {Socialism and Power in Egypt}*.

52. Rami Ginat, *Syria and the Doctrine of Arab Neutralism: From Independence to Dependence* (Portland, OR: Sussex Academic Press, 2005), 211.

53. Mahfouz, *Socialisme et Pouvoir en Égypte {Socialism and Power in Egypt}*.

54. Ibid., 103.

55. Ibid., 122.

56. Muhammad Jalal Kishk, *al-Marksiyya wa-al-Ghazw al-Fikri {Marxism and the Intellectual Invasion}* (Cairo: al-Dar al-Qawmiyah lil-Taba'ah wa-al-Nashr, 1966), 16.

57. Ibid., 50.

58. Ibid., 99.

59. Kepel, *The Prophet and Pharaoh*, 42; Musallam, *From Secularism to Jihad*, 168.

60. A. Chris Eccel, "Alim and Mujahid in Egypt: orthodoxy versus subculture, or division of labour?" *The Muslim World* 78 (1988): 203.

61. Ashmawi, *al-Tarikh al-Sirri li-Jama'at al-Ikhwan al-Muslimin: Mudhakkirat 'Ali 'Ashmawi Akhir Qadat al-Tanzim al-Sirri {The Secret History of the Muslim Brotherhood: Recollections of Ali Ashmawi, the Last Leader of the Secret Organisation}*, 77.

62. Ibid., 80.

63. Ibid., 85.

64. Ibid., 87.

65. Ibid.

66. Ibid.

67. Ibid., 89.

68. Ibid.

69. Ibid., 93.

70. Sayyid Qutb, *Limadha a'damuni? {Why Did they Execute Me?}* (Jeddah: al-Sharikat al-Saudiyah lil-Abhath wa al-Taswiq, 198), 17.

71. Ibid., 18.

72. Ibid., 28.

73. Sayyid Qutb, *Milestones* (Indianapolis, IN: American Trust, 1990).

74. Charles Tripp, *A History of Iraq* (Cambridge; New York: Cambridge University Press, 2002), 179.

75. Abdel-Malek, *Egypt: Military Society*, 148.

76. Raymond William Baker, *Sadat and After: Struggles for Egypt's Political Soul* (London: I.B.Tauris, 1990).

77. Malcolm H. Kerr, *The Arab Cold War: Gamal 'Abd Al-Nasir and His Rivals, 1958–1970*, 3rd ed. (London: Published for the Royal Institute of International Affairs by Oxford University Press, 1971), 24.

78. Sela, 'Abd al-Nasser's regional politics: a reassessment,' 188.

79. Abd al-Rahman al-Bazzaz, 'al-Dawla al-muwahhada wa-al-dawla al-ittihadiyya [The unitary state and the federal state],' in *Political and Social Thought in the Contemporary Middle East*, ed. Kemal H. Karpat (London: Pall Mall Press, 1968), 257.

80. Nissim Rejwan, *Nasserist Ideology: Its Exponents and Critics* (New York: Wiley, 1974), 131.

81. Ibid., 77.

82. Dawisha, *Egypt in the Arab World*.

83. Rami Ginat, *Egypt's Incomplete Revolution: Lutfi al-Khuli and Nasser's Socialism in the 1960s*, 85.

84. Shlaim, *The Iron Wall*, 230.

85. Sayigh, *Armed Struggle and the Search for State*, 32.

86. Muhammad Hasanayn Haykal, 'bi al-saraha [To be frank],' *al-Ahram* (Cairo, September 18, 1964).

87. Vatikiotis, *Nasser and His Generation*, 254.

88. Muhammad Hasanayn Haykal, 'bi al-saraha [To be frank],' *al-Ahram* (Cairo, January 1963).

89. Ibid.

90. The term '*isra'iliyat*', as has been previously discussed, has Islamic resonance, referring to distortions introduced into *hadith* and jurisprudence by Jews. Baha al-Din does not explain his choice of title in the book, so it is unclear whether it was intended to be perceived as such. It could also have the meaning of 'stories about Israel' or 'facts/anecdotes about Israel'.

91. Ahmad Baha al-Din, *Isra'iliyat* (Cairo: Dar al-Hilal, 1965), 7.

92. Ibid., 65.

93. Ibid., 91.

94. Ibid., 250.

95. Ibid., 7.

96. In the late 1990s, the Egyptian economist Galal Amin took issue with Baha al-Din's comparison, which the latter had restated after 1967 to explain the more recent defeat. For Amin, the implication that the Arabs were in

the same predicament they were in almost 170 years earlier played into the Israeli myth promoted after the Six-Day War, that the Arabs were, by nature, cowardly and unable to fight, and contributed to a more general Arab 'self-loathing' in the wake of the defeat. Galal A. Amin, *al-Muthaqqafun al-'Arab wa-Isra'il {Arab Intellectuals and Israel}* (Cairo: Dar al-Shuruq, 1998), 21–24.

97. Baha al-Din, *Isra'iliyat* 253.

98. Ibid., 256.

99. Ibid., 257.

100. Dekmejian, *Egypt under Nasir,* 238.

101. Ginat, *Egypt's Incomplete Revolution*, 86.

102. Ahmad Hamrush, 'al-Tariq ila Wahdat al-Quwwa al-Taqaddumiyya' [The road to the unity of progressive forces],' *Ruz al-Yusuf* (Cairo, March 14, 1966).

103. Ahmad Hamrush, 'Editorial,' *Ruz al-Yusuf* (Cairo, March 21, 1966).

104. Ahmad Hamrush, 'al-Hilf al-Islami [The Islamic pact],' *Ruz al-Yusuf* (Cairo, March 7, 1966).

105. Sayigh, *Armed Struggle and the Search for State*, 32.

106. Gamal Abdel Nasser, 'Speech to the Arab Socialist Union in Alexandria Stadium' (Alexandria, July 27, 1966).

107. Ibid.

108. See, for example, Barnett, *Dialogues in Arab Politics: Negotiations in Regional Order*, 155–159.

109. Kerr, *The Arab Cold War, 1958–1964: a Study of Ideology in Politics*, 126.

Chapter 4

1. Dawisha, *Egypt in the Arab World*.

2. Vatikiotis, *Nasser and His Generation*, 258.

3. Isma'il Sabri Abdullah, *al-Tali'a* (Cairo, July 1967), 24.

4. Ibrahim Sa'd al-Din, *al-Tali'a* (Cairo, July 1967), 39.

5. Lutfi al-Khuli, 'Editorial,' *al-Tali'a* (Cairo, August 1967).

6. Lutfi al-Khuli, 'Editorial,' *al-Tali'a* (Cairo, July 6).

7. Anwar Sadat, 'Speech to the university and higher institute professors at Cairo University,' *Anwar Sadat Chair for Peace and Development* (University of Maryland, January 8, 1971), http://www.bsos.umd.edu/SADAT/archives/speeches.htm (accessed 15 November 2007).

8. See Tareq Y. Ismael, *The Arab Left*, vol. 1 (Syracuse, NY: Syracuse University Press, 1976).

9. Sadiq Jalal Azm, *al-Naqd al-Dhati ba'd al-Hazima {Self Criticism after the Defeat}* (Beirut: Dar al-Tali'ah, 1969).

10. Sa'd al-Din Ibrahim was through the 1970s a staunch critic of Sadat's moves toward peace with Israel, but would through the 1980s evolve in a more liberal direction in which he recognised the achievements of Israel and the rights of its citizens to live in peace. He acknowledged his intellectual affinity with Sadiq al-Azm. (Interview with Sa'd al-Din Ibrahim, Cairo, August 2006.)

11. Sa'd al-Din Ibrahim, *Fi Susyulujiyat al-Sira' al-'Arabi al-Isra'ili {On the Sociology of the Arab-Israeli Conflict}* (Beirut: Dar al-Tali'ah, 1973), 80.

12. Ibid., 131.

13. Ibid.

14. Ibid., 274.

15. Azm, *al-Naqd al-Dhati ba'd al-Hazima {Self Criticism after the Defeat}.*

16. Baker, *Sadat and After: Struggles for Egypt's Political Soul*, 179–185.

17. According to his own recollections, Elmessiri's wariness towards the West had deeper roots. In his 'intellectual' autobiography, Elmessiri describes his disquiet about being a student in Alexandria in the 1950s, in particular towards the 'foreign' majority in the university. Elmessiri describes how learnt English so that he could mix in these circles even though he did not respect them on account of their detachment from the native population. See Abd al-Wahhab al-Masiri, *Rihlati Rihlati al-Fikriyya: fi Budhur wa-al-Judhur wa-al-Thamr: Sira Ghayr Dhatiyya Ghayr Mawdu'iyya {My Intellectual Journey: On Seeds, Roots and Fruits: A Subjective Non-Autobiography}*, 4th ed. (Cairo: Dar al-Shuruq, 2009), 131.

18. Sayigh, *Armed Struggle and the Search for State*, 197.

19. Ibid., 181.

20. Ibid., 252–257.

21. Ibid., 212.

22. Ibid., 250.

23. Ramadan, *al-'Alaqat al-Misriyya al-Isra'iliyya: 1948–1979 {Egyptian-Israeli Relations: 1948–1979}*, 54.

24. Anwar Sadat, 'Speech, October 7, 1970,' http://www.bsos.umd.edu/SADAT/archives/speeches.htm (accessed 15 November 2007).

25. H. Erlich, *Students and University in 20th Century Egyptian Politics* (London: Cass, 1989), 208.

26. Kepel, *The Prophet and Pharaoh.*

27. Mustafa Sa'dani, *'Adwa 'ala al-Sihyuniyya {Focus on Zionism}* (Cairo: al-Majlis al-A'la lil-Shu'un al-Islamiyah, 1969).

28. Azm, *al-Naqd al-Dhati ba'd al-Hazima {Self Criticism after the Defeat}.*

29. William Sulayman, *al-Tali'a* (Cairo, July 1967).

30. Baker, *Sadat and After*, 194.

31. Ajami, *The Arab Predicament*, 52.

32. Kishk, *al-Marksiyya wa-al-Ghazw al-Fikri {Marxism and the Intellectual Invasion}*, 6.
33. Ibid., 7.
34. Ibid., 8.
35. Ibid., 166.
36. Ibid., 164.
37. Ibid., 172.
38. Ibid., 197.
39. Ibid., 215.
40. Ibid., 220.
41. Ibid., 221.
42. Ibid., 161.
43. Ibid., 223.
44. He is not surprised that Marxists said this, but astonished that such views can find their way into print in Egypt.
45. Ibid., 230.
46. Yusuf Qaradawi, *al-Hall al-Islami: Farida wa Darura {The Islamic Solution: Obligation and Necessity}*, vol. 12 (Beirut: Mu'assasat al-Risalah, 1988).
47. Ibid., 33.
48. Ibid., 36–43.
49. Bassam Tibi, *Arab Nationalism: Between Islam and the Nation-State*, vol. 3 (New York: St. Martin's Press, 1996), 219.
50. Seale, *Asad of Syria*, 195.
51. Mustafa, *al-Nizam al-Siyasi wa-al-Mu'arada al-Islamiyya fi Misr {The Political System and the Islamic Opposition in Egypt}*, 148.
52. Ibid., 151.
53. Ibid., 153.
54. Ibid.
55. Ibid., 154.
56. Ibid., (emphasis added).
57. Ibid.
58. See Wa'il Uthman, *Asrar al-Haraka al-Tullabiyya {Secrets of the Student Movement}* (Cairo-al-Sharikat al-Misriyya li-l-tabb'a, 1976).
59. Interview with Sa'd al-Din Ibrahim, Cairo, August 2006.
60. Qustantin Zurayq, *Ma'na al-Nakba {The Meaning of the Catastrophe}*, 2nd ed. (Beirut: Dar al-'Ilm lil-Malayin, 1948).
61. Qustantin Zurayq, *Ma'na al-Nakba Mujadaddan {The Meaning of the Catastrophe Revisited}*, 1st ed. (Beirut: Dar al-'Ilm lil-Malayin, 1967).
62. Ibid., 29.
63. Ibid., 13.
64. Ibid., 84–88.

65. Ibid., 30.
66. Ibid., 65.
67. Ibid., 33.
68. Ibid., 20.
69. Ibid., 52–60.
70. Ibid., 19.
71. Ahmad Baha al-Din, *Iqtirah Dawlat Filastin wa ma Dara Hawlahu min Munaqishat {Proposal for the State of Palestine and the Dscussions Surrounding It}* (Beirut: Dar al-Adab, 1968).
72. Ibid., 19.
73. Ibid.
74. Ibid., 15.
75. Sasson Somech, 'I dream of the day when . . . ,' *Dissent* Winter (2004).
76. Raymond A. Hinnebusch, *Egyptian Politics under Sadat: The Post-Populist Development of an Authoritarian-Modernizing State* (Boulder, CO: Lynne Rienner Publishers, 1988), 117.
77. Somech, 'I dream of the day when . . .'
78. Ibid.

Chapter 5

1. Despite these departures, and though written at the height of Sadat's prestige in the wake of the October War, the Paper remained true to much of the Nasserist legacy. It is particularly striking the delicacy with which the Paper repudiates elements of the Nasser experience, such as the failure to complement social with political freedom. Also, in introducing new policy directions, the Paper frequently insists that nothing new is being said, often referring to the UAR Charter of 1961 to justify *infitah*, including its key dimension of opening up to foreign investment. Significantly, the chair of the Paper's drafting committee was Isma'il Sabri Abdullah, a Marxist, and the committee also contained the veteran leader of the Egyptian Communist Party Fu'ad Mursi. Kirk Beattie, *Egypt during the Sadat Years*, 140.
2. Anwar Sadat, *The October Working Paper* (Cairo: State Information Service, 1974), 10.
3. Ibid., 43.
4. Ibid., 52.
5. Ibid., 47.
6. Ibid., 23.
7. Ibid., 24.
8. Ibid., 54.

9. Mustafa, *al-Nizam al-Siyasi wa-al-Mu'aradah al-Islamiyah fi Misr {The Political System and the Islamic Opposition in Egypt}*.

10. Beattie, *Egypt during the Sadat Years*, 191.

11. Mustafa, *al-Nizam al-Siyasi wa-al-Mu'aradah al-Islamiyah fi Misr {The Political System and the Islamic Opposition in Egypt}*, 248.

12. Kepel, *The Prophet and Pharaoh*.

13. Egyptian migrant workers increased in number from about 10,000 in 1968 to 1.2 million in 1985. See Wickham, *Mobilizing Islam*.

14. Rafiq Habib, *l-Ihtijaj al-Dini wa-al-Sira' al-Tabaqi fi Misr {Religious Protest and Class Struggle in Egypt}*, vol. 1 (Cairo: Sina lil-Nashr, 1989).

15. Wickham, *Mobilizing Islam*, 22.

16. R.D. McLaurin, Don Peretz, and Lewis W. Snider, *Middle East Foreign Policy: Issues and Processes* (New York: Praeger, 1982), 48.

17. Islamist inroads in the GUES at al-Mansoura University in 1968 had prompted the regime to close the branch due to 'right-wing' elements.

18. Uthman, *Asrar al-Haraka al-Tullabiyya {Secrets of the Student Movement}*.

19. Wickham, *Mobilizing Islam*, 123.

20. Salwa al-Awa, *al-Gama'a al-Islamiyya al-Musalliha fi Misr: 1974–2004 {The Armed Islamic Group in Egypt: 1974–2004}* (Cairo: Maktabat al-Shuruq al-Dawaliya, 2006); Bayat, 'Revolution without movement, movement without revolution: comparing Islamic activism in Iran and Egypt.'

21. Hinnebusch, *Egyptian Politics under Sadat*, 114.

22. Sa'd al-Din Shazli, *Our Faith, Our Way to Victory* (Israel Information Centre, 1973).

23. Baker, *Sadat and After*, 247.

24. Ruth Roded, 'Bint al-Shati's Wives of the Prophet: feminist or feminine,' *British Journal of Middle Eastern Studies* 33, no. 1 (May 2006): 51–56.

25. Aisha Abd al-Rahman, *al-Isra'iliyat fi al-Ghazw al-Fikri {The Isra'iliyat in the Intellectual Invasion}* (Cairo: Ma'had al-Buhuth wa-al-Dirasat al-Arabiyah, 1975), 7.

26. Ali Jarisha, 'al-Ghazw al-fikri [The intellectual invasion],' *al-Da'wa* (Cairo, November 1976), 28.

27. Although for Kuhlah some of this third group did finance communist activities in the region such as the 'French *mutamassir* [Egyptianised] Jew' Henri Curiel, who bankrolled Egyptian communist activities.

28. Fu'ad Kuhlah, 'al-Marksiyya wa-al-Sihyuniyya wa Wahdat al-Judhur [Marxism and Zionism and their shared roots],' *al-Da'wa* (Cairo, April 1977).

29. Abd al-Mun'im Salim, 'Isra'il al-Hadir wa-al-Mustaqbal' [Israel: Present and future],' *al-Da'wa* (Cairo, November 1976).

30. Ibid., 44.

31. Abd al-Mun'im Salim, 'Isra'il al-Hadir wa-al-Mustaqbal: al-Salam 'an al-Tariqa al-Amrikiyya al-Yahudiyya [Israel present and future: Peace the American-Jewish way],' al-Da'wa (Cairo, January 1977), 57.

32. Ibid., 52.

33. Salim, 'Isra'il al-Hadir wa-al-Mustaqbal: [Israel: Present and future],' 52.

34. 'Isra'il al-Hadir wa-al-Mustaqbal: al-Salam 'an al-Tariqa al-Amrikiyya al-Yahudiyya [Israel present and future: Peace the American-Jewish way],'.

35. Salim, 'Isra'il al-Hadir wa-al-Mustaqbal: [Israel: Present and future],' 57.

36. Salim, Isra'il al-Hadir wa-al-Mustaqbal: al-Salam 'an al-Tariqa al-Amrikiyya al-Yahudiyya [Israel present and future: Peace the American-Jewish way],' 57.

37. Salih Ashmawi, al-Da'wa (Cairo, April 1977).

38. Ala' Zaydan, 'Qadiyat al-Masjid al-Aqsa Tazdat Khuturatan [The issue of the Aqsa Mosque gets more dangerous],' al-Da'wa (Cairo, August 1977).

39. Ronald L Nettler, 'Islam vs. Israel,' Commentary 78, no. 6 (1984): 28.

40. Ibid.

41. Baker, Sadat and After: Struggles for Egypt's Political Soul, 61.

42. El-Mikawy, The Building of Consensus in Egypt's Transition Process, 44.

43. Saad Eddin Ibrahim, 'Domestic developments in Egypt,' in The Middle East: Ten Years after Camp David, ed. William B. Quandt (Washington, D.C.: Brookings Institution Press, 1988), 53–54.

44. Baker, Sadat and After, 155.

45. Erlich, Students and University in 20th Century Egyptian Politics, 213.

46. Shukri, Egypt: Portrait of a President, 1971–1981; the Counter-Revolution in Egypt; Sadat's Road to Jerusalem, 390.

47. Beattie, Egypt during the Sadat Years.

48. Lutfi al-Khuli, Awraq min al-Milaff al-'Arabi: Mustaqbal al-Sira' al-'Arabi al-Isra'ili 'Am 2000 {Papers from the Arab File: The Future of the Arab Israeli Conflict in the Year 2000}, vol. 1 (Cairo: Dar al-Fikr, 1986), 91.

49. Ibid.

50. Ibid., 92.

51. Ibid., 67, 75.

52. Ibid., 78.

53. More recently, the Egyptian economist Galal Amin used a similar argument to blame violent Islamism, including an attack on Nagib Mahfuz, in Egypt on Israeli meddling. Amin, al-Muthaqqafun al-'Arab wa-Isra'il {Arab Intellectuals and Israel}.

54. al-Khuli, Awraq min al-milaff al-'arabi: Mustaqbal al-Sira' al-'Arabi al-Isra'ili 'Am 2000 {Papers from the Arab File: The Future of the Arab-Israeli Conflict in the Year 2000} 75.

55. Ibid., 60–62.

56. Ibid., 33.

57. Ibid., 64.

58. Muhammad Sid Ahmad, *After the Guns Fall Silent: Peace or Armageddon in the Middle-East* (New York: St. Martin's Press, 1976).

59. Ibid., 9.

60. Ibid., 10.

61. Ibid., 16.

62. Ibid., 25.

63. Ibid., 43.

64. Ibid., 73.

65. Ibid., 122.

66. Ibid., 118.

67. In particular, Naqash focussed on Abba Eban's 1947 translation of Tawfiq al-Hakim's *Yaumiyat Na'ib fi al-Aryaf (Maze of Justice)* and Sasson Somech's study of Nagib Mahfuz. Raja al-Naqqash, *al-Musawwar* (Cairo, December 28, 1973).

68. Mufid Shihab al-Din, al-Sayyid Yasin, and Yunan Labib Rizq, *al-Sihyuniyya wa al-'Unsuriyya al-Sihyuniyya ka Namt min Anmat al-Tafriqa al-'Unsuriyya {Zionism and Zionist Racism as a Form of Racial Discrimination}* (Cairo: Ma'had al-Buhuth wa-al-Dirasat al-'Arabiyya, 1977), 13.

69. Ibid., 15.

70. Ibid., 16.

71. Ibid., 20.

72. Ibid., 23.

73. Ibid., 24.

74. Elmessiri was, until his death in 2008, the leader of the Kifaya opposition movement in Egypt. His politics have evolved from the secular far left to what he himself described as a 'radical' Islamist position. In a discussion with the author, he suggested that one of his main contributions to Islamist discourse had been to introduce a more nuanced, scientific, perspective on Israel and Jews, due to his own background in the left. (Interview with Abdelwahab Elmessiri, Cairo, August 2006.)

75. Abdelwahab M. Elmessiri, *The Land of Promise: A Critique of Political Zionism* (New Brunswick, NJ: North American, 1977).

76. Abd al-Wahhab al-Masiri, *'Mawsu'at al-Mafahim wa-al-Mustalahat al-Sihyuni-yya: Ru'ya Naqdiyya' {Encyclopedia of Zionist Concepts and Terms: A Critical View}* (Cairo: Markaz al-Dirasat al-Siyasiyya wa-al-Istratijiyya bi-al-Ahram 1975), 13.

77. Ibid., 18.

78. Ibid., 20.

79. Ibid.

80. Ibid., 21.

81. Ibid.

82. Ibid., 22.

83. Al-Masiri, *Rihlati Rihlati al-Fikriyya: fi Budhur wa-al-Judhur wa-al-Thamr: Sira Ghayr Dhatiyya Ghayr Mawdu'iyya {My Intellectual Journey: On Seeds, Roots and Fruits: A Subjective Non-Autobiography}*, 178.

84. Usamah al-Ghazali Harb, *al-Istratijiyya al-Isra'iliyya wa-al-Muqawama fi al-'Ard al-Muhtalla' {Israeli Strategy and the Resistance in the Occupied Territory}* (Cairo: Markaz al-Dirasat al-Siyasiyah wa-al-Istirajiyah bi-al-Ahram, 1977), 148.

85. Ibid., 4.

86. Ibrahim A. Karawan, 'Identity and foreign policy: The case of Egypt,' in *Identity and Foreign Policy in the Middle East*, ed. Shibley Telhami and Michael Barnett (Ithaca: Cornell University Press, 2002), 155–169.

87. Fu'ad Zakariya, *'Abd al-Nasir wa-al-Yasar al-Misri {Abdel Nasser and the Egyptian Left}* (Cairo: Ruz al-Yusuf, 1977).

88. Ibrahim, 'Domestic developments in Egypt,' 26.

89. Ibid., 27.

90. Bianchi, *Unruly Corporatism*, 13.

91. Baker, *Sadat and After: Struggles for Egypt's Political Soul*, 31.

92. Ibid., 94.

93. Talhami, *Palestine and Egyptian National Identity*, 46.

94. Ihsan Abd al-Quddus, *Khawatir Siyasiyya {Political Dangers}*, vol. 1 (Cairo: Muntasir, 1979), 32–34.

95. Ibid., 57.

96. Ibid., 43.

97. Ibid., 55–57.

98. In his speech before the Knesset in November 1977, Sadat spoke of the psychological barrier constituting 'seventy percent of the problem.' Anwar el Sadat and Egypt State Information Service, *Speech by President Anwar El Sadat to the Knesset, 20th November 1977* (Cairo: State Information Service, 1977) 15.

99. Abd al-Quddus, *Khawatir Siyasiyya {Political Dangers}*, 85.

100. Ibid., 57.

101. Ibid., 57, 84.

102. Ibid., 134.

103. Ibid., 86.

104. Ibid., 152.

105. Ibid., 126–28.

106. Ibid., 133–35.

Chapter 6

1. Peter Kenyon, 'Israel's "cold" peace with Egypt, Jordan grows chillier,' *All Things Considered* (NPR, October 26, 2009), http://www.npr.org/templates/story/story.php?storyId=114170104 (accessed 6 February 2010).

2. Walid Mahmoud Abdelnasser, 'Islamic organizations in Egypt and the Iranian Revolution of 1979: the experience of the first few years,' *Arab Studies Quarterly* 19, no. 2 (Spring 1997).

3. Ibid., 142.

4. Denis Joseph Sullivan and Sana Abed-Kotob, *Islam in Contemporary Egypt: Civil Society vs. the State* (Boulder, CO: Lynne Rienner Publishers, 1999), 20; Fawaz A. Gerges, *The Far Enemy: Why Jihad Went Global* (New York: Cambridge University Press, 2005).

5. Ruhollah Khomeini, *Imam's Message*, vol. 14, 1981.

6. Ruhollah Khomeini, 'Imam Khomeini's Message to the pilgrims to the house of god in Mecca,' *Sahifa-yi Nur*, September 6, 1981.

7. Abdelnasser, 'Islamic organizations in Egypt and the Iranian Revolution of 1979: the experience of the first few years.'

8. Ibid.

9. Shahrough Akhavi, 'The impact of the Iranian revolution on Egypt,' In *The Iranian Revolution: Its Global Impact*, ed. John L. Esposito (Miami; Gainesville, FL: Florida International University Press), 149.

10. Ibid., 150.

11. Husni Mubarak, 'Speech of President Muhammad Husni Mubarak at the Joint Meeting of the People's and Shura Council,' October 3, 1982, http://www2.sis.gov.eg/Ar/Politics/PInstitution/President/Speeshes/000001/04010 10200000000000198.htm.

12. Ibid.

13. Ibrahim, 'Domestic developments in Egypt,' 32.

14. Anis Mansour. Quoted in Ibid., 19.

15. Albrecht, 'How can opposition support authoritarianism? Lessons from Egypt.'

16. Sullivan and Abed-Kotob, *Islam in Contemporary Egypt*, 58.

17. Ibrahim, 'Domestic developments in Egypt,' 33.

18. Awa, *al-Gama'a al-Islamiyya al-Musalliha fi Misr: 1974–2004 {The Armed Islamic Group in Egypt: 1974–2004}*.

19. Gerges, *The Far Enemy*; Kepel, *The Prophet and Pharaoh*; Johannes J. G. Jansen and Muhammad Abd al-Salam Faraj, *The Neglected Duty: The Creed of Sadat's Assassins and Islamic Resurgence in the Middle East* (New York: Macmillan, 1986).

20. El-Mikawy, *The Building of Consensus in Egypt's Transition Process*.

21. Ibrahim, 'Domestic developments in Egypt,' 44.

22. al-Jama'a al-Islamiyya bi-Misr, *Mithaq al-Amal al-Islami [Charter of Islamic Action}* (Minbar al-tawhid wa-al-jihad, 1984), 1.

23. Ibid., 55.

24. al-Jama'a al-Islamiyya bi-Misr, *Hatmiyat al-Muwajiha {The Inevitability of Confrontation}* (Minbar al-tawhid wa-al-jihad, 1987), 43.

25. The source here for the *Gama'a* is the book *al-Isra'iliyat fi al-Ghazw al-Fikri {Modalities of the Intellectual Invasion}* by the Saudi-based Brotherhood thinker Ali Garisha. Jama'a al-Islamiyya bi-Misr, *Hatmiyat al-Muwajiha {The Inevitability of Confrontation}*, 45 n.106.

26. Ibid., 52.

27. Ibid.

28. Montasser al-Zayyat, *The Road to al-Qaeda: The Story of Bin Laden's Right-Hand Man* (London; Sterling, VA: Pluto Press, 2004), 44.

29. Fawaz A. Gerges, 'The decline of revolutionary Islam in Algeria and Egypt,' *Survival* 41, no. 1 (Spring 1999): 113–25.

30. Zayyat, *The Road to al-Qaeda*, 71.

31. Ibid.

32. Ibid., 78.

33. Ayman Zawahiri, *In His Own Words: A Translation of the Writings of Dr. Ayman al-Zawahiri*, trans. Laura Mansfield (LULU, 2006), 211.

34. Ibid., 28.

35. Adel Husayn, *al-Jabha al-'Arabiyya al-Iraniyya did al-Hilf al-Amriki al-Sihyuni' {The Arab-Iranian Front against the American-Zionist Alliance}*, 1998.

36. Adel Husayn, *Ba'd Fashl al-Mufawadat ma'a Isra'il: Hal al-Harb Mumkin? Wa Kayf? {After the Failure of the Negotiations with Israel: Is War Possible? And How?}* (Kotobarabia, 2001), 41, www.kotobarabia.com.

37. Mona El-Ghobashy, 'The dynamics of Egypt's elections,' *Middle East Report Online*, September 29, 2010.

38. El-Mikawy, *The Building of Consensus in Egypt's Transition Process*, 44.

39. Maha Abdelrahman, 'With the Islamists? Sometimes… With the State? Never!: Cooperation between the Left and Islamists in Egypt,' *British Journal of Middle Eastern Studies* 36, no. 1 (April 2009).

40. Albrecht, 'How can opposition support authoritarianism? Lessons from Egypt.'

41. Ibrahim, 'Domestic developments in Egypt,' 47.

42. Abdelrahman, 'With the Islamists? Sometimes… With the state? Never!,' 45.

43. Tariq al-Bishri, *al-'Arab fi Muwajihat al-'Udwan {The Arabs Confronting Aggression}* (Cairo: Dar al-Shuruq, 2002).

44. al-Sayyid Yasin, *al-Ustura al-Sihyuniyya wa-al-Intifada al-Filastiniyya {The Zionist Myth and the Palestinian Intifada}* (Cairo: Mirit li-al-nashr wa-al-matbu'at, 2001), 10.

45. Ibid.

46. Ibid., 141.

47. Abd al-Qadir bin Abd al-Aziz, *Al-'Umda fi I'dad Al-'Udda {The Essentials of Making Ready for Jihad}*, 1988.

48. Abd al-Wahhab al-Masiri, *al-Sihyuniyya wa-al-Naziyya wa-Nihayat al-Tarikh {Zionism and Nazism and the End of History}*, 3rd ed. (Cairo: Dar al-Shuruq, 2001), 27.

49. Nazih Ayubi has defined Amin, along with Tariq al-Bishri and Adel Husayn as a 'cultural Islamist.' Ayubi, *Over-stating the Arab State*, 185.

50. Amin, *al-Muthaqqafun al-'Arab wa-Isra'il {Arab Intellectuals and Israel}*, 82.

51. Isam Aryan, 'Asl al-Qadiya [The Root of the Issue],' *al-Dustur*, November 3, 2008.

52. Isam Aryan, 'Fi Dhikrat al-Nakba al-Ula: Mas'uliyyat al-Hukam wa Mas'uliyyat al-Shu'ub' [On the first anniversary of the catastrophe: the responsibilities of rulers and the responsibilities of the people],' *al-Dustur*, May 11, 2009.

53. Al-Hayat. 'Murshid al-Ikhwan li-al-Hayat: laysa fi qamusina shay'un ismuha Isra'il [Guide of the Muslim Brotherhood: there is nothing called Israel in our dictionary], al-Hayat, October 18, 2007.

54. Ibid.

55. Usama Salih, 'Akef: we reject "Camp David" since its signing and the nuclear programme is a political smokecreen,' *al-Masry al-Youm*, November 12, 2007.

56. Ayman Nur, 'Hadatha fi Sitta Ayyam! [It happened in six days!],' *al-Dustur*, June 9, 2006.

57. Fahmi Huwaydi, 'al-Tatbi' wa Aful al-Haraka al-Wataniyya al-Misriyya [Normalisation and the demise of the Egyptian national movement],' *al-Shuruq al-Jadid*, September 29, 2009.

58. Salah al-Din Hafiz, *Karahiyya taht al-Jild: Isra'il 'Aqdat al-'Alaqat al-'Arabiyya al-Amrikiyya {Hatred under the Skin: Israel, The Complication in Arab-American Relations* (Cairo: Dar al-Shuruq, 2003), 271.

59. Ibid., 274.

60. Yusuf Qaradawi, *Fiqh al-Jihad: Dirasa Muqarana li-Ahkamihi wa-Falsafa-tihi fi Du' al-Qur'an wa-al-Sunna {The Jurisprudence Of Jihad: A Comparative Study of its Rules and Philosophy in the light of the Quran and the Sunna}* (Cairo: Maktabat wahba, 2009), 1086.

61. Ibid., 1099.

62. Ibid., 1100.

63. Imara, *Fi Fiqh al-Sira' 'ala al-Quds wa-Filistin {On the Jurisprudence of the Conflict over Jerusalem and Palestine}*, 7.

64. Ibid., 82–88.

65. Ibid., 89.

66. Ibid., 95.
67. Ibid., 108.
68. Ibid., 126.
69. Ali al-Din Hilal al-Sira' bayna al-Qanun wa-al-Fawda...wa Difa' 'an Siyadat Misr [The conflict between law and chaos...and the defence of Egyptian sovereignty],' *al-Ahram*, April 18, 2009; Andrew Wander, 'Egypt's Brotherhood backs Hizbullah in spat with Cairo,' *The Daily Star (Lebanon)*, April 24, 2009; Chris Zambelis, 'The Hizbullah trial in Egypt: A war of words in the New Middle East Cold War,' *Terrorism Monitor* 8, no. 21 (May 28, 2010), http://www.jamestown.org/single/?no_cache=1&tx_ttnews[tt_news]=36441&tx_ttnews[backPid]=13&cHash=b08e2a0a6 (accessed 1 October 2010).
70. Tarek Heggy, 'The Arab mind and the denial phenomenon,' October 5, 2005, http://www.windsofchange.net/archives/the_arab_mind_the_denial_phenomenon.php#more (accessed 1 September 2006).
71. Nevine Khalil, '"Peace offensive" hits Cairo,' *al-Ahram Weekly*, June 11, 1998.
72. al-Hayat, 'Lutfi al-Khuli: al-Rafidun li-Harakatina 'Aqaliyya wa idha Fashalna Sanabhath 'an Sigha 'Ukhra [Lutfi al-Khuli: Those who reject our movement are a minority and if we fail we will find another formula],' *al-Hayat*, March 1, 1998.
73. Amin, *al-Muthaqqafun al-'Arab wa-Isra'il [Arab Intellectuals and Israel]*.
74. For example, and for a recent supportive position, see Nabil Sharaf al-Din 'Libraliyun wa Harbajiyya [Liberals and warmongering],' *al-Masry al-Youm*, October 12, 2009.
75. Ahmad Muslimani, 'Libraliyun did al-Tatbi" 2 [Liberals against normalisation 2],' *al-Masry al-Youm*, October 5, 2009.
76. Ahmad Muslimani, 'Libraliyun did al-Tatbi" 4 [Liberals against normalisation 4],' *al-Masry al-Youm*, November 30, 2009.

Chapter 7

1. Reinhard Schulze, *A Modern History of the Islamic World* (New York: NYU Press, 2002).

BIBLIOGRAPHY

Abd al-Aziz, Abd al-Qadir bin. *Al-'Umda fi I'dad Al-'Udda (The Essentials of Making Ready for Jihad)*, 1988.

Abd al-Quddus, Ihsan. *Khawatir Siyasiyya (Political Dangers)*. Vol. 1. Cairo: Muntasir, 1979.

Abd al-Rahman, Aisha. *al-Isra'iliyat fi al-Ghazw al-Fikri (The Isra'iliyat in the Intellectual Invasion)*. Cairo: Ma'had al-Buhuth wa-al-Dirasat al-Arabiyah, 1975.

Abd al-Rahman, Awatif. *Misr wa-Filistin (Egypt and Palestine)*. Kuwait: Alim al-Ma'rifa, 1980.

Abdel-Malek, Anouar. *Egypt: Military Society: The Army Regime, the Left, and Social Change Under Nasser*. 1st ed. New York: Random House, 1968.

Abdelnasser, Walid Mahmoud. *The Islamic Movement in Egypt: Perceptions of International Relations, 1967–81*. London: Kegan Paul International, 1994.

———. 'Islamic organizations in Egypt and the Iranian Revolution of 1979: the experience of the first few years.' *Arab Studies Quarterly* 19, no. 2 (Spring 1997).

Abdelrahman, Maha. 'With the Islamists? Sometimes ... With the State? Never!: Cooperation between the Left and Islamists in Egypt.' *British Journal of Middle Eastern Studies* 36, no. 1 (April 2009).

Abdullah, Isma'il Sabri. *al-Tali'a*. Cairo, July 1967.

Abrahamian, Ervand. 'The causes of the Constitutional Revolution in Iran.' *International Journal of Middle East Studies* 10, no. 3 (August 1979): 381–414.

Achcar, Gilbert. *The Arabs and the Holocaust: The Arab-Israeli War of Narratives*. London: Saqi Books, 2010.

Aflaq, Michel. *Choice of Texts from the Ba'th Party Founder's Thought*. Florence: Cooperativa Lavoratori (Arab Ba'th Socialist Party), 1977.

Ajami, Fouad. *The Arab Predicament: Arab Political Thought and Practice since 1967*. Cambridge: Cambridge University Press, 1992.

Albrecht, Holger. 'How can opposition support authoritarianism? Lessons from Egypt.' *Democratization* 12, no. 3 (June 2005): 378–397.

Al-Hayat. 'Murshid al-Ikhwan li-al-Hayat: laysa fi qamusina shay'un ismuha Isra'il [Guide of the Muslim Brotherhood: there is nothing called Israel in our dictionary], *al-Hayat,* October 18, 2007.

———. 'Lutfi al-Khuli: al-rafidun li-harakatina aqaliya wa-idha fashalna sanabhath 'an sigha ukhra [Lutfi al-Khuli: Those who reject our movement are a minority and if we fail we will find another formula].' *al-Hayat,* March 1, 1998.

al-Alim, Mahmud Amin. *I'tirafat Shaykh al-Shuyu'iyin al-'Arab: Mahmud Amin al-'Alim {Confessions of the Shaykh of the Arab Communists: Mahmoud Amin al-Alim}.* Cairo: Maktabat Madbuli, 2006.

al-Anani, Khalil. *al-Ikhwan al-Muslimun fi Misr: shaykhukha turasi' al-zaman {The Muslim Brotherhood in Egypt: Gerontocracy against Time}.* Cairo: Dar al-Shuruq al-Dawaliya, 2007.

al-Awa, Salwa. *al-Gama'a al-Islamiyya'al-Musalliha fi Misr: 1974–2004* [The Armed Islamic Group in Egypt: 1974–2004]. Cairo: Maktabat al-Shuruq al-Dawaliya, 2006.

Amin, Galal A. *al-Muthaqqafun al-'Arab wa-Isra'il {Arab Intellectuals and Israel}.* Cairo: Dar al-Shuruq, 1998.

Ansari, Hamied. *Egypt, the Stalled Society.* Albany: State University of New York Press, 1986.

Aryan, Isam. 'Asl al-qadiya [The root of the issue].' *al-Dustur,* November 3, 2008.

———. 'Fi Dhikrat al-Nakba al-Ula: Mas'uliyyat al-Hukam wa Mas'uliyyat al-Shu'ub [On the first anniversary of the catastrophe: the responsibilities of rulers and the responsibilities of the people].' *al-Dustur,* May 11, 2009.

Ashmawi, Ali. *al-Tarikh al-Sirri li-Jama'at al-Ikhwan al-Muslimin: Mudhakkirat 'Ali 'Ashmawi Akhir Qadat al-Tanzim al-Sirri {The Secret History of the Muslim Brotherhood: Recollections of Ali Ashmawi, the Last Leader of the Secret Organisation}.* Cairo: Dar al-Hilal, 1993.

Ashmawi, Salih. *al-Da'wa.* Cairo, April 1977.

Ayubi, Nazih N. *Over-stating the Arab State: Politics and Society in the Middle East.* London: I.B.Tauris, 1995.

Azm, Sadiq Jalal. *al-Naqd al-Dhati ba'd al-Hazima {Self Criticism after the Defeat}.* Beirut: Dar al-Tali'ah, 1969.

Badawi, M. M. 'Islam in modern Egyptian literature.' *Journal of Arabic Literature* 2 (1971): 154–177.

Baha al-Din, Ahmad. *Iqtirah Dawlat Filastin wa ma Dara Hawlahu min Munaqishat {Proposal for the State of Palestine and the discussions surrounding it}.* Beirut: Dar al-Adab, 1968.

———. *Isra'iliyat.* Cairo: Dar al-Hilal, 1965.

Baker, Raymond William. *Sadat and After: Struggles for Egypt's Political Soul.* London: I.B.Tauris, 1990.

Barnett, Michael. *Dialogues in Arab Politics: Negotiations in Regional Order.* New York: Columbia University Press, 1998.

Batatu, Hana. *The Old Social Classes and the Revolutionary Movements of Iraq: A Study of Iraq's Old Landed and Commercial Classes and of Its Communists, Ba'thists and Free Officers.* Reprinted edition. Princeton, NJ: Princeton University Press, 1992.

Bayat, Asef. 'Revolution without movement, movement without revolution: comparing Islamic activism in Iran and Egypt.' *Comparative Studies in Society and History* 40, no. 1 (1998): 136–169.

al-Bazzaz, Abd al-Rahman. Al-Dawla al-Muwahhada wa-al-Dawla al-Ittihadiyya [The unitary state and the federal state].' In *Political and Social Thought in the Contemporary Middle East*, edited by Kemal H. Karpat. London: Pall Mall Press, 1968.

Beattie, Kirk. *Egypt during the Nasser Years: Ideology, Politics and Civil Society.* Boulder, CO; Oxford: Westview Press, 1994.

———. *Egypt during the Sadat Years.* New York; Basingstoke: Palgrave, 2000.

Beinin, Joel. *The Dispersion of Egyptian Jewry: Culture, Politics, and the Formation of a Modern Diaspora.* Cairo: American University in Cairo Press, 2005.

———. 'Political Islam and the new global economy: the political economy of an Egyptian social movement.' *CR: The New Centennial Review* 5, no. 1 (Spring 2005): 111–139.

———. *Was the Red Flag Flying There?: Marxist Politics and the Arab-Israeli Conflict in Egypt and Israel,1948–1965.* London: I.B.Tauris, 1990.

Berque, Jacques. *Egypt, Imperialism and Revolution.* London: Faber, 1972.

Bianchi, Robert. *Unruly Corporatism: Associational Life in Twentieth-Century Egypt.* New York; Oxford: Oxford University Press, 1989.

Binder, Leonard. *The Ideological Revolution in the Middle East.* New York; London: Wiley, 1964.

———. *In a Moment of Enthusiasm: Political Power and the Second Stratum in Egypt.* Chicago; London: University of Chicago Press, 1978.

al-Bishri, Tariq. *al-'Arab fi Muwajihat al-'Udwan {The Arabs Confronting Aggression}.* Cairo: Dar al-Shuruq, 2002.

———. *al-Haraka al-Siyasiyya fi Misr 1945–1953 {The Political Movement in Egypt, 1945–1953}.* 2nd ed. Cairo: Dar al-Shuruq, 2002.

Botman, Selma. *The Rise of Egyptian Communism, 1939–1970.* Syracuse, NY: Syracuse University Press, 1988.

Bull, Hedley. 'The emergence of a universal international society.' In *The Expansion of International Society*, edited by Hedley Bull and Adam Watson. Oxford: Oxford University Press, 1984.

Bush, Ray. 'Facing structural adjustment: strategies of peasants, the state and the international financial institutions.' In *Directions of Change in Rural Egypt*, edited by Nicholas Hopkins and Kirsten Westergaard. Cairo: American University in Cairo Press, 1998.

Carr, Edward Hallet. *The Twenty Years' Crisis 1919–1939: An Introduction to the Study of International Relations.* Edited by Michael Cox. Vol. 2. Basingstoke: Palgrave, 2001.

Churchill, Winston S. 'Zionism versus Bolshevism: a struggle for the soul of the Jewish people.' *Illustrated Sunday Herald*, February 8, 1920.

Dawisha, Adeed. *Egypt in the Arab World: The Elements of Foreign Policy*. London: Macmillan, 1976.

Dawisha, Karen. *Soviet Foreign Policy towards Egypt*. New York: St. Martin's Press, 1979.

Dekmejian, Richard H. *Egypt under Nasir: A Study in Political Dynamics*. Albany: State University of New York Press, 1971.

Doran, Michael. *Pan-Arabism before Nasser: Egyptian Power Politics and the Palestine Question*. New York; Oxford: Oxford University Press, 1999.

Eccel, A. Chris. "'Alim and Mujahid in Egypt: orthodoxy versus subculture, or division of labour?' *The Muslim World* 78 (1988): 189–208.

El-Awaisi, Abd al-Fattah. 'The conceptual approach of the Egyptian Muslim Brothers towards the Palestine Question, 1928–1949.' *Journal of Islamic Studies* 2, no. 2 (1991): 225–244.

———. *The Muslim Brothers and the Palestine Question, 1928–1947*. London: I.B.Tauris, 1996.

El-Ghobashy, Mona. 'The dynamics of Egypt's elections.' *Middle East Report Online*, September 29, 2010.

Elmessiri, Abdelwahab M. *The Land of Promise: A Critique of Political Zionism*. New Brunswick, NJ: North American, 1977.

El-Mikawy, Noha. *The Building of Consensus in Egypt's Transition Process*. Cairo: American University in Cairo Press, 1999.

El-Sa'id, Rifa'at, and Tareq Y. Ismael. *The Communist Movement in Egypt: 1920–1988*. Syracuse; London: Syracuse University Press, 1990.

Eppel, Michael. 'Note about the term effendiyya in the history of the Middle East.' *International Journal of Middle East Studies* 41 (2009): 535–539.

Erlich, H. *Students and University in 20th Century Egyptian Politics*. London: Cass, 1989.

Fandy, Mamoun. 'Egypt's Islamic Group: regional revenge?' *Middle East Journal* 48, no. 4 (Autumn 1994): 607–25.

Fiori, Guiseppe. *Antonio Gramsci: Life of a Revolutionary*. London: New Left Books, 1970.

Firestone, Reuven. *Journeys in Holy Lands: the Evolution of the Abraham-Ishmael Legends in Islamic Exegesis*. Albany, NJ: State University of New York Press, 1990.

Gerges, Fawaz A. 'The decline of revolutionary Islam in Algeria and Egypt.' *Survival* 41, no. 1 (Spring 1999): 113–25.

———. *The Far Enemy: Why Jihad Went Global*. New York: Cambridge University Press, 2005.

Gershoni, Israel. 'Haykal's Recantation of Positivism.' In *Middle Eastern Politics and Ideas: A History from Within*, edited by Moshe Maoz and Ilan Pappé, 236p. London: I.B.Tauris, 1997.

Ginat, Rami. *Egypt's Incomplete Revolution: Lutfi al-Khuli and Nasser's Socialism in the 1960s.* London: Frank Cass, 1997.

———. *Syria and the Doctrine of Arab Neutralism: from Independence to Dependence.* Portland, OR: Sussex Academic Press, 2005.

Goldberg, Ellis. 'Smashing idols and the state: The Protestant ethic and Egyptian Sunni radicalism.' *Comparative Studies in Society and History* 33, no. 1 (1991): 3–35.

Gorman, Anthony. *Historians, State and Politics in Twentieth Century Egypt: Contesting the Nation.* London: Routledge, 2003.

Gramsci, Antonio. *Selections from the Prison Notebooks of Antonio Gramsci.* New York; London: Lawrence and Wishart, 1971.

Habib, Rafiq. *al-Ihtijaj al-Dini wa-al-Sira' al-Tabaqi fi Misr {Religious Protest and Class Struggle in Egypt}.* Vol. 1. Cairo: Sina lil-Nashr, 1989.

Hafiz, Salah al-Din. *Karahiya taht al-Jild: Isra'il 'Aqdat al-Alaqat al-Arabiya al-Amrikiya {Hatred under the skin: Israel, the complication in Arab-American relations.* Cairo: Dar al-Shuruq, 2003.

Halliday, Fred. *The Middle East in International Relations: Power, Politics and Ideology.* Cambridge: Cambridge University Press, 2005.

Hamrush, Ahmad. 'Editorial.' *Ruz al-Yusuf.* Cairo, March 21, 1966.

———. 'al-Hilf al-Islami [The Islamic pact].' *Ruz al-Yusuf.* Cairo, March 7, 1966.

———. 'al-Tariq ila Wahdat al-Quwwa al-Taqaddumiyya [The road to the unity of progressive forces].' *Ruz al-Yusuf.* Cairo, March 14, 1966.

Hanafi, Hassan. *al-Din wa-al-Thawra fi Misr, 1952–1981 {Religion and Revolution in Egypt: 1952–1981}.* Cairo: Maktabat Madbuli, 1989.

Harb, Usamah al-Ghazali. *al-Istratijiyya al-Isra'iliyya wa-al-Muqawama fi al-'Ard al-Muhtalla {Israeli Strategy and the Resistance in the Occupied Territory}.* Cairo: Markaz al-Dirasat al-Siyasiyya wa-al-Istratijiyya bi-al-Ahram, 1977.

Harik, Iliya. *The Political Mobilization of Peasants: a Study of an Egyptian Community.* Bloomington; London: Indiana University Press, 1974.

Hawali, Safar. 'Ba'd al-Kutub alati Taruddu 'ala al-Afkar al-Hadima [Some books that refute destructive ideas].' http://www.alhawali.com/index.cfm?method=home.SubContent&ContentID=2128#Alam1001131.

Haykal, Muhammad Hasanayn. 'Bi-al-Saraha [To be frank].' *al-Ahram.* Cairo, September 10, 1959.

———. 'Bi-al-Saraha [To be frank].' *al-Ahram.* Cairo, January 1963.

———. 'Bi-al-Saraha [To be frank].' *al-Ahram.* Cairo, September 18, 1964.

———. *Nasser – the Cairo Documents.* London: New English Library, 1972.

———. *Sphinx and Commissar: The Rise and Fall of Soviet Influence in the Arab World.* London: Collins, 1978.

Heck, Paul L. 'Jihad revisited.' *Journal of Religious Ethics* 32, no. 1 (3, 2004): 95–128.

Heggy, Tarek. 'The Arab Mind and the Denial Phenomenon,' October 5, 2005. http://www.windsofchange.net/archives/the_arab_mind_the_denial_phenomenon.php#more.

Heikal, Mohamed Hassanein. 'Egyptian foreign policy.' *Foreign Affairs* (July 1978).

Henry, Clement M., and Robert Springborg. *Globalization and the Politics of Development in the Middle East.* Cambridge: Cambridge University Press, 2001.

Heydemann, Steven. *War, Institutions, and Social Change in the Middle East.* Berkeley: University of California Press, 2000.

Hilal, Ali al-Din. 'al-Sira' bayna al-qanun wa-al-fawda . . . wa-difa' an siyadat Misr [The conflict between law and chaos . . . and the defence of Egyptian sovereignty].' *al-Ahram*, April 18, 2009.

Hinnebusch, Raymond A. *Egyptian Politics under Sadat: The Post-Populist Development of an Authoritarian-Modernizing State.* Boulder, CO: Lynne Rienner Publishers, 1988.

Hobsbawm, Eric. *Age of Extremes: The Short Twentieth Century, 1914–91.* London: Abacus, 1995.

Hopkins, Nicholas. 'Sufi organization in rural Asyut: the Rifa'iyya in Musha.' In *Upper Egypt: Identity and Change*, edited by Reem Saad and Nicholas Hopkins. Cairo; New York: American University in Cairo Press, 2004.

Hourani, Albert H. *Arabic Thought in the Liberal Age, 1798–1939.* London; New York: Oxford University Press, 1962.

Husayn, Adel. *al-Jabha al-'Arabiyya al-Iraniyya did al-Hilf al-Amriki al-Sihyuni {The Arab-Iranian Front against the American-Zionist Alliance},* 1998.

———. *Ba'd Fashl al-Mufawadat ma'a Isra'il: Hal al-Harb Mumkin? Wa Kayf? {After the Failure of the Negotiations with Israel: Is War Possible? and How?* Kotobarabia, 2001. www.kotobarabia.com.

Husayn, Muhammad Muhammad. *al-Ittijahat al-Wataniyya fi al-'Adab al-Mu'asir: min al-Harb al-'Alamiyya al-Ula ila Qiyam al-Jami'a al-'Arabiyya {Patriotic Tendencies in Contemporary Literature: From WW1 until the Arab League}.* Vol. 2. 2nd ed. Cairo: Maktabat al-Adab, 1956.

———. *al-Ittijahat al-Wataniyya fi al-'Adab al-Mu'asir: min al-Thawra al-'Urabiyya ila Qiyam al-Harb al-'Alamiyya al-Ula {Patriotic Tendencies in Contemporary Literature: From the Urabi revolution until World War One}.* Vol. 1. 2nd ed. Cairo: Maktabat al-Adab, 1962.

Huwaydi, Fahmi. 'al-Tatbi' wa Aful al-Haraka al-Wataniyya al-Misriyya [Normalisation and the demise of the Egyptian national movement].' *al-Shuruq al-Jadid*, September 29, 2009.

Ibrahim, Saad Eddin. 'Domestic developments in Egypt.' In *The Middle East: Ten Years after Camp David*, edited by William B. Quandt. Washington, D.C.: Brookings Institution Press, 1988.

———. *Fi Susyulujiyat al-Sira' al-'Arabi al-Isra'ili {On the Sociology of the Arab-Israeli Conflict}.* Beirut: Dar al-Tali'ah, 1973.

Imara, Muhammad. *Fi Fiqh al-Sira' 'ala al-Quds wa Filistin {On the Jurisprudence of the Conflict over Jerusalem and Palestine}*. Cairo: Dar al-Shuruq, 2005.

Ismael, Tareq Y. *The Arab Left*. Vol. 1. Syracuse, NY: Syracuse University Press, 1976.

Jackson, Sherman A. 'Jihad and the Modern Word.' *Journal of Islamic Law and Culture* (Spring/Summer 2002).

al-Jama'a al-Islamiyya bi Misr. *Hatmiyat al-Muwajiha {The Inevitability of Confrontation}*. Minbar al-tawhid wa-al-jihad, 1987.

―――. *Mithaq al-Amal al-Islami {Charter of Islamic Action}*. Minbar al-tawhid wa-al-jihad, 1984

James, Laura M. *Nasser at War: Arab Images of the Enemy*. Basingstoke; New York: Palgrave Macmillan, 2006.

Jankowski, James P., and Israel Gershoni. *Egypt, Islam, and the Arabs: The Search for Egyptian Nationhood, 1900–1930*. New York: Oxford University Press, 1986.

―――. *Redefining the Egyptian Nation, 1930–1945*. Cambridge: Cambridge University Press, 1995.

Jansen, Johannes J. G., and Muhammad Abd al-Salam Faraj. *The Neglected Duty: The Creed of Sadat's Assassins and Islamic Resurgence in the Middle East*. New York: Macmillan, 1986.

Jarisha, Ali. 'al-Ghazw al-Fikri [The intellectual invasion].' *al-Da'wa*. Cairo, November 1976.

Kahin, George M. *The Asian-African Conference, Bandung, Indonesia*. Ithaca, NY: Cornell University Press, 1956.

Karawan, Ibrahim A. 'Identity and foreign policy: The case of Egypt.' In *Identity and Foreign Policy in the Middle East*, edited by Shibley Telhami and Michael Barnett. Ithaca: Cornell University Press, 2002.

Kassem, Maye. *Egyptian Politics: The Dynamics of Authoritarian Rule*. Boulder, CO: Lynne Rienner Publishers, 2004.

Kenyon, Peter. 'Israel's "cold" peace with Egypt, Jordan grows chillier.' *All Things Considered*. NPR, October 26, 2009. http://www.npr.org/templates/story/story.php?storyId=114170104.

Kepel, Gilles. *The Prophet and Pharaoh: Muslim Extremism in Contemporary Egypt*. London: Al Saqi Books, 1985.

Kerr, Malcolm H. *The Arab Cold War, 1958–1964; a Study of Ideology in Politics*. London; New York: Oxford University Press, 1965.

―――. *The Arab Cold War: Gamal 'Abd Al-Nasir and His Rivals, 1958–1970*. 3rd ed. London: Published for the Royal Institute of International Affairs by Oxford University Press, 1971.

Khalil, Nevine. '"Peace offensive" hits Cairo.' *al-Ahram Weekly*, June 11, 1998. http://weekly.ahram.org.eg/1998/381/eg3.htm.

Khomeini, Ruhollah. 'Imam Khomeini's Message to the Pilgrims to the House of God in Mecca.' *Sahifa-yi Nur*, September 6, 1981.

―――. *Imam's Message*. Vol. 14, 1981.

al-Khuli, Lutfi. *Awraq min al-Milaff al-'Arabi: Mustaqbal al-Sira' al-'Arabi al-Isra'ili 'Am 2000 {Papers from the Arab File: The Future of the Arab Israeli Conflict in the Year 2000}*. Vol. 1. Cairo: Dar al-Fikr, 1986.

————. 'Editorial.' *al-Tali'a*. Cairo, August 1967.

Kienle, Eberhard. *A Grand Delusion: Democracy and Economic Reform in Egypt*. London: I.B.Tauris, 2001.

Kishk, Muhammad Jalal. *al-Marksiyya wa-al-Ghazw al-Fikri {Marxism and the Intellectual Invasion}*. Cairo: al-Dar al-Qawmiyah lil-Taba'ah wa-al-Nashr, 1966.

Krämer, Gudrun. *The Jews in Modern Egypt, 1914–1952*. London: I.B.Tauris, 1989.

Kuhlah, Fu'ad. 'al-Marksiyya wa-al-Sihyuniyya wa Wahdat al-Judhur [Marxism and Zionism and their shared roots].' *al-Da'wa*. Cairo, April 1977.

Laroui, Abdallah. *The Crisis of the Arab Intellectual: Traditionalism or Historicism?* Berkeley; London: University of California Press, 1976.

Lerman, Eran. 'A revolution prefigured: foreign policy orientations in the post-war years.' In *Egypt from Monarchy to Republic: A Reassessment of Revolution and Change*, edited by Shimon Shamir. Boulder, CO; Oxford: Westview Press, 1995.

Lesch, Ann Mosely. 'Egyptian-Israeli relations: normalization or special ties?.' In *Israel, Egypt, and the Palestinians: From Camp David to Intifada*, edited by Ann Mosely Lesch and Mark Tessler. Bloomington, IN: Indiana University Press, 1989.

Lia, Brynjar. *The Society of the Muslim Brothers in Egypt: The Rise of an Islamic Mass Movement 1928–1942*. Reading: Garnet, 1998.

Mahfouz, el Kosherki. *Socialisme et Pouvoir en Égypte {Socialism and Power in Egypt}*. Paris: Librairie générale de droit et de jurisprudence, 1972.

Mann, Michael. *The Sources of Social Power*. Cambridge: Cambridge University Press, 1993.

Mannheim, Karl. *Ideology and Utopia: An Introduction to the Sociology of Knowledge*. London: Routledge and Kegan Paul, 1960.

al-Masiri, Abd al-Wahhab. *al-Sihyuniyya wa-al-Naziyya wa-Nihayat al-Tarikh {Zionism and Nazism and the End of History}*. 3rd ed. Cairo: Dar al-Shuruq, 2001.

————. *Mawsu'at al-Mafahim wa-al-Mustalahat al-Sihyuniyya: Ru'ya Naqdiyya {Encyclopedia of Zionist Concepts and Terms: A Critical View}*. Cairo: Markaz al-Dirasat al-Siyasiyah wa-al-Istirajiyah bi-al-Ahram, 1975.

————. *Rihlati al-Fikriyya: fi Budhur wa-al-Judhur wa-al-Thamr: Sira ghayr Dhatiyya ghayr Mawdu'iyya {My Intellectual Journey: On Seeds, Roots and Fruits: A Subjective Non-autobiography}*. 4th ed. Cairo: Dar al-Shuruq, 2009.

McLaurin, R.D., Don Peretz, and Lewis W. Snider. *Middle East Foreign Policy: Issues and Processes*. New York: Praeger, 1982.

Meijer, Roel. *The Quest for Modernity: Secular Liberal and Left-Wing Political Thought in Egypt, 1945–1958*. London: Routledge Curzon, 2002.

Mitchell, Richard P. *The Society of the Muslim Brothers*. New York: Oxford University Press, 1993.

Mubarak, Husni. 'Speech of President Muhammad Husni Mubarak at the Joint Meeting of the People's and Shura Council,' October 3, 1982. http://www2. sis.gov.eg/Ar/Politics/PInstitution/President/Speeshes/000001/0401010200 000000000198.htm.

Musallam, Adnan. *From Secularism to Jihad: Sayyid Qutb and the Foundations of Radical Islamism*. Wesport, CT; London: Praeger, 2005.

Muslimani, Ahmad. 'Libraliyun did al-Tatbi 2 [Liberals against normalisation 2].' *al-Masry al-Youm*, October 5, 2009.

————. 'Libraliyun did al-tatbi' 4 [Liberals against normalisation 4].' *al-Masry al-Youm*, November 30, 2009.

Mustafa, Hala. *al-Nizam al-Siyasi wa-al-Mu'arada al-Islamiyya fi Misr (The Political System and the Islamic Opposition in Egypt)*. Cairo: Markaz al-Mahrusah lil-Nashr wa-al-Khidmat al-Suhufiyah, 1995.

Nairn, Tom. *The Break-up of Britain: Crisis and Neo-Nationalism*. London: NLB, 1977.

Namnam, Hilmi. *al-Tarikh al-Majhul: al-Mufakkirin al-'Arab wa-al-Sihyuniyya wa Filastin (Unknown History: Arab Thinkers, Zionism and Palestine)*. Cairo: Ru'ya li-al-nashr wa-al-tawzi', 2007.

al-Naqqash, Raja. *al-Musawwar*. Cairo, December 28, 1973.

Nasser, Gamal Abdel. *The Charter: Draft of the National Charter Presented...at the Inaugural Session of the National Congress of Popular Powers on the Evening of 21st May, 1962*. Cairo, 1962.

————. 'Speech, 29 April 1954' (Nasser Institute and Bibliotheca Alexandrina, available from http://nasser.biblex.org/Data/GR09-1/speeches/1954/ 540429-1. htm) (In arabic) (accessed 10 October 2007).

————. 'Speech during visit to Gaza, 13 May 1956' (Nasser Institute and Bibliotheca Alexandrina) (accessed 10 October 2007)

————. 'Speech to the Arab Socialist Union in Alexandria Stadium,' Alexandria, July 27, 1966.

————. 'Speech to the Popular Congress in Jumhuriyya Square,' Cairo, July 22, 1955.

Nettler, Ronald L. 'Islam vs. Israel.' *Commentary* 78, no. 6 (1984): 26.

————. *Past Trials and Present Tribulations: A Muslim Fundamentalist's View of the Jews*. Oxford: Published for the Vidal Sassoon International Center for the Study of Antisemitism, the Hebrew University of Jerusalem by Pergamon, 1987.

Nur, Ayman. 'Hadatha fi Sitta Ayyam! [It happened in six days!].' *al-Dustur*, June 9, 2006.

Perrault, Gilles. *A Man Apart: The Life of Henri Curiel*. London: Zed Books, 1987.

————. 'Henri Curiel, Citizen of the Third World.' *Le Monde Diplomatique*, April 1998.

Peters, Rudolph. *Jihad in Classical and Modern Islam: A Reader*. Princeton, NJ: Markus Wiener Publishers, 2005.

Qaradawi, Yusuf. *al-Hall al-Islami: Farida wa Darura {The Islamic Solution: Obligation and Necessity}*. Vol. 12. Beirut: Mu'assasat al-Risalah, 1988.

———. *Fiqh al-Jihad: Dirasa Muqarana li Ahkamihi wa Falsafatihi fi du' al-Qur'an wa-al-Sunna {The Jurisprudence of Jihad: A Comparative Study of Its Rules and Philosophy in the Light of the Quran and the Sunna}*. Cairo: Maktabat wahba, 2009.

Qutb, Sayyid. *Limadha a'damuni? {Why Did They Execute Me?}*. Jeddah: al-Sharikat al-Saudiyah lil-Abhath wa al-Taswiq, 198.

———. *Milestones*. American Trust, 1990.

Radwan, Fathi. *Hadha al-Sharq al-'Arabi {This Arab East}*. Cairo: Dar al-Ma'arif, 1957.

Ramadan, Abd al-Azim. *al-'Alaqat al-Misriyya al-Isra'iliyya: 1948–1979 {Egyptian-Israeli Relations: 1948–1979}*. Cairo: al-Hay'a al-Misriya al-'Ama lil-Kitab, 1991.

Rejwan, Nissim. *Nasserist Ideology: Its Exponents and Critics*. New York: Wiley, 1974.

Roded, Ruth. 'Bint al-Shati's Wives of the Prophet: feminist or feminine.' *British Journal of Middle Eastern Studies* 33, no. 1 (May 2006): 51–56.

Rodinson, Maxime. *Islam and Capitalism*. London: Allen Lane, 1974.

Sa'd al-Din, Ibrahim. *al-Tali'a*. Cairo, July 1967.

Sa'dani, Mustafa. *Adwa' 'ala al-Sihyuniyya {Focus on Zionism}*. Cairo: al-Majlis al-A'la lil-Shu'un al-Islamiyah, 1969.

Sadat, Anwar. 'Speech to the University and Higher Institute Professors at Cairo University.' *Anwar Sadat Chair for Peace and Development*. University of Maryland, January 8, 1971. http://www.bsos.umd.edu/SADAT/archives/speeches.htm (accessed November 15, 2007).

———. 'Speech, October 7, 1970,' http://www.bsos.umd.edu/SADAT/archives/speeches.htm (accessed November 15, 2007).

———. *The October Working Paper*. Cairo: State Information Service, 1974.

Sadat, Anwar and Egypt State Information Service, *Speech by President Anwar el Sadat to the Knesset, 20th November 1977* (Cairo: State Information Service, 1977).

Salamé, Ghassan. *Democracy without Democrats?: The Renewal of Politics in the Muslim World*. London: I.B.Tauris, 1994.

Salih, Usama. 'Akef: we reject "Camp David" since its signing and the nuclear programme is a political smokecreen.' *al-Masry al-Youm*, November 12, 2007.

Salim, Abd al-Mun'im. 'Isra'il al-hadir wa-al-mustaqbal: sihat al-salam min hirtzil ila ishaq rabin [Israel present and future: calls for peace from Hertzl to Yitzak Rabin].' *al-Da'wa*. Cairo, March 1977.

———. 'Isra'il al-Hadir wa-al-Mustaqbal: al-Salam 'an al-Tariqa al-Amrikiyya al-Yahudiyya [Israel present and future: peace the American-Jewish way].' *al-Da'wa*. Cairo, January 1977.

————. 'Isra'il al-Hadir wa-al-Mustaqbal [Israel: present and future].' *al-Da'wa*. Cairo, November 1976.

Sayegh, Fayez A. *The Dynamics of Neutralism in the Arab World: A Symposium*. San Francisco: Chandler, 1964.

Sayigh, Yazid. *Armed Struggle and the Search for State: The Palestinian National Movement, 1949–1993*. Oxford: Oxford University Press, 1999.

Schulze, Reinhard. *A Modern History of the Islamic World*. New York: NYU Press, 2002.

Seale, Patrick. *Asad of Syria: The Struggle for the Middle East*. Berkeley: University of California Press, 1989.

————. *The Struggle for Syria: A Study of Post-War Arab Politics, 1945–1958*. London; New York: Oxford University Press, 1965.

Sela, Avraham. 'Abd al-Nasser's regional politics: a reassessment.' In *Rethinking Nasserism: Revolution and Historical Memory in Modern Egypt*, edited by Elie Podeh and Onn Winckler, xv, 365 p. Gainesville, FL; London: University Press of Florida: Eurospan, 2004.

————. *The Decline of the Arab-Israeli Conflict: Middle East Politics and the Quest for Regional Order*. New York: State Univeristy of New York Press, 1998.

Sharaf al-Din, Nabil. 'Libraliyun wa Harbajiyya [Liberals and warmongering].' *al-Masry al-Youm*, October 12, 2009.

Shazli, Sa'd al-Din. *Our Faith, Our Way to Victory*. Israel Information Centre, 1973.

Shichor, Yitzhak. *The Middle East in China's Foreign Policy, 1949–1977*. Cambridge; New York: Cambridge University Press, 1979.

Shihab al-Din, Mufid, al-Sayyid Yasin, and Yunan Labib Rizq. *al-Sihyuniyya wa-al-'Unsuriyya al-Sihyuniyya ka Namt min Anmat al-Tafriqa al-'Unsuriyya {Zionism and Zionist Racism as a Form of Racial Discrimination}*. Cairo: Ma'had al-Buhuth wa al-Dirasat al-'Arabiyah, 1977.

Shlaim, Avi. *The Iron Wall: Israel and the Arab World*. New York: W.W. Norton, 2000.

Shukri, Ghali. *Egypt: Portrait of a President, 1971–1981; the Counter-Revolution in Egypt; Sadat's Road to Jerusalem*. Middle East Series. London: Zed Books, 1981.

Sid Ahmad, Muhammad. *After the Guns Fall Silent: Peace or Armageddon in the Middle-East*. New York: St. Martin's Press, 1976.

Singerman, Diane. *Avenues of Participation: Family, Politics, and Networks in Urban Quarters of Cairo*. Princeton, NJ: Princeton University Press, 1996.

Somech, Sasson. 'I dream of the day when. . . .' *Dissent* Winter (2004).

Stein, Ewan. 'What does the Gama'a Islamiyya want now?' *Middle East Report* 254 (Spring 2010).

Sulayman, William. *al-Tali'a*. Cairo, July 1967.

Sullivan, Denis Joseph, and Sana Abed-Kotob. *Islam in Contemporary Egypt: Civil Society vs. the State*. Boulder, CO: Lynne Rienner Publishers, 1999.

Taji-Farouki, Suha. 'Thinking on the Jews.' In *Islamic Thought in the Twentieth Century*, edited by Suha Taji-Farouki and Basheer M. Nafi. London: I.B.Tauris, 2004.

Talhami, Ghada Hashem. *Palestine and Egyptian National Identity.* New York; London: Praeger, 1992.

Tammam, Husam. *Tahawulat al-Ikhwan al-Muslimun: Tafakkuk al-Idiyulujiyya wa Nihayat al-Tanzim {Transformations of the Muslim Brotherhood: fragmentation of Ideology and the End of the Organisation}.* Cairo: Maktabat Madbuli, 2006.

Tibi, Bassam. *Arab Nationalism: Between Islam and the Nation-State.* Vol. 3. New York: St. Martin's Press, 1996.

Tignor, Robert. 'Foreign capital, foreign communities, and the Egyptian Revolution of 1952.' In *Egypt from Monarchy to Republic: A Reassessment of Revolution and Change,* edited by Shimon Shamir. Boulder, CO; Oxford: Westview Press, 1995.

Tripp, Charles. *A History of Iraq.* Cambridge; New York: Cambridge University Press, 2002.

Uthman, Wa'il. *Asrar al-Haraka al-Tullabiyya {Secrets of the Student Movement}* (Cario: al-Sharika al-Misriya li-al Taba'a) 1976.

Vatikiotis, P.J. *The History of Modern Egypt: From Muhammad Ali to Mubarak.* Vol. 4. London: Weidenfeld and Nicolson, 1991.

Vatikiotis, Panayiotis J. *Nasser and His Generation.* London: Croom Helm, 1978.

Wander, Andrew. 'Egypt's Brotherhood backs Hizbullah in spat with Cairo.' *The Daily Star (Lebanon),* April 24, 2009.

Waterbury, John. *The Egypt of Nasser and Sadat: The Political Economy of Two Regimes.* Guildford, CT: Princeton University Press, 1983.

Wickham, Carrie Rosefsky. *Mobilizing Islam: Religion, Activism, and Political Change in Egypt.* New York: Columbia University Press, 2002.

Yasin, al-Sayyid. *al-Ustura al-Ustura al-Sihyuniyya wa-al-Intifada al-Filastini-yya {The Zionist Myth and the Palestinian Intifada}.* Cairo: Mirit li-al-nashr wa-al-matbu'at, 2001.

Zakariya, Fu'ad. *'Abd al-Nasir wa-al-Yasar al-Misri {Abdel Nasser and the Egyptian Left}.* Cairo: Ruz al-Yusuf, 1977.

Zambelis, Chris. 'The Hizbullah Trial in Egypt: a war of words in the new Middle East Cold War.' *Terrorism Monitor* 8, no. 21 (May 28, 2010). http://www.jamestown.org/single/?no_cache=1&tx_ttnews[tt_news]=36441&tx_ttnews[backPid]=13&cHash=b08e2a0a6.

Zawahiri, Ayman. *In His Own Words: A Translation of the Writings of Dr. Ayman al-Zawahiri.* Translated by Laura Mansfield (LULU, 2006).

Zaydan, Ala'. 'Qadiyat al-masjid al-aqsa tazdat khuturatan [The issue of the Aqsa Mosque gets more dangerous].' *al-Da'wa.* Cairo, August 1977.

Zayyat, Montasser al-. *The Road to al-Qaeda: The Story of Bin Laden's Right-Hand Man.* London; Sterling, VA: Pluto Press, 2004.

Zollner, Barbara. *The Muslim Brotherhood: Hasan al-Hudaybi and Ideology.* 1st ed. New York: Routledge, 2008.

Zurayq, Qustantin. *'Ma'na al-Nakba {The Meaning of the Catastrophe}.* 2nd ed. Beirut: Dar al-'Ilm lil-Malayin, 1948.

———. *Ma'na al-Nakba Mujadaddan' {The Meaning of the Catastrophe Revisited}.* 1st ed. Beirut: Dar al-'Ilm lil-Malayin, 1967.

INDEX